Sustainability in the Anthropocene

Postphenomenology and the Philosophy of Technology

Series Editors: Robert Rosenberger, Peter-Paul Verbeek, Don Ihde

As technologies continue to advance, they correspondingly continue to make fundamental changes to our lives. Technological changes have effects on everything from our understandings of ethics, politics, and communication, to gender, science, and selfhood. Philosophical reflection on technology can help draw out and analyze the nature of these changes, and help us to understand both the broad patterns of technological effects and the concrete details. The purpose of this series is to provide a publication outlet for the field of the philosophy of technology in general, and the school of thought called "postphenomenology" in particular. The field of philosophy of technology applies insights from the history of philosophy to current issues in technology and reflects on how technological developments change our understanding of philosophical issues. Postphenomenology is the name of an emerging research perspective used by a growing international and interdisciplinary group of scholars. This perspective utilizes insights from the philosophical tradition of phenomenology to analyze human relationships with technologies, and it also integrates philosophical commitments of the American pragmatist tradition of thought.

Recent Titles in This Series

Sustainability in the Anthropocene

Philosophical Essays on Renewable Technologies

Edited by
Róisín Lally

LEXINGTON BOOKS
Lanham • Boulder • New York • London

Published by Lexington Books
An imprint of The Rowman & Littlefield Publishing Group, Inc.
4501 Forbes Boulevard, Suite 200, Lanham, Maryland 20706
www.rowman.com

6 Tinworth Street, London SE11 5AL, United Kingdom

British Library Cataloguing in Publication Information Available

Library of Congress Cataloging-in-Publication Data Available

ISBN: 978-1-4985-8422-7 (cloth : alk. paper)
ISBN: 978-1-4985-8423-4 (electronic)

Contents

Introduction

Sustainable Technologies in the Anthropocene

Dan Bradley

This book gathers together the contributions of philosophers of technology from around the world, some at the top of the field, others emerging voices from many of the leading centers of technology production and research (Denmark, Ireland, Scotland, Israel, Brazil, and the US states of New York, California, and Washington). Their task is to discuss technology under the banner of "sustainability," which is one of our most urgent desires, and "the Anthropocene," which is one of the most pervasive and provocative understandings of the time in which we live.

We are facing an environmental crisis that threatens not only a great deal of life on the planet but also our understanding of who we are and our relation to the natural world. In the face of this crisis it has become clear that we need a more sustainable way of life. In fact the language of sustainability has become pervasive in our culture and has deeply ingrained itself in our understanding of what living a good life would entail. As Cristina Bonfiglioli, a philosopher of technology at the Universidade de São Paulo, explains in her contribution to this book: sustainability is one of the major discursive events of our time. But as she goes on to note, *sustainability* is a contested word, and it carries with it, often implicitly and unacknowledged, deep philosophical claims that are entangled with all kinds of assumptions and power relations, some of them very problematic. Thus, Bonfiglioli's contribution is perhaps the flagship chapter or at least the frame for understanding the importance of this collection of chapters. In these pages, we will not definitively decide what a sustainable life should be, but we will contribute to shaping the conversation.

The disciplines of "postphenomenology" and "technoscience" are marked, among other things, by the desire that philosophers use their talents and training to address concrete problems and to shape governmental policies and social institutions in ways that change the world for the better. Not all the thinkers in this book are explicitly connected to these traditions, but all are committed to the idea of praxis. In this vein, and in light of the ongoing environmental crisis, this timely book brings together both empirical and philosophical studies of sustainable energy and the renewable technologies associated with that movement. Thus, we hope this book does inspire *action*, but most importantly we hope it will help to make sense of ourselves and our world so that those actions will be guided by wisdom.

The book is divided into four sections: (1) Defining Sustainability; (2) Sustainability and Renewable Technologies: Sun, Air, Wind, Water; (3) Sustainability and Design; and (4) Sustainability and Ethics. The first section sets the context for our studies and opens a space for thinking sustainability in a more thoughtful way than is often the case in contemporary discussions. The next two sections are the heart of our contribution to postphenomenology and technoscience, and the chapters, here, turn to concrete examinations of particular technologies and questions of technological design in the light of our environmental crisis. The fourth section closes the book by drawing some more general implications for ethics from the intersection of the foregoing themes.

We hope this provides a helpful structure and even something of a narrative arc for reading the collection. However, by way of introduction, rather than presenting each chapter in this structural sequence, we will look to three interweaving themes that appear throughout the book and that can help us to see the chapters as part of an interrelated thematic whole. Our first hermeneutic key to this thematic unity is to notice the pervasiveness of the historical question of the relation between technology and the rise of modernity. However, this is understood not as some esoteric question for specialists; rather what is at stake is the question of our very identity as modern beings. This is revealed by our second hermeneutic key; all of the authors present in this book are well-established academics, but their writing about our environmental crisis is marked by an uncharacteristically personal quality that tells us something important about the topic. There is a kind impulsiveness, here, stemming from an urgency that sometimes overflows into recklessness, manifest in the breaking of taboos—including discussing such forbidden and impermissible topics as Sloterdijk's weather warfare, Spengler's philosophy of history, Indigenous water protectors, and a papal encyclical. This urgency reveals a common conviction that we must think carefully, open-mindedly, and critically about our actions now more than ever; however, it seems to be marked by two distinct types of motivations. The first is moved more by the "aesthetic" leveling of all things in the world to a single utilitarian value as understood through the lens of Heidegger's critique of "standing-reserve."

The second is moved more by the silencing of human voices and their loss of agency. We will suggest that these differing motivations create real tensions, but they do not have to be exclusive. In particular, an attention to Lally's theme of "ontogenesis," the bringing into being through the co-production of life and the creation of art and technology, can make this tension a productive rather than a paralyzing one and, thus, serve as a third hermeneutic key for reading the interweaving voices of this collection.

THE HISTORICAL NATURE OF THE PROBLEM: SUSTAINABILITY AND THE QUESTION OF MODERNITY

Bonfiglioli's contribution is the most explicitly historical. It also does the most to tie the discussion to the question of sustainability as a contested concept. As she tells us, "The notion of sustainability justifies and conditions the operations of the contemporary ecological discourse, constituting it as one of the main events-statements of the twentieth century." As such this concept plays a substantial role in our understanding of ourselves and what would constitute a good life. However, it is also "constituted by a tangle of technical discourses (whether legal, economic, ecological or simply administrative) and political." These often operate subterraneously, unbeknownst to us, opening some aspects of truth, while foreclosing others, and mixing yet others with dangerous illusions. These chapters do considerable work bringing to light a genealogy of these forces so that they can be understood and evaluated. This means looking to key points in history when the effects of these meanings became sedimented. Several of our chapters point to a new emphasis on *sustainability* language that emerges in the last decades of the twentieth century, notably in the *Brundtland Report* (1987), the *Rio Summit on Development and the Environment* (1992), and the *Kyoto Conference on Global Warming* (1998).

For example, in my chapter I show how the first generation of academic environmental ethicists in the mid-twentieth century believed that philosophers must use their talents and training to protect endangered ecosystems, but also that this engagement would transform philosophy, revealing the intrinsic value of the more-than-human world and overcoming the anthropocentrism of modernity. From the latter part of the twentieth century, this emphasis on intrinsic value has been increasingly criticized by "ecomodernists" who argue that the older environmentalism cannot address despair about climate change and has failed to recognize human creativity. I go on to argue that the ecomodernists are right to suggest that our philosophical anthropology must include a greater emphasis on the positive aspects of human life, but that this does not mean rejecting the original insight that nature has a goodness beyond merely instrumental value.

This sets up a central question for ethics, namely the tension between human and nonhuman sources of value, but Bonfiglioli's chapter provides a much deeper temporal horizon that reveals this contribution, as well as the others in the book, to be a part of a wider conversation about the meaning of modernity itself. She gives us a careful etymological tracing of the word "sustainability" and its cognates in French and German as well as a close reading of historical documents to show that the idea of "sustainability," as an explicitly formulated concept, first arose in response to the threat of deforestation in the seventeenth century. The increasing use of charcoal to fuel burgeoning industry and wood to build ships for trade with foreign colonies was indispensable for the mercantilist economies of early modern Europe and led to increasingly unsustainable cutting of timber. The relation between trade and war, as well as the centrality of merchant and military navies, meant that a supply of wood was a national security issue. Thus, for both Colbert's government under Louis XIV and the ministers of Charles II, developing policies for sustainable timber harvests became a major priority. These were national problems that existed in mutually reinforcing relations with the new rise of the nation-state, and these interrelations were to guide early modern thinkers in France and England and eventually Germany toward seeing nature as a supply of raw materials that need to be managed under the strict control of centralized governmental powers informed by accurate and value-free science and thus divorced from historical uses and local contexts. Thus, not only does the quest for a sustainable energy source to avert a looming crisis threaten to return us to characteristically modern views of axiology and ontology, *it was exactly the same worry that helped contribute to the rise of Modernity in the first place.*

By way of this insightful historical work, we can see that modernity and sustainability are fundamentally interwoven. So not only is the question of what sustainability means a burning contemporary issue in applied ethics, but it is fundamentally linked to our understanding of ourselves as modern. But as Bonfiglioli also points out, this version of modernity was always a contested one. If the policy disputes rose to the level of Ministers of Finance and Ministers of Defense, the real intellectual work that has shaped our understanding of sustainability was worked out by the forest managers themselves, including, most importantly, Hanns Carl von Carlowitz, who "defines and uses, for the first time in history, the term sustainability (*Nachhaltigkeit*) and its derivatives (*nachhaltige, nachhaltend*)." On the other hand, it is also from within the community of forester managers that arises determined resistance to the reduction of the forest to measurable quantities of timber, and Bonfiglioli quotes another early "Forstklassiker," who "warned that pressing the life of a forest to fit into formulas and numbers was a process that would eventually provoke a 'revenge of nature' . . . [for] 'the growth and health of forests depend on very thin and deeply hidden yarns.'"

Thus, we can see the inspiration for the environmental movement provided by Aldo Leopold, who was himself a forest manager, and John Muir in his debates with Pinchot Gifford, first chief of the US Forest Service, as a part of a deeper history in which what seem like minor debates about forest management turn out to play a central role in our understanding of ourselves in relation to nature. This means that the turn to the language of sustainability in the 1980s and 1990s is not merely a reassertion of modern values, but only the contemporary manifestation of a much longer debate about the nature of modernity that has been going on as long as modernity itself. As a further provocation Bonfiglioli mentions, almost in passing, that while "it was not until the seventeenth century that this concern took the form of explicit texts, documents, and regulations to compose public policies specifically focused on the theme," worries about environmental degradation, particularly loss of forests and soil erosion, had already preoccupied classical thinkers, including most notably *Plato*. This suggests that the debates about forest management not only play a larger role in our understanding of the contested nature of modernity, as it arises with the formation of the nation-state and mercantilism in economics and politics, but they also play a larger role in the contested role of Platonic idealism in the rise of modernity. In this vein it is intriguing that Carlowitz coins the term, *nachhaltend*, because there was no word to talk about what he wanted policy to achieve, namely a supply of timber that would be "continuous, stable and sustainable" —a desire that clearly evokes the language that Plato uses to talk about knowledge of the eternal forms as opposed to the unstable nature of finite things.

Bonfiglioli reveals a connection between the need for sustainability, particularly with regard to forest management, and the rise of modernity that is both fascinating and little known. But this is no esoteric thesis of interest only to historians. She also gives a powerful account of the way words are never univocal, but fluid sites of multiple lines of influence and values that are always amenable to change and adaptation, in which we are "being transformed into a communion in which we do not remain what we were."[1]

The contribution of Danish philosopher Lars Botin is, like mine, focused on the ethical implications of environmental philosophy, but for him, too, the question of our understanding of modernity is never far from the surface. Botin opens his chapter with a quote from the low-budget 1959 sci-fi movie *Plan 9 from Outer Space*. It has come to the attention of the Aliens that humans are about to destroy themselves and their planet, and in response to this crisis the aliens attempt to plan a way to avert the catastrophe. After the first eight plans all fail, on the ninth and final try, they awaken our dead ancestors to intervene in our destructive path; of course the results are another ridiculous failure. This is a humorous reference to a cult classic, but it points to the poignancy of the recognition of our failures to plan for the future, particularly in the face of crisis. For Botin, as for many of the thinkers in the volume, this recognition is a painful burden, but it can also lead to an intellectual humility that overcomes the single-minded focus on progress that marks some understandings of what it means to be modern. Botin's point is to open a more pluralistic reading of modernity and in fact of being as a whole. He appeals to Deleuze and Guattari's metaphor of reality as a fluid rhizome of becoming that suggests our task in living sustainably is one of "constructing, creating and shaping a framework that upholds, preserves, rejuvenates, invigorates, enhances, empowers and emancipates what it means to be human, and what it means to be together as human/technological assemblages, on this earth that we are given."

The contribution of Galit Wellner, a philosopher at Tel Aviv University, is also historical although it focuses less on deconstructing past sedimented meanings of sustainability than on linking it to contemporary events that themselves call for novelty. She thereby provides an important balance for the collection, but the intended goal remains significantly similar to the other more overtly historical contributions: namely, that of opening the meaning of "sustainability" to alternative possibilities not addressed in mainstream conversations about environmental concerns. In fact she opens her chapter writing, "Since the Brundtland Report coined the term 'sustainable development' in 1987, the word sustainability continues to be expanded and charged with new meanings. The expansions are frequently needed as we face a constant flow of changes in our environments." She points out that the Brundtland report correctly notes that "a world in which poverty and inequity are endemic will always be prone to ecological and other crises. Sustainable development requires meeting the basic needs of all and extending to all the opportunity to satisfy their aspirations for a better life."[2] This allows us to see environmental concern as merely one pillar of a just social order that also includes concern for economic well-being and equality. Wellner goes on to suggest that the transformations, or better metamorphoses, of our world brought about by digital technologies in the succeeding thirty years calls for a further opening of discussions about sustainability, this time toward a fourth pillar, that of culture, with a particular emphasis on human-technology relations, that will open a whole new context in which to encounter things. As she puts it, "Whereas, in classical postphenomenology, the world has been usually conceived as mute or simply uninteresting, the challenges of sustainable development urge us to give more attention to the role of the world in the relations between humans and technologies."

As Bonfiglioli, Botin, Wellner, and the other contributors to this volume show that "sustainability" plays a vital role in our understanding of ourselves as a modern culture, and their work is a valuable call to take up the conversation about that contested word with a series of thoughtful questions about our place in the natural world and who we hope to become. This gives perhaps the most plausible justification for the book. Our effort will not magically produce a *sustainable* society, but we are performing the ongoing work of keeping open this site of meaning and identity formation in the face of the threat of collapse under a totalizing economic program and attempting to shape our understanding of ourselves and our relation to nature in ways that are richer and more open to the possibilities of goodness and meaning.

THE PASSION OF THE PERSONAL: DISGUST AT THE FOULING OF THE WORLD/DEHUMANIZATION

The urgency of this task and the stakes involved make this discussion a deeply personal one. Thus, in this collection, we see academics writing with an uncharacteristic impulse to discuss their own personal lives—and to challenge academic taboos in other ways as well. Don Ihde, one of the early and most prominent philosophers of technology in the world, discusses solar energy with relation to the history of our scientific understanding of optical technologies and the current political climate, but the majority of the chapter describes his own personal experience with the life-enriching nature of solar power as framed by his rather poetic title, "Is it Too Late to 'Let the Sunshine in?'" The normally more reserved Jan Kyrre Berg Friis, a philosopher of technology at the University of Copenhagen, ends his chapter with a similar mingling of an appeal to the contemporary political climate and the invocation of the personal. He critiques Trump's renewed commitment to coal and then says that we must "begin regaining access to that nature of which we are inextricably a part and to give the young access to it—if not my soon to be born granddaughter may actually come to experience the end of the world as we know it."

This personal element in Ihde's and Friis's chapters is marked by political frustration and a personal poignancy. The majority of these chapters are marked by that poignancy, but in many we get the sense that this pathos is merely the outward expression of an even deeper and more intense anger: rage against the machine, rage against the loss of beauty, rage against the collapse of all possibilities into one flattened sameness.

Babette Babich is one of the premier living philosophers practicing what we might call an aesthetic method of philosophy,[3] and her contribution here is characteristically provoking and moving as a revolt against this collapse.

She wants to begin to address our environmental crisis by "talking about the weather," which as she points out is conventionally a euphemism for idle chatter, wasting time, shooting the breeze. Interestingly, environmental scientists make a dramatic point of saying that they are talking about *climate* and *not weather*, for they are real scientists not meteorologists (television personas who are known less for their predictive ability than charm, good looks, and—if internet click-bait can be trusted—wardrobe malfunctions). Climate is general and amenable to scientific study; whereas weather events are particular and therefore, in their particularity, not scientifically intelligible. So in our national discussions after a tragic storm, climatologists are careful to say that we cannot definitively attribute any one particular event to climate change, just that *in general* destructive storms are now more likely. Our science, like our corporate surveillance, moves from particular quantitative measurements to aggregate data in which the individual is suppressed for predictive power about the general. A revealing example of this comes from a controversy about an article *National Geographic* published in August 2018. They had shown a starving polar bear that they said was dying because of human-caused climate change. The picture had a powerful emotional appeal, but scientists wrote and objected that science cannot tell us if this particular bear would have suffered even if the general conditions of climate change did not hold. *National Geographic* retracted the picture.

Babich's aesthetic (*aesthenomai:* I feel) prose pulls us the other direction, toward the intelligibility of the sensuous, of the particular. She begins by referring to Luce Irigaray's work, *Heidegger and the Forgetting of Air*, where "atmosphere, breath are intimate affairs," evoking interiority and reciprocity. However, she quickly moves to Sloterdijk and his reflections on the way modern warfare reigns terror from the sky. Here, our concern is the opposite of Stephen Pinker's (discussed in the Friis's chapter), who merely counts dead bodies or rather plots numbers of the dead on abstract and quantitative graphs. For Babich, as for Sloterdijk, the aesthetics—the particularities—of the mode of death matter. For example Babich does not just tell us how many people died in the firebombing of Dresden; rather she explains that "the attackers aimed to generate a fiery central vacuum by dropping a high concentration of incendiary bombs, to produce a hurricane-like suction effect—a so-called firestorm . . . a special atmosphere capable of burning, carbonizing, desiccating, and asphyxiating at least 35,000 people in the space of one night [which] constituted a radical innovation in the domain of rapid mass killings." This is death from the sky, from one knows not where, and to which one can never respond, death that kills by taking away our very air. Chlorine gas, atomic bombs, Napalm, unmanned death drones: in this "atmosphere" no one can breathe or truly live; *ruah, pneuma, spiritus* suffocated.

These are things that we do not want to know or to think about. "Thus the backstory to all fake news concerns how what is 'fit to print' gets into print and how what is silenced is silenced. Think of Harvey Weinstein over the years, but think too of all the Harveys there have been in the entertainment industry, in academia, anywhere there is power, unmentioned scandals." Nonetheless, the aesthetic is merely "sense perception," and we cannot cut ourselves off from our senses forever. The stench of open sewers in medieval cities may have been more immediately apparent, but our stench eventually seeps its way out of the institutions where the old people are stored, out of the funeral homes where the bodies are hygienically (and discreetly) burned, and through the scent of the air fresheners—to trouble our urban paradise. And if one could walk in less than an hour beyond the reach of London coal smoke and the reek of Parisian tanneries, there are increasingly fewer places to escape the reach of modern contamination.

Here Babich ties her aesthetic critique most forcefully to the repressed aspects of modernism by summoning our despair, appealing to the rain-drenched and lifeless urbanism of *Blade Runner*, and our disgust, appealing to the liminal crossings of life and death in *Frankenstein*:

> Shelley's modern Prometheus was already a creature wrought of body parts, medical detritus, a creature, as a result, of "proud" flesh, insulted, inflamed: in stasis between necrotized tissue and still viable, still functioning organs. This condition of necrotization and inflammation is the condition of any transplant, and the drugs one takes to prevent rejection of the organ are as much to prevent the body's reaction to the decay in today's medical innovations, hearts and kidneys, lungs and livers, from cadavers, human and not (xenotransplantation) but above all skin, even faces, and limbs.

Babich is careful to pick medical applications in order to be clear that she is not just naively responding to the "yuck-factor" inherent in new technologies. It is obvious that no one would find organ transplants morally objectionable or argue that we should not do them; life-saving and life-enhancing medical technologies are the paradigmatic example of why a pure techno-skepticism is untenable. In fact, the cultural anthropologists tell us that at the far side of the cultural horizon in the transition between hunter-gather and agricultural economies, we find a group of partnerless old men; the women have accepted the harsh realities of modernity—so that their children can go to school and to the hospital.

Rather Babich points to things like the aesthetics of putting a half rotting pig heart into one's body, the yellow foam oozing from the lungs of a victim of chlorine gas, the hyperbolic excesses of Sloterdijk, or our own timid embarrassment at the mention of "conspiracy theories," to wake us up and to call us to a radical rethinking of our way of life and what we are doing to the world; "there is such a thing as Climate Change but, like Pogo looking for the enemy, we ourselves are it." At its most vacuous and formalistic, the question of "sustainability" merely tells you whether an activity could continue indefinitely, but says nothing about whether the activity should go on. Babich is showing us that the results of our modern desire to become "masters and possessors" of nature are not merely technical problems to be fixed by technical solutions (geoengineering), but neither are they merely "ethical" problems to be fixed by increasing tolerance and greater inclusivity. Rather they are deeper problems with our relation to meaning, value, and purpose. Put bluntly, our problems are revealed not only by worries about empirical data (rising temperatures) and guilt about ethical culpability (the breaking of a normative law), but also by disgust at what we are doing to the world (turning everything, including our own bodies and the very air into mere tools of power and control, without concern for their intrinsic goodness or beauty).

Friis's chapter also has an important aesthetic element as seen in the confrontation between Nietzsche's *On Truth and Lie in the Extra-Moral Sense* and Stephen Pinker's *Enlightenment Now: The Case for Reason, Science, Humanism and Progress*. What is at stake for Friis are the limits of a reductive rationality that campaigns under the banner of "progress." This does not at all mean, as Pinker would charge, that Friis is celebrating irrationalism. Rather he is appealing to a truth that transcends human capacities, a truth to which we can respond rather that one over which we exert domination and control. We have often neglected this truth in modernity, and so "what is needed is wisdom: a new type of thoughtful acting or 'letting be' that has the courage to perceive and accept humanity's place in the natural world, that is, to act truthfully to nature." For Friis this "does not mean to abandon technology or science or analytical reflection, it means to escape the one-dimensional metaphysics of scientific rationality and to add a new dimension, one of openness to being, to nature, to the human mind." Thus, we see this critique, running through many of the chapters, that certain tendencies in modernity are leveling all things into a single uniform and drab world. Friis's suggestion is that there has been a vast and colorful array of human cultures in the past and still flourishing at the margins today. None of these can we adopt whole cloth, but they can open possibilities for creative retrieval and inspiration; the example he gives here is that of the Kyoto School.

While Babich and Friis put the aesthetic method to work in rich and compelling ways, Brendan Mahoney gives us an explicit methodological defense of the aesthetic as an ethico-ontological category. He begins by drawing our attention to a proposed wind turbine farm in Nantucket Sound off Cape Cod. The local residents generally support sustainable energy; they just do not want this project so close to where they live—and on aesthetic grounds. This sounds like the worst form of "NIMBY"ism (Not in My Backyard) that Ihde so fiercely criticizes, but Mahoney thinks there is an important issue at stake. "Instead of being an objection to the disruption of their scenic views, the opponents of the project object to the potential loss of the singularity and uniqueness of Nantucket Sound. The threat of the Cape Wind Project is that it will reduce the Sound to one more industrial landscape, indistinct from and wholly replaceable by any other industrial landscape; in brief the Sound would become merely a power plant."

To support his claim, Mahoney also appeals to Heidegger's philosophy of technology. "Where [Enframing] holds sway, it drives out every other possibility of revealing" so that everything is revealed *only* as standing-reserve. In earlier epochs, one way things could appear was as resources, but that was not their essential or sole mode of being; in the modern epoch, Heidegger claims, this is no longer the case. To illustrate this point, he provides a striking image: "Nature becomes a gigantic gasoline station, an energy source for modern technology and industry." This leads Mahoney to a rather stunning result: "within the logic of Heidegger's concept of Enframing, both [burning coal and massive solar-arrays] *are ontologically indistinguishable*: i.e., they reduce phenomena to a calculable coherence of forces and challenge them forth to yield distributable and storable energy." This is quite a provocative way to put it, but many of the contributors to this volume share what seem to be compelling worries that are best expressed aesthetically. If our new "green" technologies are indeed "sustainable," in the sense of being processes that are able to continue indefinitely, what reason do we have to think they would not do it by turning everything into a cog in some horrid machine? In other words, if "sustainable technologies" are able to save the world, would it be a world whose continued existence would be worth caring about?

This is not an anthology of Heideggerian philosophy of technology, and Heidegger's work and even his name remain a flash point of contention among the contributors. That debate is too complex to enter here, but it is worth noting that those drawn to Heidegger tend to be motivated most deeply by worries about the degradation of the world, particularly as this is expressed in aesthetic terms; those opposed to him are more worried about the dehumanization of the person. In our view, as elaborated more fully below, these two moments are always related. However, the differences of emphasis can have significant philosophical implications. In this collection of chapters, the "humanist" strand may be less emphasized. We see some of its characteristic motivations in Ihde's celebration of human creativity and technological advancement, and in Wellner and Botin's critique of the neglect of economic considerations in the contemporary environmental movement, but the most insistent voice for this position comes from Thomas Jeannot, whose contribution is based on an ethics of free creation that transcends the bounds of capitalist alienation.

Jeannot's chapter is an interweaving reflection on two aphorisms (or slogans or koans—as you prefer), one from Pope Francis and the other from Karl Marx:

> There can be no adequate ecology without an adequate anthropology. —Francis

> One basis for life and another basis for science is a priori a lie. —Marx

Jeannot connects the two by saying, "I will suggest that it is possible to establish a relation between a naturalist form of humanism and a personalist form without slurring the identity of either one." It is clearly a personalist account that he thinks will provide us with the "adequate anthropology" which will open onto the possibility of an "adequate ecology," but he needs the appeal to Marx for several reasons. Perhaps the most important is the Marxian link between the alienations of capitalism and a "positivistic" reductive materialism that work together to present a natural world that has no other purpose than to be exploited.

At the heart of Jeannot's chapter is a critique of physicalism. In his reading of the contemporary literature, he finds that physicalism begins with the contradiction between human experience and truth as revealed by science, and proceeds by reducing the former to the latter. This reduction includes the repudiation of a laundry list of the illusions of ordinary experience, but particularly significant are "freedom of action" and "social agency." Jeannot thinks that a non-reductive resolution to this prima facie conflict between science and experience will have resonances with a Marxian humanism, such that overcoming "physicalism" and overcoming "economism" cannot be accomplished separately. Further, the turn to Marx helps deepen the critique of modern alienation, particularly as related to ethics. In his engagement with Amy Wendling on the topic of ideology critique, Jeannot claims: "Among the many aspects of these ruling ideas, which Wendling presents as a concrete dialectical totality, two are especially relevant to our consideration, namely, 'the turning of private property into an ontological foundation of selfhood, and the reduction of all morality to exchange value.' This is a good definition of economism." What is being lost is not only a general sense of human subjectivity and social action, but one in which the human flourishes by way of creative labor and social relations that are partially constitutive of that flourishing. Jeannot and Ihde are clearly divided by crucial metaphysical and theological differences, but they both celebrate human creativity and self-realization, and perhaps it is not a coincidence that they are both critics of the Heideggerian project.

ONTOGENESIS: THE PRO/CREATION OF NEW BEINGS

The previous section reveals a tension between the desire to account for the goodness and beauty of being in an aesthetic ontology and the desire to account for the creativity and dignity of the human person in a eudemonistic anthropology. In our view, an affirmation of the goodness of the human person and an affirmation of the goodness of the natural world are interwoven. While this integrative view may be appealing, the two concerns are often bifurcated in a contemporary milieu marked by a lingering Cartesian anti-naturalism, on the one hand, and the inversions of this dualism among some of its environmentalist and other anti-humanist critics, on the other. Thus, even thinkers who in principle affirm the compatibility of an aesthetics of being and a humanism of the person often tend to emphasize one or the other of these concerns, leading to continued tension between "shallow" and "deep" environmentalism. In this section, we will focus on a third theme that will go a long way to making this tension productive rather than paralyzing—namely, the question of coming into being, as this occurs in art, reproduction, and the emergence of new technologies.

As with the other two hermeneutic keys we have proposed, this question of re/production by which things come into being brings together many of the chapters into a common conversation, but it is particularly prominent in the contributions of Belu, Glazebrook, and Lally. Dana Belu is a philosopher of technology at California State University whose recent work includes careful and insightful philosophical reflection on the possibilities and abuses of reproductive technologies, work that thereby provides practical and empirically grounded guidance for the practice of ethical reproductive medicine. With regard to our current theme, the critical element in her work provides an important check on a naïve encomium to genesis. Re/production can involve serious abuses of our ethical responsibilities by turning human beings into mere resources in a logic of fungibility by which each individual's characteristic way of being is made transparent before an indifferent logic of resource utilization. Strikingly, she shows how this logic is indifferent to the differences between humans and nonhumans.

Like Babich, Danu appeals to the aesthetics of medical technologies, not only to enter directly into debates surrounding the applied ethics of the issue, but also to make a wider point about the increasing reduction of all things to resources available for technical manipulation. Belu's point of critique is the way that in contemporary medical practice, women are set up as extractable resources in the service of reproductive technologies, in particular through gestational surrogacy. In this practice a donated ovum is fertilized with a sperm via IVF and then implanted into a womb. Her focus is on the experience and treatment of the woman who acts as the gestational surrogate. But in the course of this discussion she brings up the fact that while currently a woman is needed to donate the ovum, with new techniques researchers have recently been able to extract and develop a potentially viable one from the tissue of an aborted fetus. This would "produce biologically motherless babies, babies whose mothers were never born, 'unborn mothers.'" Belu's point is not merely to shock us with the strangeness of this practice, but to point us to an underlying logic. She recognizes that there are important ethical issues to think through here, for example, "the thorny issue of informed consent is bypassed altogether since . . . there is no woman to consult." But the wider point is not limited to this context only.

> We see how the potential reproductive energy contained in this stock—that is, in the ovarian tissue of the dead fetus—is extracted, challenged forth so that, as Heidegger stated, "the energy concealed in [its] nature is unlocked, what is unlocked is transformed, what is transformed is stored up, what is stored up is, in turn, distributed, and what is distributed is switched about ever anew." The procedure dispenses with the woman as subject and with the egg as object so that they both "disappear into the objectlessness of standing-reserve."

Belu develops this line of thought more fully in *Heidegger, Reproductive Technologies and the Motherless Age*.[4] In her chapter for this collection, she emphasizes the significance of her work for an environmental philosophy. The key insight that she uses to link the two is that the same modern logic, which makes all things available for manipulation, turns both persons and nonhuman beings into mere resources. "Unlike a resource, a rational subject defines herself through individual acts of reflection and autonomous choice. As such she is not interchangeable with other subjects or with objects, *but an object is not necessarily fungible, either* [my emphasis]." On Belu's reading, it is not a coincidence that energy use becomes the central focus of our environmental crisis. For the modern drive for efficiency "places an uncritical value on the reduction of all things to resources available on demand. Resource optimization, flexibility and storing become dominant, self-sufficient goals. Thus, a constant ordering as 'continuous attack' discloses a world of uniform and replaceable entities whose potential is 'stored up.'" Here Belu shows us how the modern logic of resource optimization crosses the human/nonhuman divide and implicitly points to an overcoming that would see their interweaving in a more positive light.

Trish Glazebrook is a philosopher deeply influenced by Heidegger but also by neo-Marxian critiques of global capitalism, and her contribution can be read in dialogue with Jeannot's but also with Belu's work as part of a rich and ongoing discussion about the relations between technology, economics, philosophy of science, and ontology. As we saw above, the Heideggerian critique centers on the worry that all things are being turned into standing-reserve (*Bestand*). It is at this central point that Glazebrook makes her pivot toward an economic critique. She tells us, "I prefer to translate '*Bestand*' as '*resource*' because the *Gestell* of technology is a revealing that challenges and sets upon nature as something that can be exploited." The question of the similarities and differences between Glazebrook's notion of exploitation and Belu's notion of fungibility is an important one that takes us beyond the scope of this introduction. Here we can only note that both take us to a common reduction of the human and nonhuman world, as this "also reduces human being to an exploitable resource."

For Glazebrook this common reduction of the human and nonhuman to a logic of resource becomes the basis for a reversal that values all life. In a moving dialectical opposition, she writes, "the current global struggle is an ontological battle between oil, structuring profit in the *Gestell* of capital, and water structuring life," and calling on the wisdom of the indigenous water keepers she ends with the invitation that we be "awakened from the *Gestell* of capital into a hydrontology that values life as an end in itself."

Irish philosopher Róisín Lally follows in this vein making the question of ontogenesis thematically explicit, but she attempts to extend the notion of a non-reductive coming into being to include humans and nonhuman life, but also nonliving beings. Coming into being requires a unifying intelligibility that delimits the thing and allows it to stand out against the flux of time. In modern philosophy, we regard this creative activity as a product of the human faculties of understanding and will. In recent work, Lally shows how these nominalist tendencies are not characteristic of modernity as such, but rather emerge from a particular strand of late-medieval thought. As an alternative, she turns to the work of Aristotle for whom a thing's *telos* allows it being independently of the human mind. However, Aristotle's ontology is limited to living organisms (and perhaps elements) and therefore has little to say about technological beings. To remedy this, she calls on Gilbert Simondon's creative re-interpretation of causality to talk about ontogenesis in a way that includes nonliving things.

This provides a method for helping us to better understand both the distinction and the evolutionary tension between ancient technology and advanced modern technology such as wind turbines. For like Babich, Friis, and Botin, Lally argues that climate is not merely an engineering problem. Rather, thinking ontologically, with a special attention to genesis, reveals engineers as generally working at the second stage of the individuation of sustainable technologies. Ontogenetically, she calls on artists and designers to be a part of the search for sustainable technologies at the moment of their incipient becoming in response to changed situations, such as our own. Artist Rebekah Wilkins-Pepiton shares this interest in the emergence of beings in their interweaving of history, materiality, and intelligibility. Lally's ongoing interest in the crossing of image and word, line and meaning, is manifest in her collaboration with Wilkins-Pepiton, whose contribution of the cover painting becomes a visual/philosophical collaboration of the kind they both cultivate. The work, "Ontogenesis in the Anthropocene," is made from copper and horse chestnut ink on handmade paper, created from combat fatigues. It explores our current, collective, and ongoing relationship with the natural world, integrating many of the threads at work in this collection and beginning the re-traversal from text to the elemental that it hopes to inspire.

This book reveals many problems in our rhetoric of "sustainability." After reading it, we are clear about how deeply tied it is to some of the most problematic aspects of modernity and some of the most pernicious power structures at work today. However, the overall sense does not seem to be one that would counsel abandoning the word. Rather as these authors point out, it is a contested word with fluid and multiple meanings. Sustainability can be used to describe a situation that merely may be prolonged indefinitely, but it also resonates with a much greater range of meanings and stems from a rich source. Bonfiglioli gives its proximate formation in early modernity as a clearly articulated concept, but natural language can betray its users by carrying a prehistorical richness they did not intend. *Sustainability* comes from *sustinere*, a word with as multiple and ambiguous a range of meanings as you could hope to find. One of its meanings is "put off, defer, delay." We could surely connect this with the post-structuralists' notion of *différence* to suggest that the word "sustainability" itself resists the reduction of its use to one final and irrevocable sedimentation. More negatively, the reassuring language of sustainability can lead us to "putt off" and "delay" the important task of thinking deeply about ourselves and our relation to nature. This book attempts to combat that latency in the language of "sustainability." But *sustinere* also means "to hold back, to check, to restrain." Our contribution points out forces and ways of thinking that must be checked in order to open a space for thinking and a more pluralistic relation to nature. We can link this meaning to Friis's appeal to the notion of *wu wei*. However, our contribution is not ultimately limited to critique. *Sustinere* also means "to protect and to guard," but most fundamentally it means "to bear up, to uphold." Our discussion of sustainability suggests that the environmental crisis calls not only for reflection on how to allow the processes of nature to continue, but also for ways to uphold the natural world—and our participation in it—as meaningful and good, so that we can, as Botin puts it, treat the world as a gift. Our contributors do this movingly, and for that gift we are grateful.

NOTES

1. Hans-Georg Gadamer, *Truth and Method* (New York: Bloomsbury Academic, 2013), 387.

2. Ibid., 41–42.

3. Along with Luce Irigaray, Julia Kristeva, Richard Kearney, John Sallis, Alphonso Lingis, and others.

4. Dana Belu, *Heidegger, Reproductive Technology & The Motherless Age* (New York: Palgrave Macmillan, 2017).

Part I

DEFINING SUSTAINABILITY

Chapter 1

Sustainability

A Single Word and a World of Meanings

Cristina Pontes Bonfiglioli

What is the minimum amount of land capable of sustaining the soil structure of a slope during torrential rains? What is the maximum number of people that an interpretive trail in a forest preservation area can receive, without there being a high environmental impact around the trail and in the preservation area itself? What is the maximum amount of chemical pollution that a lake or a river can receive before the toxicity threatens every organic life within it? How many individuals in a wildlife population (whether salmon, crabs, whales, elephants, jaguars, seals, or caribou) or native plants (especially trees such as cedar, oak, rosewood, or chestnut) can be killed/felled without endangering the species they represent? What is the maximum amount of organic matter from human-related activities that can be dumped into a lake without leading it to artificial eutrophication? What is the maximum amount of herbicide that can be used without endangering the farmer who applies it, the groundwater that will receive it from the drainage of rainwater, and the consumer of the fruits and vegetables it helps to grow? Similarly, what is the quantity of cultivable varieties that can be grown together in order to avoid the indiscriminate use of pesticides but with the advantage of ensuring food safety for consumers? Also, what is the maximum amount of particulate matter suspended in the air or the concentration of ozone during the winter that can be borne by the inhabitants of a city, with no incidence much higher than the average hospital admissions or even of the average mortality in the period?

All these questions seem to point to mathematical and statistical equations, capable of accurately and safely defining what is conventionally called *carrying capacity* (Odum, 1971),[1] and later, *resilience*. The latter was born in Materials Science and Engineering and refers to "the ability of metal [or any solid material] to absorb energy when elastically deformed, and then to return it when it is unloaded."[2] The concept of *resilience* is important for several

3

engineering specialties, such as materials engineering, mechanical engineering, and metallurgy, but it was through the engineering branches linked to the management of natural resources—forest engineering, agricultural engineering, and aquacultural engineering—that the term has gained the significance later appropriated by the Ecology of Ecosystems:

> *Resilience* is the capacity of a system to absorb disturbance and reorganize while undergoing a change so as to still retain essentially the same function, structure, identity, and feedbacks. . . . The focus is on the dynamics of the system when it is disturbed far from its modal state. The notion of speed of return to equilibrium leads to what has been termed "engineering resilience."[3]

In fact, as Veiga (2010) points out, "Until the 1980s, the adjective 'sustainable' was a jargon of agronomists, foresters or fishermen, to evoke the possibility of an ecosystem remaining robust and stable (resilient), despite being attacked by some human exploitation."[4]

Today, it is also possible to use another derived term, but with a broader meaning: *biocapacity* or *biological capacity*. This notion is also related to the idea of resilience and, consequently, sustainability:

> Biocapacity measures how biologically productive land is. It is measured in "global hectares": a hectare with the world average biocapacity. Biologically productive land includes cropland, pasture, forests, and fisheries. 16% of the world's biocapacity is in Brazil.
>
> The biocapacity of a territory is affected by physical conditions and people's actions. A pertinent example of this is Iraq, the Mesopotamian marshes were once part of the fertile crescent. Much of this marshland has been drained and become desert. Trade sanctions and social upheavals also reduce people's ability to use land productively. Iraq's land is now estimated to be the least productive in the world.[5]

This notion of a predictability that could be granted by numerically quantifiable measurements for establishing an absolute and unique limit of carrying capacity (resilience) or for determining the biocapacity of a cultivable area—whether fish farming, agricultural production, livestock, or forestry—is the central idea, embedded in the rather broad and often vague meaning of the word "sustainability."

This perception that the term sustainability has a broader meaning than that of resilience or carrying capacity comes, in fact, from the appropriation it underwent during the 1980s. From the institutional point of view—that is for the many international agencies within which a formal speech about the environment or environmental issues is politically validated and characterized as an official ecological discourse based on multilateral conventions and agreements—the term sustainability first appears in the document *Our Common*

Future or the *Brundtland Report* (1987). The history that could be traced from this point onwards would only account for the many official meetings of the various UN bodies that have assisted the process of legitimizing and fixing the term in the media and the global society. Another "historical beginning," with much deeper cultural roots, will look to the origins of the term sustainability in forest management. As we shall below, in 1713, Hanns Carl von Carlowitz (1645–1714) published *Sylvicultura oeconomica* in which he defines and uses, for the first time in Western history, the term sustainability (*Nachhaltigkeit*) and its derivatives (*nachhaltige, nachhaltend*). Carlowitz is considered by many the founder of the field of knowledge today established as forest engineering and also the creator of the modern meaning of the term sustainability.

It is therefore clear that the idea of sustainability and its derivation, the notion of sustainable development, are the result of a semantic convergence of several scientific concepts, originated from engineering, ecology and liberal economics. The theoretical constructs and techniques that support the notion have been developed and implemented as practices of both business and public management of the so-called natural resources since the seventeenth century. Despite its technical origin, the adequacy or normalization of the use of the terms sustainability and sustainable development, and its consequent spread through the modern Western world, is due to multilateral political processes that reach the peak of their characterization during the second half of the twentieth century, and in particular the creation of the World Commission on Environment and Development (the Brundtland Commission). As Veiga (2006) warns:

Since 1987, an intense process of legitimation and normative institutionaliza tion of the term "sustainable development" has begun to take hold. It was in that year that Gro Harlem Brundtland, the president of the World Commission on Environment and Development, characterized sustainable development as a "political concept" and a "broad concept for economic and social progress." What gave rise to this expression was the debate mainly American in the 1960s—that polarized "economic growth" versus "environmental preservation," wholly impregnated by an apocalyptic fear of "demographic explosion," mixed with danger of nuclear war.[6]

Thus, the central meaning attributed to the term sustainability includes the human perception about the risk of the scarcity of natural resources—mainly related to humankind's survival—and the need to spare them for future generations. This highlighted the threat of introducing a *barbarism*[7] into society that would effect a breakdown of governance due to the devastating effects of environmental disasters worldwide—which could destabilize the hegemonic economic and financial system. In response, the notion of sustainability seems a logical, practical, "obvious" and central solution, from a technical, political, and cultural point of view. The term also seems to operate as the engine of a new contemporary metanarrative,[8] that of the "quest for sustainability," which, being institutionalized by the UN and its various agencies and in particular the UNEP (United Nations Environment Program), makes it acceptable and desirable to promote public policy initiatives or technological innovations that, in turn, create and legitimize new terms or synonyms that govern our discourse such as green economy, environmental governance, green procurement, ecosystem management, renewable energy, low carbon economy, and climate neutrality.

The genealogy approach to the term sustainability implies assuming and accepting that both terms—*sustainability* and *sustainable development*—cannot be thought outside the socioeconomic and cultural context that invented them.[9] It is of fundamental importance to recognize that the context to which we refer to is the symbolic construction of a speech on "Nature" that has a particular history, and thereby it becomes possible to reinvent these concepts and take hold of them and use them to force us to think (Deleuze, 1994)[10] and evaluate or direct our actions regarding the pressing socio-environmental issues of our time.

It is precisely this attempt to construct a conceptual map that contains the "different meanings that the idea took in the course of the ages" together with the discursive formations (Foucault, 1969)[11] constituting the genealogy of the term sustainability, that is, all the texts and the concepts of thinkers who helped to build this idea, that Djalali and Vollaard (2008)[12] present in a graphic showing the many different and connected parts of the metanarrative about the history of the ecological thinking system.

Their graphic illustrates the interlocking of countless utterances, represented by various fields of cultural expression. From the *logocentric* (Derrida, 1967)[13] point of view, there are, at the center of the graph, modern philosophers, physicists, economists, natural scientists, biologists, and other modern and postmodern thinkers whose names are "plotted" on colored confluence lines. Above and below this central area of the graph, there are the discursive formations characterized by a lesser emphasis of the *logos* and a greater appeal to the *pathos*, to use a traditional pair of opposites in the Western philosophy. Movie titles, electronic and computer games, science fiction, and fiction novels follow the timeline at the bottom edge of the graph, while the titles of major works and architectural projects accompany the timeline by the top edge of the chart. Those are aesthetic and cultural products that interconnect their discursive effects with the central area of the figure.

The graph undoubtedly points to the immense complexity[14] that comes with the noun, which has been established as an iconic word of the modern world and understood as a synonym for the idea of a planetary ecological unity that has to be conquered or attained. Sustainability can be either a civilizing goal;

a motivation for civil society organizations; a technological challenge for the industry; a political dispute in UN bodies; a marketing target for consumption; and a desired public image of virtually all contemporary corporations, whether governmental or private. It is this polyvalence of the term that stuns and inspires us, but also makes it so hard to make sense of what we mean by "sustainability" and what cultural, historical, and political work it is doing.

My main contribution, here, is to look to the principles, notions, and concepts that made possible the theoretical foundation of the word sustainability during the seventeenth century and thereby to uncover significant meanings that the term, often covertly, still carries. From this process of formal conceptualization, it is possible to see its appearance in mercantilist Europe inside a school of thought dedicated to the "well managing of natural resources" for any nation. This new approach to the public administration of natural resources has been institutionalized over the following centuries through the increasingly efficient development of scientific practices and methodologies applied to the growth or maintenance of European forested areas.[15] These practices would lead, much later, to the emergence of environmentalism.

This is complicated because "environmentalism" has at least two different historical trajectories, both independent of sustainability. Environmentalism was first used in the early 1900s specifically as a new approach to human behavior that would counter the prevailing overemphasis on genetics and the corresponding neglect of the social environment.[16] But it soon came to describe an ethical approach to the relations between humans and everything that is alive on Earth. In this use it inherited a tradition of respect for the nonhuman world present in various places, such as German romanticism and American transcendentalism; it also appears, later, in Albert Schweizer's *Ethics* (1875–1965); in the Pinchot versus Muir controversy and the origins of the Sierra Club in the United States; in the ecosophy of Arne Naess (1912–2009) and in the thought of Rachel Carson (1907–1964).

Thus, it is in this way that we perceive the possibility of assigning to the word sustainability a use as a synonym of *ecology* and *ecosystem* and even *environmentalism* as a whole, and by way of this "semantic migration" to generate other meanings in fields of knowledge as diverse as political ecology, environmental justice, conservation biology, environmental law, ecological economics, environmentalism[17] and, of course, sustainable development. In these uses, it amalgamates the knowledge and often obfuscates the controversies present in and among the ecological and economic sciences (biogeography, conservation biology, human ecology, phytosociology, ethology, forest sciences, agronomy, political economy, and fishing engineering), philosophies about environmental ethics and the law of nature, ecological economics theories, and legal texts and treaties. All the disciplines construct and constitute the discursive operations characteristic of the experience of living the so-called environmental or ecological crisis, which is increasingly evident at this beginning of the twenty-first century.

"SCARCITY AS THE MOTHER OF INVENTION": THE EMERGENCE OF SUSTAINABILITY AS AN IDEA AND AS A WORD

Seventeenth-century Europe saw the strengthening of mercantilism and the development of the territorial acquisitions obtained during the Age of Exploration. England, the Netherlands, Italy, Germany, and France had high economic growth thanks to the set of measures that guaranteed great control and intervention of the state in the economy. Such practices were based on the accumulation of precious metals, trade protectionism, the guarantee of raw materials for the growing manufacturing industry and strong incentive to foreign trade based on surplus production.

The period saw a renewed interest in public administration among the leading European monarchies, which were politically mobilized by the English Restoration and the policies implemented by King Charles II from 1660 onward and by the French mercantilism of Jean-Baptiste Colbert (1619–1683), adviser to King Louis XIV (the "Sun King"), Intendant of Finance and Secretary of the Royal Navy.

It was also within this framework of references that the first ideas arose about the relevance that science and technology could have for the development of the Modern National States that had been established during the fifteenth century and for the progress of civilization as a whole. The South African professor of history Jacobus A. Du Pisani makes the point thus:

> Western modernity and the belief in progress are almost synonymous. During the Renaissance ideas of cyclical recurrence were propagated, but Reformation thinkers recovered their belief in the linear progress of humanity. In 1683 the French scientist Fontenelle first articulated the Great Idea of Progress, i.e., "that mankind with the new science and improved technology had entered on a road of necessary and unlimited progress." During the Enlightenment and its aftermath (1750–1900) the idea of progress reached its zenith in the Western civilization and as a result of the work of Turgot, Condorcet, Saint-Simon, Comte, Hegel, Marx, Spencer and many others became the dominant idea of the period. The link between progress, and modern, empirical, and exact science was consolidated and the conviction that science was the golden avenue to the future and would give humankind mastery over nature grew stronger.[18]

This interweaving of science, technology, belief in progress, and European imperialism was soon to effect the deep roots of the crisis with which we are still living, and by the mid-seventeenth century, all the great monarchies begin almost simultaneously to glimpse the first signs of an energy crisis due to the scarcity of wood for shipbuilding and civil construction, for remodeling of damaged vessels, and the supply of charcoal to the nascent manufacturing industry and metallurgy. The German intellectual historian, Ulrich Grober, whose work I follow closely in this section, notes in particular the link between "sustainability" and national security: "Timber was a strategic resource. Most of the new manufactures would heavily depend on sufficient and reasonably-priced charcoal. The continual growth of foreign trade, a decisive element of the mercantilist economy, was impossible without an efficient merchant navy. Commerce was considered a form of warfare. It demanded protection by an armada of war vessels."[19]

Pisani makes the links with our contemporary situation explicit:

Georg Agricola,[20] a German mining engineer, described the negative impacts of woodcutting and mining on wildlife as early as the 16th century. [But] by the 18th century, because of the massive consumption of wood for ship-building, mining and many other purposes, a shortage of wood became a very real danger in Europe. Fears that such a shortage would threaten the basis of people's existence stimulated a new way of thinking in favor of the responsible use of natural resources in the interest of the present and future generations, very similar to the thinking behind sustainable development today.[21]

In England, John Evelyn (1620–1706), renowned writer and landscaper at the court of King Charles II, had been nominated in 1662 by the Royal Society,[22] an institution he had helped found two years earlier, to lead a team of noble experts of the time designated to deal with the issue of wood reduction available for shipbuilding at the request of the British Royal Navy's high commissioners. According to Grober,

Those fears were not unfounded. Since 1500, Britain had been continually losing much of her woodlands and house-building material. New glass factories and ironworks consumed huge amounts of charcoal, their only fuel. During the Civil War (1642–1651) many of the traditional feudal laws and customs protecting the woods had collapsed or were abandoned. As the countryside was more and more deforested, a potentially disastrous resource crisis came in sight.[23]

On February 16, 1664, Evelyn presented to the king, the Royal Society, and the public his work, *Sylva, or a Discourse of Forest Trees and the Propagation of Timber in His Majesties Dominions*. Since then, the book has been reprinted with revisions and extensions numerous times, and it is widely recognized as a seminal publication in the field of forestry management. Grober points out that "the book became a seventeenth century bestseller, and instigated, according to Evelyn's remarks in later editions, the planting of millions of trees all over England. It tackled the timber problem in a way that certainly went beyond the schemes of the Royal Navy."[24]

The work is a comprehensive essay on dendrological knowledge of the time. It combined detailed descriptions of numerous tree species such as oak, elm, beech, holly, and cedar, with precise instructions on how and when to plant, transplant, prune, and fell trees to enhance the beauty of forests and the market value of hardwoods. Evelyn's passionate motto was "Let's get up and do it!" inspired by examples of successful forest recovery and conservation projects in Europe at the time, such as the Forest of Nuremberg, in Germany; the Montello Forest, in northern Italy; and legislation in Luxembourg, which did not allow a farmer to log a hardwood tree without being forced to plant another in its place. Evelyn describes practices of landowners in France and Germany who divided groves, woodlands, and forests into eighty partitions, logging only one of them a year to ensure that no hardwood was felled in less than eighty years, and makes other recommendations to elucidate a comprehensive theory of the primary methods of sustained-yield forestry. Evelyn cites a wide variety of sources, ranging from the Bible to classical Greek and Roman authors such as Pliny, the Elder, Virgil, Ovid to his literary and theological contemporaries such as Nikolaus Cusanus, Philipp Melanchthon, and William Shakespeare, but the modern thrust of his position is clear.

From his survey and his personal experience as a court landscaper, Evelyn deduces some applications. He recommends, for example, the displacement of the metallurgical industry of Old England to the densely forested territories of New England, that is to say, the North American colonies. However, for Grober, Evelyn's central appeal—and the *leitmotiv* of his book—is to consider the problem of the interests of future generations, that is, the problem of posterity. For Evelyn, each generation is *"non sibi soli natus,"*[25] that is, it is born not only for itself, for its own survival and growth, but also with the responsibility to ensure the prosperity of future generations. In this sense, Evelyn develops the ethics of a responsible and prudent society: "men should perpetually be planting, that so posterity might have Trees fit for their service . . . which it is impossible they should have, if we thus continue to destroy our Woods, without this providential planting in their stead, and felling what we do cut down with great discretion, and regard to the future."[26]

In the same period that Evelyn published *Sylva*, the France of Louis XIV was also beginning to face the same problems concerning the scarcity of natural resources essential for the maintenance of their economic development. According to Grober, "Historians of forestry estimate that in the few decades since the beginning of the 17th century, the size of the woodlands in France had diminished from about 35% of the nation's territory to roughly 25%."[27] The alarm sounded in 1661. The young Sun King, preoccupied with the *"rétablissement de la navigation"* (the restoration of navigation) in his own country, understood the problem—and expressed it in a handwritten statement—*"combien il était nécessaire de faire un bon ménage des bois"* (how necessary it is to make good management of forests), leading him to intervene and interrupt the sale of timber from royal lands.[28]

Author of several economic practices specific to French mercantilism, Jean-Baptiste Colbert was also responsible for the radical improvement of the supply of hardwood and forest supplies. As Secretary of the Treasury and the Merchant and Naval Navy, but primarily as the king's trusted man, Colbert was responsible for implementing an impressive *réformation des forêts* (forest reform) because he believed that France would perish due to the imminent shortage of hardwood. Until 1661, the French navy was virtually nonexistent, while its great British and Dutch rivals already possessed advanced naval forces. Louis XIV and Colbert recognized this weak point in their national strategy, and so they decided that shipbuilding would become a priority. Thus, to ensure the supply of oak and other hardwoods to newly constructed yards, the devastation of the country's forests needed to be halted or dramatically minimized as soon as possible.

The management reform was personally supervised by Colbert and began in 1662 with an investigation into the condition of the royal forests. This initiative resulted in a general inventory of the forested regions of the crown. Over the next few years, a vast collection of reports and statistical data was gathered, providing a detailed study of the location, and the number of forested areas, species and ages of trees, areas authorized for pasture, the rights for cutting/felling of trees, and the monetary value of logging. The picture revealed what the royal government considered a severe abuse of the king's property; through the unscrupulous activity of corrupt officials and the illicit appropriation of cutting rights, the illegal clearing of forests had become commonplace procedure, and the once substantial timber resources had been significantly reduced.[29] The forested areas of the crown were relentlessly overexploited by speculators, timber merchants, and residents adjacent to the forests, small feudal lords, the low landowning nobility, as well as by beggars, small animal breeders, and poor landless people.

Once the bleak picture became more evident, a set of measures was designed to put an end to such abuses and to ensure the government's strict control and power over the royal forests. In this way, Colbert sought the restoration and conservation of the forested areas of France, reducing the pressure of use in order to adapt the consumption of hardwood to the capacity of maintaining the forests. The motto *"La réduction des usages à leur possibilité"* (the reduction of the use for the possibility of them [the forests, themselves, and the future generations]) was promoted as a severe directive. Limiting regulations were created, directing the foresters in the silviculture system to leave untouched trees under ten years old and a number of ancient mother plants.[30] The final outline of the *"grande ordonannce forestière"* (the major ordinance on forestry) included many bureaucratic details, specifying the minimum age of foresters in the silviculture system, levying fines for vagrancy and criminal fires, and so on. The decisive reforms were to (1) replace ineffective officers by competent foresters who obtained jurisdiction over private or public forests; (2) reduce herding in forests; (3) reorganize the system of sales of hardwood; (4) establish strict control over the use rights of forested areas, especially the general abolition of the old right to freely use firewood.

Grober points to the clear and obvious contrast between Colbert's methods of administration and Evelyn's strategy of mobilizing his own social group, the landowners of the British nobility. However, despite this difference, the preamble to the French text shows of very similar commitment to the idea of responsibility for future generations: *"Il ne suffit pas d'avoir rétabli l'ordre et la discipline, si par de bons règlements on ne les assure pour en faire passer le fruit à la posterité"* (It is not enough to restore order and discipline if through proper regulations one cannot be sure to pass the fruit to posterity).[31] The new *ordonnance* came into force in 1669 and was an immediate success. Over the next ten years, real revenues from hardwood sales increased considerably. However, the triumph was not long-lasting. Enforcing the new rules and overseeing the procedures adopted became *"un veritable travail des Sisyphe"* (a truly Sisyphean task). Due to the apathy and neglect of the French public administration, economic individualism and the strength of old customs, *"la grande réformation des forêts"* had some effect, but it was not able to establish a truly sustainable supply of timber. Unfortunately, on the eve of the Revolution of 1789, there were fewer forested areas in France than in 1669.

Strongly influenced by cameralism, which took extremely elaborate forms there, Germany also saw with concern the risk of declining forests and the harmful effects on the economy this could have. Grober points out that the transport of hardwood from the distant forests in the Erzgebirge Mountains for use as charcoal in the mines and the steel mills located in the foothills had become a vital issue for the economy of the country. The areas surrounding the mining towns were totally stripped of groves and forests due to long periods of over-logging. "In 1665, a year after the publication of *'Sylva,'* while Colbert's *'grand réformation'* was well underway, Carlowitz set off for his 'grand tour' of Europe. [. . .] He was in Leyden, the Dutch bastion of early 'European Enlightenment' when Spinoza's pantheistic philosophy which claimed the identity of God and Nature (*deus sive natura*) was the talk of the town."[32] In 1770, Carlowitz returned from his European tour, and for the next thirty years he worked as a senior government official for the administration of the Saxon silver mines in Freiberg. Significantly, he had "two important sources and models: a folio-sized book published in 1664 in London, John Evelyn's *Sylva*, and Jean-Baptiste Colbert's *Ordonnance* of 1669, concerning the royal forests of France."[33]

In 1713, Carlowitz published his work *Sylviculture eoconomica: Anweisung zu wilden Naumzucht (Sylviculture eoconomica: Instructions for the Cultivation of Native Trees)*. In this book,

> Carlowitz criticizes the contemporary short-termed way of thinking which was centered solely on making money: woodland was being cleared because agriculture seemed more profitable than forestry. The common man had no motivation to plant trees, knowing he would not harvest them in his lifetime. He wasted timber, thinking the supplies were inexhaustible. Once the forests were ruined, however, the revenues would cease for many years to come. In the name of apparently quick profits, unrepairable damage had been done. [, , .] Against the devastation of the forests, *Sylvicultura oeconomica* puts up the strict rule: "*Daß man mit dem Holtz pfleglich umgehe*" [that we use timber with care, p. 87]. The term "*pfleglich*" is—according to Carlowitz—an "age-old term" meaning "*oeconomically*," but also indicating the need to care for the renewal of forests that had been cleared. *A balance should be reached between renewal and cutting, so that timber could be used forever, continuously and perpetually.*[34]

Crucially for this paper, Grober also argues that while Carlowitz made us of the traditional term "*pfleglich*," he felt that it did not fully express the idea that we must use natural resources moderately and with an eye to the far future. In discussing how to achieve this type of conservation that would guarantee the continuous, stable and sustainable use of hardwoods (*wie eine sothane Conservation und Anbau des Holtzes anzustellen, daß en eine continuirlle beständige und nachhaltende Nutzung gebe*[35]), Carlowitz uses the term "*nachhaltend*" or "*nachhaltig*," with the current modern meaning, for the first time in history.

Other essential aspects of Carlowitz's work are the ways he conceptualizes what he means by "Nature." Carlowitz characterized the natural environment as "mild" and "gentle" Mother Nature, mentioning the "power of the sun to give life," the "wonderful vegetation," and the "admirable spirit who provides food for life from within the soil." Carlowitz places the outer appearance of the trees in a context of fundamental form, "the signature and constellation of the sky beneath which they bloom and green," with its "matrix," the Mother Earth and its natural work. Nature, for Carlowitz, is "unspeakably beautiful" and unfathomable, maintaining aspects unrelated to Man. However, he believed it was possible to "read the book of Nature" (*wie die Natur spielet*) and "find the way Nature behaves" through experiments.[36]

Grober further indicates that the way Carlowitz thinks economics in his book is closely related to Protestant morality. Carlowitz states that since Man no longer inhabits the Garden of Eden, he can no longer rely on nature as a provider of eternal abundance. Instead, Man must come to and help with Nature (*mit ihr agiren*). Like Evelyn before him, Carlowitz cites passages from the book of Genesis from which he extracts words that serve to this day as a formula for sustainability:

> "Abad" and "schamar," "dress" and "keep" the soil. In Luther's translation, which the pious Lutheran Carlowitz was familiar with: "Bebauen und bewahren," cultivate and preserve. Here are the fundamentals of ecological economics: Recognizing that there are limits to the use of natural resources, man must not act against nature ("wider die Natur handeln"). Instead, he must "follow" her and be a true housekeeper with her offerings. Every lavish, wasteful and harmful use of nature, the over-use, the ruinous exploitation is sinful.[37]

The devastation of forests had been halted. The new management system of time and space in a forest, however, had led to a drastic reduction of biodiversity. The anthropic *"Normalwald"* (normalized/ordered forest) had to be as homogeneous as possible: a monoculture. The mosaic of an untouched forest had become the checkered pattern of an orderly hardwood plantation. In 1841, Gottlob König, a resident of Thuringia (central Germany) and a *"Forstklassiker,"* warned that pressing the life of a forest to fit into formulas and numbers was a process that would eventually provoke a "revenge of nature." As Grober explains, for König "the growth and health of groves and forests depend on very thin and deeply hidden yarns." His warning was directed against the deep arrogance of his fellow foresters, but especially against the new laissez-faire liberalism that tried to make the highest possible yield of hardwood (and thereby financial gain) the ultimate goal of forestry. Grober also points out that there were long and intense disputes, many of which are still ongoing today, needed to reestablish and strengthen the idea that *Nachhaltigkeit* depends on the natural regenerative capacity of ecosystems, which must include a multiplicity of functions. Forests are not mere plantations or farms of hardwood. They are also habitats of plants and wildlife and areas for the protection of watersheds.

It is important to remember, also, that in the same period works on the problem of population growth begin to gain the attention of the rulers:

> In the 18th century, concern about population growth and its consequences for the consumption of resources started surfacing. Authors such as Matthew Hale and William Petty had already in the 17th century drawn attention to this issue. However, the most famous work in this regard, *Essay on the principle of population as it affects the future improvement of society*, by Thomas Robert Malthus, was published in 1798. He stated that because it threatened to outstrip food production the increase in population had to be restricted.[38]

In this way, the worries of high modernism about national security and stability related to the effect of resource use on military strength and economic production are linked to sociological questions of consumption and demography as well as population biology.

In conclusion, it is possible to identify the beginning of the use of the term sustainability associated with the public administration of natural resources, such as the forests of the nation-state, including those which were located overseas, that is, in the colonies. Therefore, the maintenance of those natural resources for present and future use had become paramount in the seventeenth century. Thus, sustainability is a question that goes right to the heart of the meaning of modernity and arises concomitantly with it. Further, there is a fundamentally ambiguous nature of this sustainable/modern worldview. On the one hand, there is planning for the rational use of forest resources, either as raw material for vessels or as an energy source, corroborating the understanding that nature is seen from a utilitarian and commercial point of view, aimed at anthropocentric interests. On the other hand, if not as dominant, there is also a concern that replanting aims to establish a certain degree of "forest health," aiming at the future well-being of human populations as well as biodiversity or the values of the existence of landscapes. Landscapes begin to be seen as natural beauties and the species within them are seen as living beings with the right to peaceful existence. This conflict of opposite meanings continued to participate in the construction of the notion of sustainability even later when the *Ecosophy* and *Deep Ecology* movements appeared in the mid-twentieth century.

In any case, it is important to note, especially from the contributions of Grober, that the idea of sustainability and the modern use of the term have been around for more than 350 years, being strongly linked to the area of public administration, to the advent of forestry engineering, and, more specifically, to the management of natural resources for the present and the future economic interests of a nation. Thus, it is not excessive to assume that the genealogy of the notion of sustainability is intimately interwoven with the genealogy of the forestry sciences, the biological sciences, the ecological sciences, and modern philosophy, along with the more recognizable environmental movement itself, understood as the countercultural tendencies born in the decade of the 1960s in the last century.

SUSTAINABILITY AS THE POSSIBILITY
OF NEW COGNITIVE STRATEGIES

The attempt at tracing the origins of the word sustainability and relating it to the history of the modification of the word's original meaning show us how remote and ancient aspects can constitute and transform ways of seeing and perceiving nature. Depending on the social and cultural contexts, nature is sometimes perceived as an extension of the divine or mystic power that connects the existence of all living things. Other times, nature seems to be reduced, represented, and referred to the set of natural resources from which we attain our survival needs. In this sense, nature is merely the environment where the evolution between modes of production of human wealth happened as well as the inhabited place where we can measure the consequences of our economic growth. Then, ideas such as the risk of the scarcity of raw materials and the decrease of the quality of life for humans due to the increase of contamination and pollution finally appear. Nevertheless, as contemporary as these ideas seem, the perception of nature or the natural environment as a habitat that can be destroyed or that can lose quality for life is by no means new.

Thus, it is possible to assume that the notion of preservation of resources as a way to ensure a minimally possible and comfortable existence for future generations has existed since ancient civilizations. This conclusion is confirmed by McCormick who points out:

> Although the environmental movement is a postwar phenomenon, environmental destruction has a long lineage. Nearly 3,700 years ago, Sumerian cities were being abandoned as the irrigated lands that had produced the world's first agricultural surpluses became increasingly saline and waterlogged. Nearly 2,400 years ago, Plato bemoaned the deforestation and soil erosion brought to the hills of Attica by overgrazing and cutting of trees for fuelwood. In the first century Rome, Columella, and Pliny the Elder warned that poor husbandry threatened crop failures and soil erosion. By the seventh century, the complex Mesopotamian irrigation system built 400 years before was beginning to break down under the strain of mismanagement. Population growth meanwhile was sowing the seeds of the tenth century collapse of the Mayan civilization. Shipbuilding for the fleets of the Byzantine Empire, of Venice and Genoa and other Italian maritime states, reduced the coastal forests of the Mediterranean. Air pollution from coal-burning so afflicted medieval England that by 1661 the diarist and naturalist John Evelyn was deploring the "Hellish and dismal Cloud" which made the City of London resemble "the Court of Vulcan . . . or Suburbs of Hell, [rather] than an Assembly of Rational Creatures."[39]

So, what is new about referring to all these contexts related to the worries about the quality of our natural environment using one common word—sustainability? The challenge of investigating processes by which the transformation of a term happens lies not only in the semantic or linguistic questions that guide the investigation. There is a problem related to the root of a term in the language in which it was first created, but there are also the processes by which the term suffered transformations in other languages. These transformations were not only related to transcriptions, translations, or adaptations of the original word. They are intrinsically related to political and economic processes in a particular time of history. This aspect of the investigation shows that words and their meanings have only apparent stability: the meaning of a term works in the very open game of meanings, which are historically, politically, and culturally built. This conclusion allows thinking of the broad network of conceptual nodes relating words, meanings, and their uses in the social fabric that is constituted by people and their discursive operations. Since words do not have a single, stable, or permanent meaning, it is in the revision and re-reading of literary, philosophical, and scientific texts that the historicity and complexity of a pluralistic and polysemic conception allow us to understand how a word is reconstructed and always modified during the process of its sociocultural use. Such is the case with the word sustainability.

We have focused here on the historical transformations of sustainability. It seems to me that one of the most interesting contemporary intersections of meaning occurs between sustainability, economics, and the concept of entropy in contemporary physics, particularly as this is worked out in Veiga's reading of Georgescu-Roegen, which suggests that to live sustainably we will have to shift away from an economic system addicted to growth.[40] This, however, would require another chapter to address more fully. Here, by pointing out the various ways in which the term sustainability has been linked to different contexts over time, we are content to have gathered the main historical elements of this broad network of meanings. Some of them are politically fixed in specific languages; others are still openly contested. These disputes can be seen in action in different fields of knowledge that still try to legitimize different meanings for sustainability, whether broader or narrower, scientifically grounded, poetically transformed in metaphors, or economically commodified.

Thus, considering all this, on the one hand, it is possible to say that the term sustainability seems to carry one of the most controversial political disputes for symbolic power in Western culture. This internal dispute is the clash of discursive (and narrative) forces, that is, of different modes of expression of power-knowledge (Foucault), and the practical aspects of survival implied in everyday life. Power-knowledge is set in motion by contemporary society with the help of different information and technological means used for the fast distribution of contents, typical of the twenty-first century. However, at the same time, knowledge has become questionable, and its validation and legitimation, that is, the source of its power, are being disrupted by the same information and technological means that once were thought to empower transparency and public decision-making.

On the other hand, by having a multidisciplinary genealogy together with such technologically mediated abundance of data, the term sustainability operates in a way that goes beyond boundaries demarcated or claimed by purist ideologues from any specific area of knowledge. In this sense, the invention and the fixation of the term sustainability in the contemporary culture are processes linked to a series of contributions from several fields of knowledge whose intense set of references and bundles of relations make it impossible to find a final or unique version of the idea within this broad, diverse, and rich map of meanings and discursive relations. Hence, the emergence and fixation of the term sustainability is not only a social, historical, and cultural choice but also a data computing process. In this way, the concept map for the term can be thought of as an ecological process if we consider "ecological" as a metaphor for "network" as suggested by Capra[41] and Latour.[42] From the cognitive point of view, meanings within languages can be nodes in a broader web of meanings, as in Machado,[43] or in a sociotechnical network, as in Lévy.[44] So, the term sustainability could be the name we would give to this network whose meanings operate distinct discursive regimes, all of them related to human survival on the planet, particularly as related to our production of wealth and pollution.

The nodes of this network maintain continuous streams of remission, which in their turn appropriate or derive new meanings. Thus, it is in this network of meanings that it is possible to make concrete ethical decisions and rationally guide our behavior in ways that are conducive to a healthier and more just relation with our environment. For example, we may say that a construction company has sustainable practices on the basis of its decisions regarding the production and treatment of solid wastes, the use of renewable resources as sources of energy for construction, or that the water used in the construction site is recycled by greywater systems. It is also possible to discuss whether the construction project foresees the consumption of reusable water for the future building or if the construction company ensures sustainable practices because it compensates for its carbon dioxide emissions by planting large native trees elsewhere. All this operates as a set of "good practices" which can be grouped under the term sustainability, although it is not known precisely how to measure the efficiency of these practices and their results and present them in a quantitative comparison that would definitely show the absolute advantages of such practices. That is why it is still so challenging to have cradle-to-grave studies which would be used for decision-making regarding sustainability. There are many other aspects involved, and a measurable unit is always incomplete from the perspective of the urbanized environment, especially concerning the values displayed in this network of meanings, such as the importance of reducing waste and pollution, but also of generating jobs and guaranteeing the safety of workers, just to mention a few. The genealogy of sustainability reminds us that ecological thinking can never be reduced to the execution of an algorithm; rather we must always act in an irreducibly complex discussion about values and meanings that remain contested.

This discursive and operative constitution of the term sustainability in its contemporary setting is its actualization[45] as a complex concept, and this includes diversity concerning the original significations of the word. The invention and continuity of the word sustainability appear as a result of a particular context, a set of significant possibilities that is not detached from a social, political, economic, and cultural reality: in particular the white, urban, Western, and Christian European man. Our main concern is to open the promise of and discussion about adding new meanings and contexts to its current network. How can discursive regimes committed to the maintenance of the original contexts that helped create the term and its network of meanings be overcome by the appearance of new contexts capable of giving new meanings to the term, in order to allow the irruption of broader, more diverse, and inclusive networks of meanings, in such a way that it becomes obsolete to ask the question "What is sustainability?" as if we expected a single answer. Then, it will become more productive to focus on the following questions: How does sustainability work? What social processes and changes does it potentialize? What social and cultural interactions does it allow—not only between groups of people and communities but also between discursive formations (between distinct sets of power-knowledge) or between the social groups that work in urbanized spaces? What new cognitive symbioses among social groups does it allow? What new technical and technological procedures to advance social relations does it encourage? How does sustainability contribute to making our social systems rich in complexity that helps them thrive, increasing its networking abilities through informational or communicative processes? Does the notion of sustainability force us to think or act by repeating crystallized cultural values, only advocating for human survival and future generations to the detriment of the elements that constitute what has been called the "natural environment"? Is it possible to think of sustainability as a scenario from which "reactive forces and active forces come together to potentiate the permanent reinvention of the world by mobilizing creative modes of existence?"[46]

Constituted by a tangle of technical discourses (whether legal, economic, ecological, or merely administrative) and political discourses, and based on the notion of unity, enclosed in both the updated meaning of the word *ecology* and the word *ecosystem*, the notion of sustainability justifies and conditions the operations of the contemporary ecological discourse, which transforms it into one of the main discursive events[47] of the twentieth century.

We understand, therefore, that the main characteristic of the term sustainability is precisely its plasticity of meaning. Although originally coined from a technical reference in the field of forestry engineering during the seventeenth century, its significance is given in the contemporary world by the way it extrapolates; widens; merges; causes anastomoses in language, discourses, narratives; abusing derivations by metonymy, analogy, or metaphor—even from fields of knowledge as far removed from the social sciences or from cultural anthropology as from physics or chemistry—inciting the becoming of concepts from other areas of knowledge, problematizing prevailed modes of existence.

This process of mutation or reinvention of the word itself continually brings us back to the existence of a network of meanings and concepts that constitute streams of intensities for a complex set of discursive formations. These, in turn, also interact in a reticular way, referring to each other, continuously, in an operational game that generates appropriations, sometimes undue, sometimes not strict, sometimes forced, and sometimes innovative. It is this fluidity that defines and guarantees the longevity of the term and its relevance as a contemporary motto. That is why sustainability is, at the same time, a reasonable goal and a romantic dream.

ACKNOWLEDGMENTS

The author would like to acknowledge that the first version of this chapter was written for the book *Redes digitais e sustentabilidade: as interações com o meio ambiente na era da informação* organized by researchers Massimo Di Felice (PhD), Julliana Cutolo Torres (PhD) e Leandro Key Higuchi Yanaze (PhD) from Átopos Research Center at the School of Communications and Arts of the University of São Paulo (USP). The book was published by Annablume Editora, in 2012, in São Paulo, SP, Brazil. This chapter is an updated version of the text and its first translation into English. The author would also like to thank Dr. Dan Bradley and Dr. Róisín Lally, from Gonzaga University, and Lexington Books for this invaluable opportunity.

NOTES

1. E. P. Odum, *Fundamentals of Ecology* (Philadelphia, PA: W. B. Sandeurs, 1971).

2. F. Campbell, *Elements of Metallurgy and Engineering Alloys* (ASM International, 2008), 206.

3. From a postphenomenology perspective, it is interesting to note that the passage continues, "because of the possibility of multiple stable states, when considering the extent to which a system can be changed, return time doesn't measure all of the ways in which a system may fail—permanently or temporarily—to retain essential

functions." B. Walker, C. S. Holling, S. R. Carpenter, and A. Kinzig, "Resilience, adaptability and transformability in social—ecological systems," *Ecology and Society* 9, no. 2 (2004): 5. Retrieved from http://www.ecologyandsociety.org/vol9/iss2/art5/.

4. Original Portuguese passage: "Até os anos 1980, o adjetivo "sustentável" era jargão de engenheiros agrônomos, florestais ou de pesca, para evocar a possibilidade de um ecossistema permanecer robusto e estável (resiliente), apesar de agredido por alguma exploração humana." José Eli Veiga, "Sustentabilidade equivocada—gerações futuras e o discurso de hoje" (*Folha de São Paulo*, September 5, 2010), Retrieved from https://www1.folha.uol.com.br/fsp/ilustrissima/il0509201004.htm.

5. Biocapacity, *WordMapper.org*. Retrieved from http://archive.worldmapper. org/display.php?selected=321.

6. J. E. Veiga, "Como pode ser entendida a sustentabilidade," in *Desenvolvimento Sustentável—o desafio do século XXI*, ed. J. E. Veiga (Rio de Janeiro, RJ: Garamond, 2006), 113.

7. By barbarism, we mean the collapse of the human and their regression to meaningless violence. Original Portuguese passage: "o colapso do humano e sua regressão a uma violência despida de significado." Jean-François Mattéi, *A barbárie interior: ensaio sobre o i-mundo moderno* (São Paulo, SP: Editora UNESP, 2001).

8. Jean-François Lyotard, *The Postmodern Condition: A Report on Knowledge* (Minneapolis: University of Minnesota Press, [1979] 1984).

9. In this sense, a genealogical study of the term sustainability would need to make an effort to visit a large set of enunciations and statements (Foucault, 2006, *The Archeology of Knowledge*) which constitute this "speech about the environment" or about "Nature." In order to understand the wide network of relationships and remissions created by this ecological discourse, it would be necessary to approach, for example, the texts that constitute the "natural history" attributed to Aristotle (384 BC–322 BC), Theophrastus (372 BC–287 BC), and Pliny the Elder (AD 23/24–79), through the natural systematics of Linneu (*Systema Naturae*, 1735), and also addressing the notions of natural selection and adaptation established by Darwin in *The Origin of Species* (1856); the construction of principles of plant and animal biogeography by Wallace (*The Malay Archipelago*, 1869); the invention of the notion of holism, by Jan Christiaan Smuts (*Holism and Evolution*, 1926); the notion of biological systems, developed by Ludwig von Bertalanffy (*General Theory of Systems*, 1952). In addition, one would have to deal with the social construction of many concepts: from the concepts of thermodynamic systems and entropy, including Sadi Carnot (*Reflections on the Motive Power of Fire*, 1824) and Rudolf Clausius (*On the Moving Force of Heat and the Laws of Heat which may be Deduced Therefrom*, 1850); of the invention of the word ecology, thought to substitute for the terms "biology"/"natural history," proposed by Haeckel (*Gennerelle Morphologie der Organismen*, 1866) and whose appearance in turn suffered remissions of philosophy (Spinozist monism), biology (Darwin's evolutionary theory of species), and German romanticism (Schelling and *Naturphilosophie*); and the notion of civil rights advocacy, implicated in the works of authors of American transcendentalism, especially Thoreau and his work *Walden* (1848). There would still be a demand to cover the economic theories that deal with issues of development and sustainability with varying degrees of intensity.

10. G. Deleuze, *Différence et repetition* (Paris: PUF, 1968), trans. as *Difference and Repetition*, by Paul Patton (New York: Columbia University Press, 1994).

11. M. Foucault, *The Archaeology of Knowledge*, trans. A. M. Sheridan Smith (London and New York: Routledge, [1969] 2002).

12. A. Djalali and P. Vollaard, "The complex history of sustainability: An index of trends, authors, projects, and fiction," *After Zero* 18 (December 2008). Retrieved from http://issuu.com/archis/docs/thecomplexhistoryofsustainability/1?mode=a_p.

13. J. Derrida, *Of Grammatology*, trans. Gayatri Chakravorty Spivak (Baltimore, MD & London: Johns Hopkins University Press, [1967] 1997).

14. See also E. Morin, *La Méthode*. 6 Volumes (Paris: Editions du Seuil, 1977; 1980; 1986; 1991; 2001; 2004).

15. Most of the forest technologies and techniques currently employed in timber production carried out by sustainable management strategies originate in this period.

16. According to Jamieson, the term *"environmentalism"* is much more recent than *sustainability*, and its meaning is not related to the notion of preservation of the so-called natural landscapes. As he puts it, "The term 'environmentalism' was coined in 1923, to refer not to the activities of John Muir and the Sierra Club, but to the idea that human behavior is largely a product of the social and physical conditions in which a person lives and develops. This view arose in opposition to the idea that a person's behavior is primarily determined by his or her biological endowment. These environmentalists championed the 'nurture' side in the 'nature versus nurture' debate that raged in the social sciences for much of the twentieth century. They advocated changing people by changing society, rather than changing society by changing people" Dale Jamieson, *Ethics and Environment: An Introduction* (New York: Cambridge University Press, 2008).

17. In Brazilian academic discourse, there is a tendency to use the term *"ecologism"* as synonymous with "deep ecology," which advocates a break with the modes of production and consumption of advanced capitalism and is thus considered subversive and radical, as opposed to the term, *environmentalism*, which refers to corporate or governmental ecological discourse and is thus the appropriate ecological discourse for the institutions of the hegemonic economic system. These differences of signification appear in Layrargues, 2000; Viola and Leis, 1991; and Leis, 1991. Such a technical distinction seems to be related to the theoretical and political dispute between Gifford Pinchot (1865–1946) and John Muir (1838–1914), begun in 1896, due to the first decision to allow sheep grazing in reserves forests. Pinchot was then head of the US Forest Service and trained in Europe between 1889 and 1890 at the École Nationale Forestière in Nancy, France, in the period of expansion of German cameralism and national forestry schools, whose theoretical foundation was the work of Carlowitz. Thus, via Pinchot, these ideas came to dominate the platform of the North American conservation movement, especially after the split between Pinchot and Muir.

18. Jacobus A. Du Pisani, "Sustainable development—historical roots of the concept," *Journal of Integrative Environmental Sciences* 3, no. 2 (2006): 83–96. Retrieved from http://dx.doi.org/10.1080/15693430600688831.

19. Ulrich Grober, "Deep roots: A conceptual history of 'sustainable development' (Nachhaltigkeit)," *Research Gate* (2007): 13. Retrieved from

https://www.researchgate.net/publication/254461192_Deep_roots_A_conceptual_
history_of_ 'sustainable_development'_Nachhaltigkeit.

20. G. Agricola, *De re metallica*, translated from the first Latin edition of 1556 by Herbert Clark Hoover and Lou Henry Hoover (New York: Dover, 1950).

21. Pisani, "Sustainable development," 85–86.

22. The Royal Society of London for Improving Natural Knowledge, also known as the Royal Society, is an association of specialists focused on the promotion of science in general. It is considered one of the oldest of such associations. Initially proposed to be a place for research and debate, it now acts as the scientific advisor to the British government, receiving financial assistance from parliament to fund research and encourage scientific endeavors. The continued relevance of this society highlights, once again, the tight link between the rise of modern science, technological innovation, and the interests of those in charge of political economy—and our indebtedness to this legacy.

23. Grober, "Deep roots," 8.

24. Ibid., 9.

25. "*Homo non sibi soli natus, sed patriae.*" Cicero, De Finibus 2.45, adapted. "Man was born not only for himself, but for his country."

26. Evelyn, 1664 as cited in Grober, "Deep roots," 11.

27. Ibid., 13–14.

28. Ibid., 12.

29. Situations like this continue to happen in practically all the tremendous forested areas of the planet. A study on the matter can be found in Drigo, Isabel Garcia (2010) *As barreiras para a implantação de concessões florestais na América do Sul: os casos de Bolívia e Brasil.* Tese de Doutorado. Programa de Ciências Ambientais da Universidade de São Paulo. São Paulo, SP, Brasil.

30. Mother plants, also called mother trees, are of vital importance to a forest, because they are older trees with a high capacity of producing seeds that will disperse far away and that can also be used for new artificial tree plantings, which help the process of reforestation.

31. Devèze, 1962, p. 55 as cited in Grober, "Deep roots," 15. M. Devèze, Une admirable reforme administrative: La grande reformation des forêts royales sous Colbert (1662–1680). *Annales de L'École Nationale des Eaux et Forêts de la station de Recherche et Expériences.* Nancy, École Nationale des Eaux et Forêts, 1962 (Citation's reference).

32. Grober, "Deep roots," 17.

33. Ibid., 8.

34. Ibid., 18–19.

35. Carlowitz, 1713, as cited in Grober, "Deep roots," 19.

36. Carlowitz, 1713, pp. 20–39 as cited in Grober, "Deep roots," 20–21. This aspect of Carlowitz's thinking may be, as pointed out by Grober, a reflection of his contact with the thinking of Spinoza, to whom God and nature coincide as immanent identities. According to Naess, for Spinoza, God, as the cause, cannot be distinguishable from what the particular things of the world themselves cause, except conceptually. In this way, Spinoza places a relationship of dependence between God and the

things of the world. God is nothing without the essences of particular things, and these, in turn, are also helpless without God. Without our essence, there is no God, and without God we are nothing; see Naess, "Spinoza and Attitudes toward Nature," in *The Selected Works of Arne Naess*, ed. A. Drengson (Dordrecht: Springer, [1969] 2005). In addition to Spinoza, it is necessary to take into account the *Sturm und Drang* literary and musical movement, a paramount intellectual approach of the beginning of romantic thought, between the 1760s and 1780s, which influenced almost all thinkers in the most diverse areas of knowledge in the later eighteenth century.

37. Grober, "Deep roots," 20.

38. Pisani, "Sustainable development," 86.

39. J. McCormick, *Reclaiming Paradise. The Global Environmental Movement* (Bloomignton: Indiana University Press, 1991), vii.

40. Veiga, "Como pode ser entendida a sustentabilidade."

41. F. Capra, *As conexões ocultas. Ciência para uma vida sustentável* (São Paulo, SP: Cultrix, 2002).

42. B. Latour, *Jamais fomos modernos. Ensaios de antropologia simétrica* (Rio de Janeiro, RJ: Editora 34, 1994), 34.

43. N. J. Machado, *Epistemologia e Didática* (São Paulo, SP: Cortez, 1995).

44. P. Lévy, *A inteligência coletiva* (São Paulo, SP: Loyola, 1998).

45. G. Deleuze e F. Guattari, *O que é filosofia?* (Rio de Janeiro, RJ: Editora 34, 1992), 34.

46. S. Rolnik, Arquivomania. Comunicação Oral. Mesa 3: abstrações-concreções. *Seminário Internacional Emoção e Imaginação. Os sentidos e as imagens em movimento.* SESC Vila Mariana. São Paulo, 30 Mar. a 1º Abr. 2011.

47. M. Foucault, *A arqueologia do saber* (Rio de Janeiro, RJ: Forense Universitária, [1969] 2005).

BIBLIOGRAPHY

Campbell, F. *Elements of Metallurgy and Engineering Alloys.* ASM International, 2008.

Deleuze, G. *Différence et repetition.* Paris: PUF, 1968. Translated as *Difference and Repetition* by Paul Patton. New York: Columbia University Press, 1994.

Djalali, A. and P. Vollaard. "The complex history of sustainability: An index of trends, authors, projects, and fiction." *After Zero* 18 (2008).

Foucault, M. *The Archaeology of Knowledge.* Translated by A. M. Sheridan Smith. London and New York: Routledge, [1969] 2002.

Grober, Ulrich. "Deep roots: A conceptual history of 'sustainable development' (Nachhaltigkeit)." *Research Gate* (2007). https://www.researchgate.net/publication/254461192_Deep_roots_A_conceptual_history_of_'sustainable_development'_Nachhaltigkeit.

Jamieson, Dale. *Ethics and Environment: An Introduction.* New York: Cambridge University Press, 2008.

Mattéi, Jean-François. *A barbárie interior: ensaio sobre o i-mundo moderno.* São Paulo, SP: Editora UNESP, 2001.

McCormick, J. *Reclaiming Paradise: The Global Environmental Movement.* Bloomington: Indiana University Press, 1991.

Odum, E. P. *Fundamentals of Ecology.* Philadelphia, PA: W. B. Sandeurs, 1971.

Pisani, Jacobus A. Du. "Sustainable development—historical roots of the concept." *Journal of Integrative Environmental Sciences* 3, no. 2 (2006): 83–96.

Rolnik, S. Arquivomania. "Comunicação Oral. Mesa 3: abstrações-concreções." *Seminário Internacional Emoção e Imaginação. Os sentidos e as imagens em movimento.* SESC Vila Mariana. São Paulo, 2011.

Veiga, José Eli. "Como pode ser entendida a sustentabilidade." In *Desenvolvimento Sustentável—o desafio do século XXI*, edited by J. E. Veiga, 109–172. Rio de Janeiro, RJ: Garamond, 2006.

Veiga, José Eli. "Sustentabilidade equivocada—gerações futuras e o discurso de hoje." *Folha de São Paulo*, 2010.

Walker, B., C. S. Holling, S. R. Carpenter, and A. Kinzig. "Resilience, adaptability and transformability in social-ecological systems." *Ecology and Society* 9, no. 2 (2004). https://www.ecologyandsociety.org/vol9/iss2/art5/.

Chapter 2

Is This the End?

Jan Kyrre Berg Friis

INTRODUCTION

In 1878 Nietzsche published *On Truth and Lie in the Extra-Moral Sense*. What he wrote—as painful as it sounds—rings truer than ever as we face an increasing number of extreme weather events, famine, and overpopulation of the Earth. And yet, we keep on trotting along that fictional trail of industrial and economic progress concocted by our rationalist Enlightenment forefathers, today a doctrine embedded into every fabric of human life, guarded by some of the largest corporations and most powerful politicians alike. Nietzsche forcefully reminds us of the ultimately illusory nature of this "progress":

> Once upon a time, in some out of the way corner of that universe which is dispersed into numberless twinkling solar systems, there was a star upon which clever beasts invented knowing. That was the most arrogant and mendacious minute of "world history," but nevertheless, it was only a minute. After nature had drawn a few breaths, the star cooled and congealed, and the clever beasts had to die.[1]

Further, I will discuss some inadequacies of the interrelated ideas of sustainable development and progress. These development ideas have had, and still have, a tremendous influence on the Anthropocene. As a counterpoint, I will present a view of environmental philosophy that is tentative, probably naïve, yet at least an alternative that may help regenerate mankind's partly forgotten relationship with nature.

Sustainable development is believed to be the solution to the environmental crisis and also a way out of the poverty crisis for the developing countries of the world. The World Commission on Environment and Development

(WCED), better known as the Brundtland report, titled "Our Common Future" from 1987, is the most applied definition of sustainable development, and its solution to the poverty crisis is continued economic growth. As a definition of sustainability, the report has been much criticized.

A common problem at the base of both ideas is an absolute faith in rationality—this includes humanity's faith in its ability to achieve continuous technological and scientific development and its belief in continued commercial competition to nurture economic growth. The core problem is how we can now relate to nature as a source from which we can satisfy humanity's needs now that we have become so conscious of how scarce these resources have become.

The ideas of progress and sustainable development are just that—ideas. But in modern times, these ideas have become particularly effective as the underlying ground on which political decisions are made, and they are infused into almost all current economic thinking. As functional social realities, as the hegemonic political reality, as the basis for industrial-technological innovations, and as the dominant worldview, they are manifest in every corner of human existence and as such have become categorical for our thinking and behavior, for trade, communication, and industry.

I would like to speak out and declare that our current state is unnatural. We act against what we are; we deny the living forces that create us, as Gerard Kuperus has compellingly put it.[2] These ideas represent no natural reality; rather, they are our own creations, and they have led us on a path of destruction on a massive scale.

What have we lost by introducing the endless possibilities of industrial and personal economic development into the mind-set of modern Europeans, Americans, and Asians? We have lost nature! What is needed is wisdom: a new type of thoughtful acting or "letting be" that has the courage to perceive and accept humanity's place in the natural world—that is, to act truthfully to nature.

FROM SUSTAINABILITY TO SUSTAINABLE DEVELOPMENT OR PROGRESS

There is an intimate relationship between the idea of sustainable development and the belief in infinite progress.

The Brundtland report defines sustainable development as "development that meets the needs of the present without compromising the ability of future generations to meet their own needs." It was formulated during the Stockholm Conference in 1972, where Maurice Strong was the secretary general. Strong has described the machinations of this conference in his book *Where on Earth Are We Going?*. This was the first time that the idea of sustainable development was discussed in an international political forum.

Stockholm 1972 was the grand meeting place between developed and developing countries with an agenda addressing what developed countries perceived as the most pressing environmental problems—namely, air and water pollution and the deterioration of the urban environment. According to Strong, this initial agenda was met with distrust and antipathy from the representatives of the developing countries. Developing countries were concerned with economic growth as a means to deal with the poverty problem in their own countries, and they were not going to accept any measures protecting the environment that would constrain their own economic development or progress. As the "Sustainability" article on thwink.org argues, "Most of (the developing countries) would gladly exchange a little pollution for the benefit of economic growth." The developing countries made it absolutely clear that their concerns had to be addressed at the conference if they were going to take part in any formulation of future actions to be taken.

One could mention that developed countries like in the Europeans, the United States, and Japan had at this point in time already had two decades of unprecedented economic growth that paved the way for optimism about the prospects of rising living standards worldwide. It was also now that the environmental crisis started to become generally more noticed. As Du Pisani points out, Western economists were aware of the sustainability problems related to the massive consumption of resources, yet it was assumed that when resources became scarce, new technologies could economize the scarce input.

In Stockholm, Maurice Strong revised the agenda, which now called for redefinition and expansion of the concept of the environment (nature and nature's resources) to link it directly to economic development and thus to the concerns of the developing countries. Environmental sustainability became linked with poverty and the need for economic growth; thus, the ground was laid for future conflicts and unavoidable tradeoffs. During the Stockholm Conference, the concept of environmental ethics transformed into the global consensus-formulation: "sustainable development"; in other words, this was a transformation that went from tackling the problems such as pollution on a global scale and the social, economic, and environmental impact of the escalating population growth, which were originally intended to challenge the values of progress to a new reaffirmation of those values. As Du Pisani writes, the new concept of sustainable development has since Stockholm become a vehicle for economic growth, reverting back to the old idea of progress, which is "that civilization has moved, is moving, and will continue to move in a desirable direction"[3] as seen in the interweaving of scientific and technological, and even moral advancement.

The reversion to progress thinking has become a ground for disagreement. Sustainable development—progress—has for many become the ground for delusion and a struggle with the limitations of rationality. On one side of the debate, advocates of growth defend present political and economic powers; on the other are those who believe that environmental awareness must inspire political critique. Defenders of growth believe that humankind always will find new ways to create resources should the natural ones become scarce. They have argued for decades that the birthrate would be lowered, agricultural productivity would increase, new low pollution energy sources would see the light of day, and because of this there would still be more than enough raw materials for industry, while the developing countries would double their income per capita. Some predictions have been realized during the last thirty years, others not.[4] These same voices now argue that growth will result in a cleaner environment, a stable population level and social and economic equality. Environmentalists that subscribe to the notion of progress argue that there has been a continual enlightenment in public attitudes toward the environment and that this enlightenment will eventually lead to the salvation of the environment.[5]

Among those who still hail progress and compare it to certain Enlightenment ideas is Steven Pinker. In *Enlightenment Now: The Case for Science, Reason, Humanism, and Progress*, Pinker argues that it is the promise of science and technology, human potential, and human rationality that is the hallmark of true progress, while anti-progress intellectuals are siding with Gowdy who declares that "there is no convincing argument for past human progress and no reason to believe that it will occur in the future."[6] The anti-progress group stresses that progressivism cannot promise any continuous improvements of the human condition because the idea was based on human hopes and aspirations rather than human limitations or potentialities, and thus we need to free ourselves from all notions of progress in order to focus on "making do with what we have rather than placing our hopes in some future material or ethical utopia."[7]

PROGRESS OPTIMISM VERSUS THE INTELLECTUALS: THE PINKER CASE

In 1982, shortly before his death, the micro-biologist and influential environmentalist, René Dubos said in an interview:

> Man does not have any idea where he is taking himself or the dangers involved. I have been reading predictions of the future by those who believe they can predict what the world of tomorrow is going to be like. In all cases, the future of which they speak is merely a grotesque extension of the present—simply more and more loading of our environment with the waste product of an industrial civilization. In my opinion, there is no chance of solving the problem of pollution—or the other threats to human life—if we accept the idea that technology is to rule our future.[8]

If not to rule our future, technologies are certainly going to be a major part of how we believe we may influence the direction of the ongoing environmental crisis. The question is, who gets to define progress or what counts as development? If the development of technologies continues to be guided by economic interests instead of social and environmental issues, such as the substitution of fossil fuels and coal with renewable energy technologies, we will all face even more severe social and environmental problems in the near future. It is decision-makers, politicians, and the media who have to persuade the world to change to cleaner energy technologies and to require that corporations pay the environmental costs associated with their profits.

Since World War II, it has been the economists that are the fiercest proponents of progress and the philosophers and historians—the so-called intellectuals—who are the pessimists. In diagnosing the attitudes of the latter group, Francis Fukuyama claims, "the horrific sequence of events in the first half of the century, including two world wars, the rise of Nazism, Stalinism, and the Holocaust, and finally, the turning of modern natural science against humankind in the form of military technology and environmental damage, engendered a tremendous pessimism concerning the existence of a coherent and progressive historical process."[9] This is a different version of the "grotesque extension of the present" into the future that René Dubos talked about. Not everyone is convinced, perhaps least of all Steven Pinker. According to Pinker, journalistic habits, cognitive biases, and the intellectuals, who suffer from "progressophobia," are bringing out the worst kind of pessimism and negativity.

This is a treacherous argument, however, and can be flipped around—for instance economists William Wimsatt and Jeffrey Schank[10] state that "'progress' became a tool for justifying the free market, for colonial domination and exploitation of non-Western 'primitive' societies, and for the manipulation and exploitation of our natural and biological environment." Gowdy comments that "today, with pessimism about the future running ever more rampant, the notion of progress is all but dead among intellectuals."[11] The anti-progress "intellectuals" are many and Pinker provides a blacklist of some of these "prophets of doom," as he calls them. On top of the list is Friedrich Nietzsche, the thinker that Pinker hates more than anyone else. He is followed by Heidegger, Adorno, Edward Said, and in all twenty-eight intellectuals, including Pinker's Nemesis the philosopher John Nicholas Gray—who has stated that "humans . . . cannot destroy the Earth, but they can easily wreck the environment that sustains them."[12]

Pinker is himself in favor of only a few Enlightenment thinkers, whom he updates with the addition of statistics, experiments, and causal theory, or the pursuit of truth or facts by the rational theories and methods of the natural sciences. In *Enlightenment Now*, he uses over a hundred graphs to prove his point, which is that the world is constantly progressing. Due to science and technology, the market economy of the West, and certain virtues of a godless humanism, the world is getting better, healthier, more tolerant, richer, and happier, and there is less war, less crime, and less illness. Pinker had previously thought that in an earlier book, where he used the same graphs (now updated), that these would convince people about the marvelous times to come. People were not convinced, to Pinker's dismay, and according to Pinker, it is due to the fact that the resistance to the idea of progress runs deeper than our appetite for statistical truths. It is the intellectual culture of today that is not equipped to deal correctly with the negativity bias—we "need" bad things: "Always predict the worst, and you'll be hailed as a prophet."

According to Pinker, the truth is only found in some parts of the Enlightenment history; Kant, Locke, even modern thinkers such as Russell provide it, but never Nietzsche, Hume, or any renaissance thinker. Truths—or facts—are only found among those that believe in reason and the blessings of progress.

Pinker's view on rationality is, thus, extremely one dimensional. In my view, there is more to a human being than being rational. Even Pinker himself points out that humans are not that rational, and he does this by referring to numerous cognitive biases that explain why some people are blocked from believing in progress. Cognitive biases must, therefore, be something very bad. Nevertheless, we have to ask, what if a bias is a natural phenomenon? What if, as Nietzsche insists, irrational instincts (biases) are preconditions of self-understanding? Why are we not convinced by Pinker's graphs? Is not letting the rational take the lead equal to letting the blind lead the shortsighted? To paraphrase Eça de Queirós: Are those solely acting according to reason alone happier by never wavering from this path? It must be a difficult task to keep this inflexible and emotionless attitude toward the world—perhaps they are only appearing as inconsolatory and within they are only inconsolable?

We know very well that the metaphors with which we, for the most part, think about the world are not always real depictions of the world. Even conscious slow analytical or reflective thinking must be counted among the instinctive activities. Think about it, thinking itself—in both cognitive systems, fast or slow—must be an instinctual activity! This is an activity that in actuality always is a "thinking-for-us," and over which we have no absolute conscious or willed control. It is an activity that is informed or "theory-laden"; it is informed by training—that is, embodied skills and experiences—and it is also informed by the individual's social background, family, traditions, education, and its relation to specific contexts. We are only consciously aware of thoughts in the past tense; we never grasp the activity itself, which is the mind acting in the present interpretatively. All reflecting, all rational analytical work if you like, is just a secondary loop around that same "axis" of the preconscious interpretative act that is always now relative to the speed of sensuous perceptions and its processing (0.3–0.5 sec).

Therefore, all technological developments that have taken place during the last hundred years are due to human ideas materializing during work within specific contexts and that are generated from the act of intuition. We also see that during the same time span, science and rational thinking do not triumph over ideology although practitioners of that ideology claim to act rationally and the ideology itself to be rational.

What all this means is that Pinker's defense of progress is intimately related to the ideologies of political economy. Economic progress falls into two parts. First, there is what is called "economic growth." This area of study is concerned with the continuous increase in wealth in the advanced countries. The other is "economic development." This area deals with "underdeveloped economies" that strive to reach the type of growth we have in the developed economies of the Western industrialized type of society.[13] Economics depends on combining factors of production—labor, materials, land, and capital—to satisfy the demand for goods and services. As Peter Mould writes, "Economic development occurs when a community does not use all its resources to meet consumption needs but devotes a surplus . . . to some profitable or productive investment in agriculture, manufacturing, transport or community services . . . there must also be profitable opportunities."[14] In order to have economic growth, there must be law and order, there has to be an efficient and flexible form of economic organization, people must have the necessary skills and a sympathetic attitude toward the economic system, and there has to be an infrastructure of transport, distribution, and financial services.

Progress is arguably one of the most persistent metaphysical ideas of the West. The populations of the West are living in an age when a matured philosophy of plenty has made sure that the foundation for ever more use and accumulation is rock solid, and as such progress or sustainable development has no foreseeable end. Progress understood as optimism about the future is a belief that almost everyone, across the modern political spectrum, condones. Paul Virilio expresses this succinctly when he writes, "I have always been convinced that everything that will determine the novelty, the originality of tomorrow, is already present at the moment, concealed in the everyday vision of each person, which accounts for this constant will to practise perspicacity worthy of my desires for change and renewal."[15]

Progress, economy, technology, science, politics, and human ingenuity are intimately linked. As a modern culture we are marked by a characteristic belief in a gradual and cumulative improvement in knowledge. As Steven Best and Douglas Kellner write, "Technology is fundamental to the adventure of evolution, promoting ever greater and more rapid waves of scientific innovation, social transformation, and economic advancement. Modernity was fuelled by perpetually revolutionizing science, industry, and technology via the printing

press, factory system, steam engine, railroad, airplanes, automobiles, communications media, and culture industries."[16] J. B. Bury said that the idea of progress
is a synthesis of the past and a prophecy of the future.[17] And Edward Copleston,
who became provost of Oriel College in 1825, said that "the pursuit of wealth
. . . is, to the mass of mankind, the great source of moral improvement."[18]

To pursue progress thinking yet at the same time being painfully aware
that the Earth's biosystem is finite must be a complicated and disconcerting
affair. It is an issue of opposites that are difficult to synergize. Free-market
capitalism is the drive for material production and consumption; it raises living
standards, but only for the few. Yet, the environmental problems are global.
Market economics has brought more progress than any other force in history.
Globalization has escalated the risks, and what is thought to be rational among
individuals is increasingly irrational for society. Giubilini and Savulescu give a
great example of the moral human.[19] We are to suppose we have an empty cup
we want to bin. I have decided, in light of the environmental crisis, that I shall
recycle the cup. I know my moral commitment; still, I have problems making
up my mind because I don't know exactly what material the cup is made of; I
don't know either whether the waste of a particular bin is destined to an efficient recycling industry. There is a lot of information that needs to be gathered,
and I just don't have those resources at hand. So, I just throw the cup into one
of the bins; it may be the right bin, but it may also be the wrong bin. Giubilini
and Savulescu write that this is quite telling of human nature: humans are often
incapable of making choices consistent with our own moral or rational goals,
particularly when we have little or no time to make the decision. We see that
our moral lives are not purely rational, and Pinker cannot point to a couple of
graphs that would inform our reflected decision and where there would be no
place for emotive and or intuitive judgments.

There is a problem to think, as Pinker does, that progress can be projected
indefinitely into the future—we simply lack the relevant wisdom to know
how we are affecting the future. Whether the engineers and scientists will
be able to come up with technologies that will solve the climate crisis in
the future we cannot know, no matter how many graphs are drawn. Will the
graphs enable the engineers' developing sustainable technologies to stop the
world from warming up, to reverse temperatures so that the ice on the poles
stops melting and sea levels rising? Can we predict what the consequences of
these new technologies will be? Will technologies or rational arguments stop
seven billion people from producing children at the same increasing rate as
today (which is 2 percent per annum)? Will technologies be able to handle
the shortage of food, hunger epidemics, mutating viruses? The point being the
amount of information about what may happen in the future is overwhelming
and we cannot access it, for it is in the future.

Du Pisani underscores further the problems caused by the crisis, by
what he has termed the "ecocide"—which is the destruction of the natural

environment. First of all, the uncontrolled population increase aggravated several other problems—especially in the developing countries: overcrowding, uncontrolled urbanization, housing shortages, slum conditions, and governments unable to provide medical and educational services to fast-growing populations. And it has become increasingly difficult to feed the populations. This means, in light of Stockholm and the new sustainable development definition that was to enable developing countries to economic growth, there is an increasing pressure on Earth's resources. The "intellectuals" that Pinker complains about are in fact almost all aware of this development and warn about it. The problem is that the West and the developing and overpopulated countries in Asia have become cultures of maximization, sustainability is but a word.

What is needed is overwhelming namely, a change in political and economic thinking. To change the economy and politics means first and foremost a radical transformation of social structures, particularly with regard to how they interact with nature; it means to change attitudes and habits concerning our private economy; it means a new and different knowledge of how we shall exchange goods, grow food, and harness energy. We can begin by questioning, like Nietzsche did, our values and purposes. From a more critical angle we can ask, where does the excitement for what's to come, come from? Are we able to deal with the answer honestly? There need to be, in the words of Daniel Sarewitz, "an awareness of how science and technology—and the continual remaking of the world that they provoke—interact with and influence the sources of value in people's lives."[20] In promoting change, we must believe that the transformation people have to undertake, for instance by removing some of the many polluting items that today are generating our material wealth, would itself be a source of human betterment—something like a deconstructive progress.

TRUTHFULNESS-TO-NATURE

We may agree with Spengler's postulation that "decline follows progress,"[21] according to which there are five movements in history that are featured in every culture:

1. From intuitive and rural societies enveloped in myth to a bloated urbanism accompanied by a practical, materialistic outlook;
2. From a poetically and mythically expressed sense of community to a prosaic individualism;
3. From a spring of dream-like feelings of fullness through a summer of consciousness in which philosophy displaces religion to an autumnal rationalism that leads to a winter of utilitarianism;

4. From a vigorous cultural primitivism through a period of great masters to a formalistic pretentiousness;
5. From a politics of patriarchal chivalry through aristocracy to a decline into economism and democracy.

The picture Spengler draws of his time "has a certain plausibility about it," Dannhauser says, "which is significant to our time as well."[22]

With this in mind, we can ask, what should guide the development of sustainable technologies? The answer is clearly related to the need for renewable energies and, thus, new technologies offering solutions that will successfully substitute for the fossil fuels, particularly petroleum and coal. Nevertheless, Nietzsche wrote in the 1870s that "if mankind is not to destroy itself . . . there must be discovered, as a scientific criterion for ecumenical goals, a knowledge of the conditions of culture, which surpasses all previous levels of such knowledge." These ecumenical goals were thought to unify all lesser goals and serve as what Zarathustra called "the meaning of the Earth."[23] However, in *Beyond Good and Evil*, Nietzsche had only scorn for those calling for a "return to nature." For what does that actually mean beyond human intentions and goals? Is it possible to adjust what fuels human intentions and goals? Can we somehow at least locally realign our intentions and goals to the state of the Earth and take, for instance, the following statistics seriously: the five warmest years on record have all come in the 2010s; the ten warmest years since 1998.[24] Are we willing to turn our scientific, technological, economic, social, human, and individual goals around so that we truly can live sustainably—that is, with some considerable material sacrifice and a new acknowledged truthfulness-to-nature as our imperative? If so, this would mean, again as Nietzsche pointed out, that we have come to embody the courage of the conscience which admits to the reality of the environmental crisis and that makes us act accordingly. It does not mean to abandon technology or science or analytical reflection; it means to escape the one-dimensional metaphysics of scientific rationality and to add a new dimension, one of openness to being, to nature, to the human mind. In other terms, can we discover simpler ways of living? Once, in early modernity, philosophy was able to shape a culture. Can it again? What would it take to change, to think, to perceive, and to live differently, for all of us to preserve whatever nature is left for us? Because we are talking about nature—because we are it.

According to Edwin Mansfield, most societies of the past had economies that were not progressive[25]—in other words, to rephrase John M. Gowdy, in the past, the purpose was not to pursue an economic policy to ensure a robust and steady increase in gross national product.[26]

Let's face it, the reason why nature is giving up on us is human greed, which is not an absolute, but rather the psychological conditioning of consumer mentality generated by the manufacturers of goods that must be sold and a culture in which progress is measured by the growth in consumer spending. Over the last hundred years, the ruthless elimination of any culture not based on market economies and the transformation of human societies and habits to a single model have made us more vulnerable because of the worldwide reliance on the same technology and the same market mentality.[27] Yet, there is a growing sense that we cannot exist in isolation from the natural world. As Gowdy states, "As individuals, we have experienced a substantial loss of information as to how to survive in the natural world without an ever-larger array of exosomatic artifacts."[28] There is a growing uniformity of human culture that is solely dependent on technological advances—and in spite of these, an enormous amount of the human population remain poor. We know now that an economy that is not embedded in a due regard for the natural world is disastrous throughout the biosphere in indiscriminate and ultimately unsustainable ways. We get the sense that we are losing our sense of the human as a species—without which it will perish as miserably as a fish out of water.[29]

However, human cultures have not always been globally uniform. Japan of the past is one case at hand. For instance, the philosophy and practice of the Zen Buddhists—all three schools Rinzai, Soto, and Pure Land— have their focus on human capabilities and their relationship with nature. It is a "thinking" very different from ours of the West, not about accumulating riches or uncritical consumption but realizing one's own true nature.

Human will is born out of nature and vanishes into nature—it is a nature that is withdrawn from rationalization and abstractions, yet it remains everywhere present, says Koichi Tsujimura.[30] It is being itself and being true. Nature means "freedom" and "truth," which is at bottom an insight into our own "emptiness" or transience of being. "Truth" is not the same as episte mological truth. Epistemological truth, with its glorification of the fact, is the human ability of "knowing" abstractly—that is, the human ability to form metaphors—but these metaphors do not touch any concrete reality; they are, in Nietzsche's words, anthropomorphizing nature. Knowing, as we use the verb, is a way of calculating as a means to master nature. The truthfulness that we strive for and the truth in knowing contradict each other. As Breazeale writes, "There is a manifest incompatibility between the desire to free oneself of all illusions, to settle for nothing else than ideal certainty in questions of truth, and the need for life-preserving fictions, which apparently must be believed to be true if they are to serve their intended function."[31] Truth which is life affirming has become subordinated to abstract methodological assessments of the world as it is "in itself" and preferably independent of the knower—where humans believe they clearly are on the "outside" with special access to the "inside of things."

The Kyoto School, including Tsujimura, has used the thinking of Zen Buddhism, Meister Eckhart, Heidegger, and Nietzsche to emphasize that only by taking a step back from the overthinking mind can we get a glimpse of the non-dualistic nature comprising body and mind as well as humanity and nature. This means that to enable a seeing-through, we first have to let go of all representing, producing, adjusting, altering, acting, making, and willing, according to Tsujimura. For instance, prior to "seeing a tree," we place ourselves before the tree and the tree presents itself to us. The representing disappears since there is no distinct "I think" at that moment—the tree stands where we stand—"the donkey looks into the well and the well looks into the donkey." This is a released representing and a leap onto the ground upon which we truly live and die. In our own world of ambition, in the world of progress economy, with the aid of technologies and the sciences, and our trust in sustainable development, we have somewhat "drawn the curtain"—as Heidegger would put it—on this ground. Thus, we miss this concreteness of living now, that is, to this literal ground upon which we tread and where there are no individual truths, as Okochi Ryogi writes, because the term the individual is itself an error to use at this primordial level.

Nature cannot, or should not, be defined solely by science—it is not most fundamentally physis or natura, that is, in modern usage, a conception of nature as an objectified resource. Nature is the spontaneous being of all things. However, it is not desired that we should rid ourselves of science and technology; instead, as Nietzsche says, we should master them. Our world cannot subsist without science and technology, but presently as a way of thinking and practice it is no longer the sustainable way. Scientific thinking as it is practiced today is only in part capable of dealing locally with pollution, but not with overpopulation; it can handle the invention of alternative energy resources, but is probably not able to halt the overharvesting of the Earth's natural resources.

We cannot travel back in time. But we can turn to a tradition that allows us to reappropriate its wisdom for the sake of the future.[32] A key concept of this wisdom is "wu wei," which means "non-interfering" and in practice means to live in accordance with nature—which by Lao Tzu was regarded as the highest moral and most natural way of life. This means living locally—"small is beautiful" as E. F. Schumacher said it—practicing inaction in the sense that all human activity is a letting be and human life takes its lead from nature.

This is a willed "naïve" way of living that is quite different from developmental progress thinking. Perhaps it is utopian; perhaps as a culture we are too dominated by one version of modernity to allow the possibility for any other, yet there remain minority traditions that still might speak to us of another way, particularly to those willing to listen. In a world as modern as our own Vincent Van Gogh was able to listen. He wrote to his brother Theo in 1888:

> In looking at Japanese art we encounter people who are apparently wise, intelligent, and even philosophical. How do they spend their time? Do they try to calculate the distance between the earth and the moon? No! Do they study the politics of Bismarck? Not that either. They study a single blade of grass. . . . But this blade of grass gradually allows them to draw and paint plants of all kinds, all seasons, landscapes with all kinds of mountains and fields, and eventually even animals and human beings. This is how they spend their lives. But life is too short for us to be able to paint everything. . . . Believe me, they live amidst nature as if they were themselves flowers. Isn't what these Japanese teach us, in fact, true and genuine religion?[33]

Human tendency is always to wander astray—we are aimlessly drifting between hope and despair for the future. Humans are the true homeless of the world; we conceal ourselves behind concepts and beliefs that make up cultures, sciences, and civilizations—abstractions that conceal the ground on which we tread, the air we breathe, the water we drink. As Heidegger states, "Everything else is no longer a superstructure, but merely a run-down annex."[34]

On August 1, 2018, it became clear that we have already spent the natural resources of the Earth for the whole of 2018; we had reached what has been termed the "Earth Overshoot Day." This year it is one day earlier than last year, according to Global Footprint Network (WWF). We are fishing more fish, using more clean water, cutting down more forests—we are basically draining the body of blood faster than ever before. We all know that some of the natural sciences and engineering disciplines have to become earmarked for this purpose only—to save the planet—but overall change—change that really matters—is possible only if the mind-set changes too, if attitudes and practices are altered as humans transform their ways. Today the real threat is still energy in the way of fossil fuels. We have seen some progress and valiant efforts, for example, when Al Gore managed to persuade India to abandon the implementation of over 400 coal-fueled power plants—the emission from which would have equaled what everyone else on the planet had managed to reduce. But big money corporations generally have politicians and decision-makers in their pocket, and Donald Trump's recent reintroduction of commercial fossil fuels and coal markets is a tremendous step backward. This is not merely a technical problem. The true challenge for the sciences, the engineers, the politicians, the economists, and even philosophers and educators is to regain access to that nature of which we are inextricably a part and to give the young access to it—if not my soon to be born granddaughter may actually come to experience the end of the world as we know it.

NOTES

1. F. Nietzsche, *Philosophy and Truth—Selections from Nietzsche's Notebooks of the Early 1870's*, ed. Daniel Breazeale (Humanity Books, 1979).

2. G. Kuperus, "An Ecology of the Future: Nietzsche and Ecological Restoration," in *Ontologies of Nature*, eds. G. Kuperus and M. Oele (Springer International Publishing AG, 2017).

3. J. A. Du Pisani, "Sustainable Development—Historical Roots of the Concept," *Environmental Sciences* 3, no. 2 (2006): 87.

4. Ibid., 90.

5. J. M. Gowdy, "Progress and Environmental Sustainability," *Environmental Ethics* 16, no. 1 (1994): 41.

6. Ibid.

7. Ibid.

8. *New York Times*, "On René Jules Dubos," 1982, https://www.nytimes.com/1982/02/21/obituaries/rene-dubos-scientist-and-writer-dead.html.

9. F. Fukuyama, "On Writing a Universal History," in *History and the Idea of Progress,* eds. Melzer, Weinberger, and Zinman (Cornell University Press, 1995), 14.

10. Gowdy, "Progress and Environmental Sustainability," 42.

11. Ibid.

12. J. Gray, *Straw Dogs: Thoughts on Humans and Other Animals* (Granta Books, 2002), 12.

13. S. Pollard, *The Idea of Progress: History and Society* (Penguin Books, 1971), 188.

14. P. Mould, "Science, Technology and Economic Development in the Third World," in *Science and the Making of the Modern World*, ed. J. Marks (Heinemann Educational, 1983), 430.

15. P. Virilio, *Negative Horizon* (Continuum, 2005), 29.

16. S. Best and D. Kellner, *The Postmodern Adventure: Science, Technology, and Cultural Studies at the Third Millennium* (Routledge, 2001), 149.

17. Mould, "Science, Technology and Economic Development," 4–5.

18. E. F. Schumacher, *Small is Beautiful: A Study of Economics as if People Mattered* (Vintage, 1993), 27.

19. A. Giubilini and J. Savulescu, "The Artificial Moral Adviser: 'The Ideal Observer' Meets Artificial Intelligence," *Philosophy and Technology* 31 (2018).

20. D. Sarewitz, "Science and Happiness," in *Living With the Genie*, eds. Lightman, Sarewitz, and Desser (Island Press, 2003), 189.

21. W. J. Dannhauser, "Nietzsche and Spengler on Progress and Decline," in *History and the Idea of Progress*, eds. Melzer, Weinberger, and Zinman (Cornell University Press, 1995), 130.

22. Ibid., 125–127.

23. D. Breazeale, "Introduction," in *Philosophy and Truth—Selections from Nietzsche's Notebooks of the Early 1870's*, edited and translated by Daniel Breazeale (Humanity Books, 1979), xxiv.

24. Climate Central, http://www.climatecentral.org/gallery/graphics/the-10-hottest-global-years-on-record.

25. E. Mansfield, *Microeconomics* (W. W. Norton, 1991), 9.

26. Gowdy, "Progress and Environmental Sustainability," 43.

27. Ibid., 47.

28. Ibid., 48.

29. K. Sale, *Rebels Against the Future* (Perseus Publishing, 1996), 266.

30. K. Tsujimura, "Martin Heidegger's Thinking, and Japanese Philosophy," *Epoché* 12, no. 2 (2008).

31. D. Breazeale, "Introduction," in *Philosophy and Truth—Selections from Nietzsche's Notebooks of the Early 1870's*, edited and translated by Daniel Breazeale (Humanity Books, 1979).

32. O. Ryogi, "Nietzsche's Conception of Nature from an East Asian Point of View," in *Nietzsche and Asian Thought*, ed. G. Parks (University of Chicago Press, 1991), 212.

33. Ibid., 208.

34. Ibid.

BIBLIOGRAPHY

Best, S. and D. Kellner. *The Postmodern Adventure: Science, Technology, and Cultural Studies at the Third Millennium.* London: Routledge, 2001.

Breazeale, D. "Introduction." In *Philosophy and Truth—Selections from Nietzsche's Notebooks of the Early 1870's*, edited and translated by Daniel Breazeale, xiii–xlix. Amherst, NY: Humanity Books, 1979.

Climate Central. http://www.climatecentral.org/gallery/graphics/the-10-hottest-global-years-on-record.

Dannhauser, W. J. "Nietzsche and Spengler on Progress and Decline." In *History and the Idea of Progress,* edited by Arthur M. Melzer, Jerry Weinberger, and M. Richard Zinman, 117–133. Ithica, NY: Cornell University Press, 1995.

Du Pisani, J. A. "Sustainable Development—Historical Roots of the Concept." *Environmental Sciences* 3, no. 2 (2006): 83–96.

Eça de Queirós. *The Maias*. Manchester, UK: Carcanet Press Limited, 1993.

Fukuyama, F. "On Writing a Universal History." In *History and the Idea of Progress,* edited by Arthur M. Melzer, Jerry Weinberger, and M. Richard Zinman. Ithica, NY: Cornell University Press, 1995.

Giubilini, A. and J. Savulescu. "The Artificial Moral Adviser: 'The Ideal Observer' Meets Artificial Intelligence." *Philosophy and Technology* 31 (2018): 169–188.

Global Footprint Network (WWF). https://www.footprintnetwork.org/.

Gowdy, J. M. "Progress and Environmental Sustainability." *Environmental Ethics* 16, no. 1 (1994): 41–55.

Gray, J. *Straw Dogs: Thoughts on Humans and Other Animals*. London: Granta Books, 2002.

Heidegger, M. *What is Called Thinking?* Translated by Fred D. Wieck and J. Glenn Gray. New York: Harper & Row Publishers, 1968.

Kuperus, G. "An Ecology of the Future: Nietzsche and Ecological Restoration." In *Ontologies of Nature*, edited by G. Kuperus and M. Oele, 201–218. New York: Springer International Publishing AG, 2017.

Lao Tzu. *Tao Te Ching*. Translated by Gia-Fu Feng, Jane English, and Toinette Lippe. New York: Penguin Random House, 1989.

Lightman, A. "The World is too Much with Me." In *Living With the Genie: Essays in Technology and the Quest for Human Mastery*, edited by Allan Lightman, Daniel Sarewitz, and Christina Desser, 287–303. Washington, DC: Island Press, 2003.

Mansfield, Edwin. *Microeconomics*. New York: W. W. Norton, 1991.

Mould, P. "Science, Technology and Economic Development in the Third World." In *Science and the Making of the Modern World*, edited by J. Marks. Portsmouth, NH: Heinemann Educational, 1983.

New York Times. "On René Jules Dubos." 1982. https://www.nytimes.com/1982/02/21/obituaries/rene-dubos-scientist-and-writer-dead.html.

Nietzsche, F. *Philosophy and Truth—Selections from Nietzsche's Notebooks of the Early 1870's*. Edited and translated by Daniel Breazeale. Amherst, NY: Humanity Books, 1979.

Nisbet, R. *History of the Idea of Progress*. New York: Basic Books Inc, 1980.

Pinker, S. *Enlightenment Now: The Case for Reason, Science, Humanism, and Progress*. New York: Viking, 2018.

Pollard, S. *The Idea of Progress: History and Society*. New York: Penguin Books, 1971.

Ryogi, O. "Nietzsche's Conception of Nature from an East Asian Point of View." In *Nietzsche and Asian Thought*, edited by G. Parks, 200–213. Chicago: University of Chicago Press, 1991.

Sale, K. *Rebels Against the Future*. New York: Perseus Publishing, 1996.

Sarewitz, D. "Science and Happiness." In *Living With the Genie: Essays in Technology and the Quest for Human Mastery*, edited by Allan Lightman, Daniel Sarewitz, and Christina Desser, 201–218. Washington, DC: Island Press, 2003.

Schumacher, E. F. *Small is Beautiful: A Study of Economics as if People Mattered.* New York: Vintage, 1993.

Strong, M. *Where On Earth Are We Going?* Canada Edition. New York: Vintage, 2001.

The World Commission on Environment and Development. *Our Common Future.* 1987. http://www.un-documents.net/our-common-future.pdf.

Tsujimura, K. "Martin Heidegger's Thinking and Japanese Philosophy." *Epoché* 12, no. 2 (2008): 349–357.

Virilio, P. *Negative Horizon.* New York: Continuum, 2005.

Part II

SUSTAINABILITY AND RENEWABLE TECHNOLOGIES: SUN, AIR, WIND, WATER

Chapter 3

Is it Too Late to "Let the Sun Shine in"?

Don Ihde

Right now the biggest fires in history are burning in our most Western states, and the media are printing articles suggesting that we may have now reached a "tipping point" from which it is too late to stop global warming. Of course, everyone, other than a rabid climate denier, knows that a wise environmental action would be to cease using fossil fuels and to develop and use only renewable fuel sources.

This chapter will include some autobiographic and postphenomenological observations about solar power as an energy source. Historically and politically this is, hopefully, a temporarily bad time for the United States regarding governance, particularly with regard to the environmental policy. The current government—bound to "save" fossil fuels, the steel industry, and other once dominant nineteenth-century energy sources—is doing everything possible to retard, stop, and return to an earlier industrial style of energy production. While coal is probably too uneconomical and thus will see its influence dwindle, the invention of fracking is allowing other fossil fuels to be even more readily available. I will here simply assert that I oppose this tendency; and having myself installed and used a solar system, I will eschew a political analysis for a postphenomenological account of this experience.

Many of my readers already know part of the story: in 1961, I purchased fifty-six acres of land in Weston, Vermont, built a log cabin (about Heidegger Hut size), and spent summers there until 1974, with no power other than kerosene lamps. At that point, I began to build a three story Saltbox house up a hill from the cabin; located now in an enlarged sixty-eight-acre property, but far from a town road and power source, it, too, lacked electricity. By this date, I was no longer a graduate student and had moved to Stony Brook University on Long Island and was busy writing, with two books published and more on the way. Mechanical typewriters had exceeded their shelf life and were now

a part of the past in my writing history, and so—my first solar experience—
a solar-powered laptop was my technology for producing books from 1974
onward. The house, the largest in my life to date, took many summers to
complete, but remained without electricity. Eventually, my wife, Linda,
began to dislike the smell of kerosene lamps; I had grown up with these as a
boy long ago in Kansas, and simply took the smell as "normal," but the winter
treks over three to five feet of snow, lacking a plowed road, did take a toll,
and so we agreed to "modernize." We planned for halogen lamps and a solar
source which would allow me to add a printer to my laptop for books. As we
researched solarization, itself a stimulating learning experience, we learned
that there were many different sizes and degrees of solar technologies then
available. The cheapest and tiniest technologies were homemade, of a small
number of solar panels with special batteries and just a few devices for light-
ing, but our engineer also showed us fully autonomous, space-age systems
which used battery systems such as those for Moon voyages, inverters to run
high-demand AC appliances, even washing machines and vacuum cleaners,
and large banks of solar panels backed up with automatically starting genera-
tors in case of long sunless periods. These were obviously very expensive
set-ups, but since Jimmy Carter had recently been voted out, subsidies for
solarization that had abounded under his administration disappeared, and
many larger companies were forced to sell their solar panels at a discount,
thus, making them temporarily financially accessible for ordinary use.

We opted for six panels on our roof and six golf cart batteries, and to our
surprise once we sat down and did a list of what we desired—me word pro-
cessor, printer, lights, she lights, CD player, radio—we found that they all
were DC, hence an AC inverter which could have added much more expense
to the system was not needed. We were delighted to discover that ambient
light was all that was needed to charge the system. We could hear (slight
sound) the relays "click on" at first light and "off" by about 10 a.m. when full.
We had a gas generator just in case; however, in the years of operation we
never once used it to fill the system. We used the generator occasionally for
a hair dryer, vacuuming, or ironing; otherwise solar provided our needs and
with no utility bills. "Insolation," the name for ambient light, we discovered
was best in the winter when snow cover magnified the available light. The
system was flawless and had cost us less than 10 percent of what it would
have cost to run a power line in from the nearest road and power source. To
this day, I regret not solarizing both our LI house and the subsequent Vermont
house traded for our previous Saltbox in Vermont. This is particularly viable
now that the utility companies have lost a battle to be required to "buy back"
solar generated electricity in New York, thus allowing a solar-powered house
to run the meter backward for much of the summer and to provide lower costs
for electricity at other times.

In countries that favor renewables, Germany for example, solar is already economically on a par with natural gas and the other less expensive fossil fuels. Indeed, in parts of northern Europe, due to subsidies and friendly regulations, meters often run backward, and so solar energy users get electricity which is far cheaper than fossil fuels. The usual objection to developing renewable technologies relates to sunless days for solar and windless days for turbines—but for those who are technically savvy, these are infrastructure problems to be solved, and many areas are already solving them. For example, smart transmission systems which draw from large regions mitigate local sunless or windless areas through spatial transmission from *where* power is available to where it is not, and improved storage technologies can provide temporal transmission from *when* power is available to when it is not. An interesting example of the latter is already underway in the US Southwest. A three billion dollar re-working of Hoover Dam will turn the previously hydro-electrical (also non-fossil) system into a giant "battery." Water flowing from the dam will be re-pumped into the lake behind the dam to be re-used for storage release in low sun and wind times, returning to hydroelectric generation.

Other possibilities include repurposing spaces closer to the energy use to serve a dual function. We already do this by putting solar panels on roofs, but there is a Chinese development underway which will use super-highways for solar system beds. Their highway construction, with much thicker cement beds, and extremely large surfaces, can then directly feed into electric vehicles (cars and trucks) with plenty of left-over power for highway side villages along the way. I think of this development every time Linda and I drive from Manhattan to our Vermont place, 235 miles of freeway for solar panels!

But the greatest shortcoming of solar power relates to current cell design. Most solar cells rely upon a silicone layer which draws power only from a limited range of electromagnetic spectrum light. The best power percentage runs to 27.7 percent of the light spectrum, with an average of 22.2 percent. Since 2009, experiments have been started with perovskite layers which theoretically could raise the total insolation power of solar cells to 30 percent of the spectrum or more, a considerable improvement. Admittedly, early developments were unstable, but recently rather than seconds of short lasting power, capacities are now approaching far greater stability and already last for thousands of hours. Once reaching commercial viability with lowered construction costs, such tandem cells would lower the cost of solar energy far below any other current energy source. If combined with political support such as occurred under Carter, Clinton, and Obama, solar would be the most economical of all current electricity sources.

The history of optical technologies in earlier science history also gives hope. Prisms, which led to discoveries that white light is made up of a color spectrum, go back to the seventeenth and eighteenth centuries, and the field of optics of which they are a part lie at the heart of the rise of modern science. The nineteenth century developed spectroscopy which has become central to biology and astronomy. These are the technological predecessors for today's experimentation of light spectra such as those on solar cells. Once science learns how to capture more of the spectrum, solar cells will become more and more efficient, and there is more than enough solar radiation to take care of human demand.

This chapter admittedly focuses only upon solar energy. Wind energy is the other partially developed source of renewable power. While I will not deal with this source here, it is worthwhile noting that its eager reception in Europe is counter-matched by much counter-rejection in the United States. A great deal of this difference is due to how the economics are presented. In Europe much wind power is locally aimed, so that in many Northern European countries power sources are *local*, whereas in the United States much wind power is capitalistically owned by large corporations. Thus, every Danish village wants its local and often subsidized wind power source, whereas, in contrast, in Vermont much local opposition is "NIMBY"—not in my back yard—opposed. I have to admit, each time I fly into the Netherlands and Denmark, I see more and more wind turbines, which reminds me that at home I hope in vain to see offshore wind farms—and feel the frustration of delay.

REFERENCE

It is my habit to regularly read *Science*, *Scientific American*, *The Economist*, *New York Times Science Section*, and other sources which regularly produce short articles on technoscience topics. As noted, I have followed developments in perovskite solar cells since their invention in 2009.

Chapter 4

Talking Weather from
Ge-Rede to Ge-Stell[1]

Babette Babich

WEATHER TALK

Talking about the weather was until recently a cliché expression for time wasting, idle chatter, what Heidegger calls Gerede. Today's talk of global warming seems altogether different. Yet Heidegger's analysis of Ge-Stell also permits a complex reading of the mobilization of popular opinion, total- ized as he knew this to have been in his own political era. Here it is useful to take up the question of its current totalization along with a reflection on today's "climatic regimes," as Bruno Latour has recently spoken of these. For his part, Peter Sloterdijk uses the language of atmoterrorism, and although his analysis draws on long-standing events from the twentieth century, he is virtu- ally alone in so doing. And if Sloterdijk alludes to Luce Irigaray's *Heidegger and the Forgetting of Air*, Irigaray herself refers more to interiority—that is, yoga and breath.[2] Indeed, most references to atmosphere, breath, are intimate affairs. If, in *Minima Moralia*, Adorno alludes to shame, the embarrassment not only of needing breath, of vulnerability and exposure, but also the awful pain that one is (still) able to breathe (this is the survivor's culpability[3]), Sloterdijk's reflections on what he calls "explication" ask us to review what we continue to take for granted. And Sloterdijk crosses academic and other lines by reminding us that the United States' use of drones for assassination (which became standard military practice with Obama) is a terrorist practice by definition.[4] Weather militarization is on the same continuum.

As opposed to Sloterdijk, when scholars such as Andrew Ross, Ackbar Abbas or Michael Taussig reflect on the weather, they carefully avoid talk- ing about political or military issues. Abbas's brief essay, "Adorno and the Weather: Critical Theory in an Era of Climate Change,"[5] concerns neither Adorno nor the weather (Abbas begins with Beckett for the first few pages), yet Abbas does manage to suggest that concern with the weather is a rich person's/first world concern, as if the poor might be pleased to ride to hell in a handbasket if some advantage could be grubbed (an argument which discovers, as public intellectuals in the age of Trump likewise argue, that capitalist investors and the indigent share the same mind-set).

Taussig, writing on "Wind and Weather,"[6] invokes William Dampier's assessment of winds.[7] Taussig's account is mostly unburdened by hermeneutics, a clear advantage of analytic or mainstream ethnography, as result he can limit himself to reflecting on weather truisms. Drawing on Ross's *Strange Weather*,[8] Taussig argues that what had been a word—for example, *mana*—evolves over time: "we talk about the weather as a way of avoiding talking about anything else."[9] Here it should be noted, similarly in an ecological and similarly ethico-political context, that Alasdair MacIntyre had earlier elaborated the same argument of contextual translation, and Taussig silently echoes MacIntyre's reflection on the word *taboo* as MacIntyre discusses, rather more ethno-hermeneutically, environment (and land values), convention, and meaning in *After Virtue*.[10] It is what things are called, as Nietzsche says—this is the key to his "philosophy of science"[11]—that makes all the difference.

Sloterdijk knows how the names we give or do not give to things work in the media. Talk today is of global warming and $CO2$ levels but not chemtrails, HAARP, or weather control. Geoengineering enters discussion as a future option, rather than as already deployed and for some time. Thus, the back story to all 'fake news' concerns how what is "fit to print" gets into print and how what is silenced is silenced. Think of Harvey Weinstein over the years but think too of all the Harveys there have been in the entertainment industry, in academia, anywhere there is power, unmentioned scandals.

If Bruno Latour has for some time been telling us that 'we have never been modern,' his recent reflections concern the weather, if they also recall the complexities of his earlier work on Pasteur and laboratories and agricultural economies and centralization,[12] that is, to use the language of Latour's actor-network theory, microbes quite as literal micro-actors, and turning more environmentally, if still on the same continuum, to reflections on climactic regimes in *Facing Gaia*.[13] By contrast, Sloterdijk documents the inception of our all-too-real modernity, complete with Žižekian expectorations, beginning with the battle of Ypres, including the why and the how of gas warfare in World War I, down to the day and the year:

> April 22, 1915, when a specially formed German "gas regiment" launched the first, large-scale operation against French-Canadian troops in the northern Ypres Salient using chlorine gas as their means of combat.[14]

Sloterdijk carries his question through two world wars and beyond, including the firebombing of Dresden, the nuclear attacks on Hiroshima and Nagasaki, but also the deployment (and denial while none the less deploying) of weather control in Vietnam.[15]

In Sloterdijk's spherical analysis, "terror from the air" is the escalation of modern warfare as wars of action-at-a-distance, now "the de facto norm for 'air battles,'" as "one-sided, irreciprocable air strikes."[16] Today's ongoing wars, the ones we Americans stand for, be these wars declared and not, are "ex-plicated" at a distance. Sloterdijk is one step beyond the rhetorical question concerning wars that do or do not "take place," as Jean Baudrillard put it:[17] past, present, and future. In this way, Sloterdijk frames his discussion of the "militarization of weather," variously, in the third of his trilogy *Spheres*: *Schäume* and earlier as *Luftbeben*, or *Terror from the Air*.[18]

Sloterdijk's invocation of Jacob Taubes (and Gnosticism) with reference to Heidegger and Adorno reminds us of Marinetti's celebration of what the Italian futurist describes as the "beauty" of gasmasks, a stylized provocation made still more clearly with Sloterdijk's discussion of the battle of Ypres and the aesthetics of yellow foam that is characteristic of fatal lung damage.

These are difficult topics and Sloterdijk takes his points a little further than we are accustomed to seeing in professors of philosophy who are usually fast students of convention. To tell the story of war in the age of its technological reproduction, its escalation, as a "force multiplier" (to quote the Pentagon),[19] Sloterdijk explains the technique involved at Ypres at some visceral length but, more technically, he goes on to describe the firebombing of Dresden, by contrast with the ice of the January 2018 "Bomb Cyclone," an end of the world in fire: a "blast furnace effect,"

> The attackers aimed to generate a fiery central vacuum by dropping a high concentration of incendiary bombs, to produce a hurricane-like suction effect—a so-called firestorm.[20]

The result of these "surgical" bombing effects was the production of

> a special atmosphere capable of burning, carbonizing, desiccating, and asphyxiating at least 35,000 people in the space of one night [which] constituted a radical innovation in the domain of rapid mass killings.[21]

In this continuum, Hiroshima and Nagasaki are force "multipliers" of the Dresden tactics deployed by Winston Churchill and Bomber Harris. Beyond mere escalation, ex-plication articulates Ge-Stell, corresponding to "the scandal of Being taken to its dark limits."[22] Here it is what we do not say that is the key as all of this takes place against a backdrop of official silence consummate censorship. Sloterdijk's language of making "radioactivity explicit" contrasts with the expressly inexplicit—occupation censorship entailed that the mention of even the deployment of the bombs would be prohibited in Japan until 1952. And if one can deny an atom bomb, trumpeted in lock step on the front page of every newspaper in the United States,[23] denying chemtrails overhead is a piece of proverbial cake. Such silencing thus continues to accompany explication (nor do we the consumers worry over much about microwaves or cellphone radiation, or indeed genetically crisped apples and salmon, or the consequences of taking our gas and heat from pipelines and fracking our water). In consequence we have a "radically new level of latency."[24]

Sloterdijk focuses on "atmospheric explication"—including current weather manipulation (and it is routine for academics, especially as academics, to deny as "conspiracies," "fake news," anything but the official story on anything from JFK to 9/11, think only of the process theologian contra the received view on this, David Ray Griffin,[25] or indeed the very idea of weather control, including HAARP, chemtrails, etc.). And every academic smiles, as if it were an unquestionable article of faith (faith?) that the government could not, would not be involved in any such thing.

Among public philosophers only Sloterdijk talks weather manipulation for military purposes. And pointing to such a thing is problematic, given that, as Sloterdijk writes,

> Built-in to the premises of weather weapons research is a stable moral asymmetry between US acts of warfare and every potential act of warfare: under no other circumstances could there be any way to justify investing public funds in the construction of a technologically asymmetrical weapon of an evidently terrorist nature. Democratically legitimizing atmoterrorism in its advanced form requires a concept of the enemy that gives the use of means for the enemy's special ionospheric treatment an air of plausibility.[26]

Sloterdijk's point concerns HAARP, citing, as already noted, the US Department of Defense's 1996 publication entitled "Weather as a Force Multiplier: Owning the Weather in 2025,"[27] naming the 1990s a decade of military escalation not only "previously unthinkable but, largely unbeknownst to the public, in the possibilities of atmoterrorist intervention,"[28] including the logical implications of the use of drone warfare under Obama (and normalized in a Hollywood movie, which normalization is an important function of the film industry, in this case, an otherwise forgettable film starring Helen Mirren and Alan Rickman, *Eye in the Sky* [2015]), in which quite "far from providing the antidote for terrorist practices, the stratification of weaponry works toward their systematization."[29] Thus, Sloterdijk observes,

The fact that the dominant weapons systems since World War II, and particularly in post-1945 US war interventions, are those of the air force, merely betokens the state-terrorist habitus and the ecologization of warfare.[30]

For Sloterdijk Air-design is the technological response to the phenomenological insight that human being-in-the-world is always and without exception present as a modification of "being-in-the-air."[31]

Thus, Sloterdijk highlights the difference between phenomenologists who "explicate human dwelling in its global atmospheric conditions" and Irigaray's material insight "that Heidegger's concept of *Lichtung* be bracketed and replaced by a meditation on air."[32]

At stake here is the state of what Heidegger called "the question,"[33] as questioning is transformed *as a possibility* in the wake of technology. If we need critical theory to recall this possibility, we are still trying to catch up to the intersection in thinking between Heidegger and Adorno, as Sloterdijk maintains, just to begin to be able to explicate "highly explicit procedures." Thinking being, we can forget to bring the "stars down to earth" such that, for Sloterdijk, "any thinking that stays phenomenological for too long turns into an internal water color which in the best of cases fades into non-technical contemplation."[34]

THE NEW "MODERN PROMETHEUS"

The allure of the titan's gift to us, we creatures of lightning and blood and titanic ash, so Mary Shelley suggests in the alternate title of her 1818 novel, *A Modern Prometheus*,[35] technology is the engine of ambition and the promise of freedom. The ideal of the tool, the modern gadget, contemporary technology signifies possibility and potential, to the extent, as Günther Anders wrote in a parallel with Adorno's reflections on breath in *Minima Moralia*, of "shaming us"—how we might we measure up to the robots to come, assuming as might well assume that they will one day 'pass' as human,[36]—leaving us to dream of a post-human, transhuman condition beyond the human, Anders argued that we feel inadequate by comparison with the orderly *Ge-Stell* of the tool, any tool, the inveigled array that is part and parcel of *Zeug*, as Heidegger writes in *Being and Time*. This might be called "the Prometheus effect" following Anders' first reflections on "the antiquatedness of humanity" in *Die Antiquiertheit des Menschen* in 1956, an effect since transmogrified into transhumanism and the cargo-cult aspirations of the same.[37] Like Adorno, who raised the question of our complicity in genocide,[38] Anders went on to raise the question of our complicity in the ongoing violence of nuclear power plants as these are, as the political theorist Langdon Winner more prosaically argues, alluding to Clausewitz, the continuation of bombs "by other means."[39]

Shelley's modern Prometheus was already a creature wrought of body parts, medical detritus, a creature, as a result, of "proud" flesh, insulted, inflamed: in stasis between necrotized tissue and still viable, still functioning organs. This condition of necrotization and inflammation is the condition of any transplant, and the drugs one takes to prevent rejection of the organ are as much to prevent the body's reaction to decay in today's medical innovations, hearts and kidneys, lungs and livers, from cadavers, human and not (i.e., xenotransplantation),[40] but above all skin, even faces,[41] and limbs. It is significant that, not unlike Shelley's early nineteenth-century vision, Ridley Scott's 1982 *Blade Runner* shows us a dark world of barely integrated cyborgs; filthy urban landscapes; decaying apartment building infrastructure, complete with ongoing rain, environmental catastrophe.

Even if we have not read Adorno, we *live* the culture industry: the consummate *Ge-Stell* of digital media including the all-encompassing imaginary that is the screen. In films and television series, beyond the vistas of the "bad future," we know the souk-style, third, and off-world markets of scavenged tech debris presumed fetishized as valuable raw materials;[42] *Star Wars* fans are redeemed by holographic projections, *what's the diff: robot lover, hologram lover*, the same bad-tech, apocalypse-as-the-new-Western schematism of the 1981 *Road Warrior* is still dominant in *Blade Runner 2049*, where— such is the market—it is capitalism itself, with all its rules, legal claims, and copyright that, *mirabile dictu*, provides sanctuary, immune to both surveillance "terror from the air," in the separate independent and therefore sovereign *corporation* headed by Deckard's daughter with the prototype replicant Rachael, Dr. Ana Stelline—one almost needs to add © as this corporate security is secured, inviolate[43]—living in a bubble, the better to be safe from the air and its terrors, as she is there, a high-level game designer, techcrafting custom memories™ essential to Neander Wallace's replicants™.

We are sure that Heidegger has missed the point, we need no god: we need the right tech, the right entrepreneur, cue Elon Musk, or, as he has been disgraced, whoever's next. And yet, even scholars focused on technology and sociology of knowledge, conversant with digital media, and theorists of artificial intelligence (AI) and robot sex and robot rights seem unaware of the rather more prosaic bubble in which we live—and on the terms of which we publish. Thus, it is not possible to buy anything one might desire in the supermarket market: rather it is only possible to buy just what is available there. Thus, Rupert Sanders's 2017, *Anime*-inspired film, *Ghost in the Shell* offers a similarly dystopian vision of full body replacement (the conceit here is that only the brain need be transplanted to a 3-D printed body, computer operating systems and minds swappable to the extent of plug and play, viral co-infection, in a stripped down world). In *Black Mirror*, special effects work better if one assumes no wetware and a soft brain upload as upgrade, or, inasmuch as *Black Mirror* specializes in ending badly, an irrevocable downgrade.

EXPECTORATIONS

Adorno had early argued a good bourgeois point Facebook now makes obvious:

> The notion that every single person considers themselves better in their particular interest than all others, is as long-standing a piece of bourgeois ideology as the overestimation of others as higher than oneself, just because they are the community of all customers. [The source of "likes"] Since the old bourgeois class has abdicated, both lead their afterlife in the Spirit [*Geist*] of intellectuals, who are at the same time the last enemies of the bourgeois, and the last bourgeois. By allowing themselves to still think at all vis-a-vis the naked reproduction of existence, they behave as the privileged; by leaving things in thought, they declare the nullity of their privilege.[44]

We dedicate our minds to social media, life-on-line, cell phones and ear buds, ignoring the possibilities that thereby our minds can be subject to strictures of "control" by those same means of the "culture industry," whether that is understood via Benjamin and Adorno and Heidegger on the work of art or by reviewing the use of music as a different kind of military "air-conditioning," as does Friedrich Kittler and others. Sloterdijk takes the latter point to reflect that because

> infrasonic waves affect not only inorganic material but also living organisms— in particular the human brain, which operates in these low frequency zones— HAARP includes the prospect of developing a quasi-neurotelepathic weapon capable of destabilizing the human population with long-distance attacks on their cerebral functions.[45]

Perhaps it is time to bring Heidegger and Adorno together, highlighting their shared focus on phenomenology and technology for the sake of a critique of reason, cynical and otherwise. Talking weather, daring to question events such as "polar vortices," "bomb cyclones,"[46] or obvious or manifest things such as chemtrails and so on, risks not only, and it is no minor risk, speaking truth to power but, and this is worse for academics, an invitation to mockery as what Sloterdijk calls "a form of incitement to blasphemy."

As our insurance policies spell it out for us: losses caused by weather are not covered as these are covered as the term "act of God" signifies a technical exclusion:[47] "the principle of the weather is like that of birth and death: it comes from God and from Him alone."[48] Thus, we opt to talk about climate change or invoke the Anthropocene rather than question already ongoing geoengineering or weather manipulation.

And there is such a thing as climate change, but like Pogo looking for the enemy, we ourselves are it. More specifically, we are the very deliberate, the very anthropogenic, cause both directly and indirectly, deliberate and incidental. If Anders, via Goethe, had already highlighted the problem of geoengineering with his discussion of the sorcerer's apprentice as *Verschlimmbesserung*, Sloterdijk clarifies: "Nowadays what human beings meet in the weather are their own expectorations—become atmospherically objective—of their own industrial-chemotechnical, militaristic, locomotive, and tourist activities."[49] Buried in this list, it is important to highlight "militaristic." Describing the "miasmatic air quality in public spaces near cemeteries, slaughtering yards, and cloacas," Sloterdijk foregrounds a certain consciousness, even broaching "black meteorology," a chemtrail reference:

> A theory of special man-made precipitations which deals with the way that aircraft unfold airspace and are deployed for atmoterrorist and para-artillery purposes.[50]

Beyond Heidegger and Adorno, beyond Sloterdijk, we are still in the wake of modern technology and all its force multiplying effects, we still need to ask after questioning.

NOTES

1. Heidegger's concern with the elusive *Ge-* in his analysis of *Ge-Stell* reflects upon *Gebirge* in the examples he gives in addition to both *Gefahr* and Gelassenheit in Heidegger, *The Ister*, p. 44. See further Babette Babich, "Constellating Technology: Heidegger's *Die Gefahr*/The Danger," in Dimitri Ginev and Babette Babich, eds., *The Multidimensionality of Hermeneutic Phenomenology* (Frankfurt am Main: Springer, 2014), pp. 153–182.

2. See Luce Irigaray, *Heidegger and the Forgetting of Air*, trans. Mary Beth Mader (Austin: University of Texas Press, 1999) as well as Luce Irigaray, *Between East and West: From Singularity to Community* (New York: Columbia University Press, 2002) and see, further, the contributions to Lenart Škof and Emily A. Holmes, eds., *Breathing with Luce Irigaray* (London: Bloomsbury, 2013).

3. "There is no exit from the entanglement. The only responsible option is to deny oneself the ideological misuse of one's own existence, and as for the rest, to behave in

private as modestly, inconspicuously and unpretentiously as required, not for reasons of good upbringing, but because of the shame that when one is in hell, there is still air to breathe." Theodor Adorno, *Minima Moralia. Reflexionen aus dem beschädigten Leben* (Frankfurt am Main: Suhrkamp, 1969), p. 36.

4. See on the question of air a little further: Babette Babich, "Heidegger and Hölderlin on Aether and Life," *Études Phénoménologique, Phenomenological Studies* 2 (2018): 111–133.

5. Ackbar Abbas, "Adorno and the Weather," *Radical Philosophy* 174 (July/ August 2012): 7–13.

6. Michael Taussig, *My Cocaine Museum* (Chicago: University of Chicago Press, 2009), p. 45 and ff. See for a useful discussion of models as such in the current context of climate chang, particularly shore erosion as well as nuclear waste storage, Orrin Pilkey and Linda Pilkey-Jarvis, *Useless Arithmetic: Why Environmental Scientists Can't Predict the Future* (New York: Columbia University Press, 2007) in addition to Babette Babich, "Hermeneutics and Its Discontents in Philosophy of Science: On Bruno Latour, the 'Science Wars,' Mockery, and Immortal Models," in *Hermeneutic Philosophies of Social Science* (Berlin: de Gruyter, 2017), pp. 163–188.

7. Milner's book *Pinpoint* offers a similar prehistory of "dead reckoning" in the same context of the South Seas, although focused on GPS. See Greg Milner, *Pinpoint: How GPS Is Changing Technology, Culture, and Our Minds* (New York: Norton, 2016).

8. Andrew Ross, *Strange Weather* (London: Verso, 1991).

9. Taussig, *My Cocaine Museum*, p. 45.

10. See Alastair MacIntyre, *After Virtue: A Study in Moral Theory* (Notre Dame, IN: University of Notre Dame Press, 2007), p. 105.

11. See Babette Babich, *Nietzsches Wissenschaftsphilosophie* (Oxford: Peter Lang, 2010) and "Towards a Critical Philosophy of Science: Continental Beginnings and Bugbears, Whigs and Waterbears," *International Journal of the Philosophy of Science* 24, no. 4 (December 2010): 343–391.

12. Bruno Latour, *The Pasteurization of France*, trans. Alan Sheridan and John Law (Cambridge, MA: Harvard University Press, 1988). Note that a relevant if complementary discussions may be found in Richard Lewontin's *Biology as Ideology* (New York: Harper, 1990) as well as, perhaps most saliently, in Ludwik Fleck's *The Genesis and Development of a Scientific Fact*, with an introduction by Thomas Kuhn (Chicago: University of Chicago Press, 1981) if also most significantly, as a book that made—and broke—science and technology studies, Bruno Latour and Stephen Woolgar, *Laboratory Life: The Construction of Scientific Facts*, with an introduction by Jonas Salk (Princeton, NJ: Princeton University Press, 1986 [1979]).

13. Bruno Latour, *Facing Gaia: Eight Lectures on the New Climatic Regime* (London: Polity, 2017).

14. Peter Sloterdijk, *Terror from the Air*, Amy Patton and Steve Corcoran (Los Angeles: Semiotext(e), 2009 [2002]), p. 10.

15. It's a practice that has yet to cease, but weather control and weaponization may be the least of it. One can 'prime' reception by speaking in January 2018 of a "Bomb Cyclone" as the technical term for the assault on the Eastern coast of the

United States. See Alan Blinder, Patricia Mazzei, and Jess Bidgoodian cover page, "'Bomb Cyclone': Snow and Bitter Cold Blast the Northeast," *New York Times*, January 4, 2018. For an analysis of the poltical use of newspaper headlines and cover pages, with respect to World War I, see David S. Bertolotti, "The Atomic Bombing of Hiroshima," in Bertolotti, *Culture and Technology* (Bowling Green: Bowling Green State University Press, 1984), pp. 81–112. Today, an ongoing issue would be both the weaponized climate bomb and the nuclear threat, thanks to Trump who, and here he does not differ, despite the unpopularity of saying so, from Hilary Clinton, who, to quote her campaign speeches, made her intentions to keep the nuclear option "on the table" perfectly clear.

16. Sloterdijk, *Terror from the Air*, p. 51.

17. See Jean Baudrillard, *Intelligence of Evil or, The Lucidity Pact* (London: Bloomsbury, 2013 [2004]) in addition to his influential but more cited as a horror notion than actually read *La Guerre du Golfe n'a pas eu lieu* (Paris: Editions Galilée, 1991).

18. There are multiple efforts to disseminate this: see Peter Sloterdijk, *Sphären. Plurale Sphärologie: Band III: Schäume* (Frankfurt a/M: Suhrkamp, 2014); *Luftbeben. An den Wurzeln des Terrors* (Frankfurt am Main: Suhrkamp, 2002), available as *Terror from the Air*.

19. See the US Department of Defense 1996 document: "Weather as a Force Multiplier: Owning the Weather in 2025." Thus, Sloterdijk dares heresy by adverting to public documents available from the US Department of Defence (the United States long ago learned that the best way to conceal its motives was to hide them in plain sight: thus the organization of opposition to terror by terrorist means is justified and no one notices any kind of contradiction).

20. Sloterdijk, *Terror from the Air*, p. 54.

21. Ibid., p. 66.

22. Ibid., p. 64.

23. See, again, especially the illustrations of the same front pages in Bertolloti, *Culture and Technology*, pp. 81–112.

24. "The long concealed, the unknown, the unconscious, the never-known, the never-noticed and imperceptible, were forthwith forced to the level of the manifest becoming indirectly noticeable in the form of peeling skin and ulcers, as if they were the result of an invisible fire." Sloterdijk, *Terror from the Air*, p. 64.

25. The language of concession compounds any issue of discussion. No academic, to my knowledge, other than Sloterdijk, talks about weather control or weaponization, and when it is discussed it is neutralized as "geoengineering" as if we were in the middle of a sci-fi story and could geoform the world overnight rather than doing the geoengineering we have always been doing (ordinary anthropocene slash-and-burn or what we call gardening) and certainly as opposed to the explicit military application of such experiments included interventions. The fact that this is done fazes no one: act of god, we say. Hence in the parallel taboo case of 9/11, the process theologian, who better to speak truth to power, David Ray Griffin did raise sustained questions about 9/11, in a range of some thirteen books. Here I cite just one: *The New Pearl Harbor Revisited: 9/11, the Cover-Up, and the Exposé* (Northampton, MA: Olive Branch

[Interlink Books], 2008). But although Patrick Aidan Heelan, a philosopher and a scientist (and a theologian), read Grifin's work and found his arguments persuasive and told me so, Heelan himself did not write about Griffin and to my knowledge, no one has seriously engaged Griffin's work simply because it is anathema for a scholar today to talk about 9/11 according to anything other than received narrative. If, in philosophy of science, one simply fails to cite outlier views, the practice works across the field (Don Ihde pioneered this to great personal success and advantage in philosophy of technology). The author has thus written essays about this in philosophy of science, with respect to the sociology of models, including weather, social science, what have you. But all of it is so much talking into the wind as colleagues read increasingly narrowly and selectively. This means that if you "dare" to say such things, one's colleagues know better than to engage what is said thereby to give "airtime" to the subject. This has a name in German—it is what happened to Nietzsche's first book on tragedy which was never criticized by colleagues in professional journals as much it was simply ignored, a silencing that is still in effect to this day—*Todtschweigerei.*

26. Sloterdijk, *Terror from the Air*, p. 51.

27. Ibid., p. 64.

28. Ibid.

29. Ibid., p. 53.

30. Ibid.

31. Ibid., p. 93.

32. Ibid. As Sloterdijk here cites Irigaray: "It is not light that creates the clearing but light comes about only in virtue of the transparent levity of air. Light presupposes air." Luce Irigaray, *The Forgetting of Air in Martin Heidegger*, trans. Mary Beth Mader (Austin: University of Texas Press, 1999), p. 166.

33. See, for a recent focus on Heidegger and the question as such, Babette Babich, "On Heidegger on Education and Questioning," in Michael A. Peters, ed., *Encyclopedia of Educational Philosophy and Theory* (Singapore: Springer 2017): 1641–1652.

34. Sloterdijk, *Terror from the Air*, pp. 93–94.

35. Shelley, *Frankenstein or a Modern Prometheus*, p. 1818.

36. This is a rich and complicatedly separate topic, but, for an introductory discussion with further references, see Babette Babich, "On Passing as Human and Robot Love," in Carlos Prado, ed., *Technology is Changing Us for Better or Worse* (Santa Barbara, CA: Praeger, 2019).

37. See for a critical discussion Nick Bostrom, "In Defense of Posthuman Dignity," *Social Epistemology Review and Reply Collective* 6, no. 2 (2017): 1–10 but see also Steve Fuller's and Veronika Lipinska's instructively titled: *The Proactionary Imperative* (Frankfurt am Main: Springer, 2014) as well as the contributions articulating several sides of the debate on transhumanism (using Nietzsche as lens) in Yunus Tuncel, ed., *Nietzsche and Transhumanism: Precursor or Enemy?* (Cambridge, MA: Cambridge Scholars, 2017).

38. See the various contributions to Ryan Crawford and Erik M. Vogt, eds., *Adorno and the Concept of Genocide* (Amsterdam: Brill, 2006).

39. For discussion of Anders on violence and nuclear power, see Babette Babich, "La violenza della violenza," in Michaela Latini, Alessandra Sannella, and Alfredo

Morelli, eds., *La grammatica della violenza Un'indagine a più voci* (Milan: Mimesis Editioni, 2017), pp. 83–98.

40. See for a discussion of this theme, including xenotransplantation, the final section of Babette Babich, "Ivan Illich's *Medical Nemesis* and the 'Age of the Show': On the Expropriation of Death," *Nursing Philosophy* 19, no. 1 (2018): 1–14, see here pp. 11–13.

41. Al Lingis has an important and disquieting reflection on the phenomenology of medical practice as lived for recipients of face transplants. Personal discussion.

42. The dream of recycling for profit and world salvation, which is also a software metaphor for those who cannot write code and are thus compelled to cut and paste hunks of what does work, defects included.

43. This is not a matter of benevolence but prescience and refusal to be bought out by Neander Wallace's corporation.

44. Adorno, *Minima Moralia*.

45. Sloterdijk, *Terror from the Air*, p. 68.

46. These terms are from newspaper accounts, see for a discussion, Kevin Loria, "A 'bomb cyclone' and 'polar vortex' are headed for the East Coast—here's what those weather terms actually mean," Business Insider, 3 January 2018. Online. https://www.businessinsider.com/what-bomb-cyclone-and-polar-vortex-mean-term-origin-2018-1?r=US&IR=T. Accessed 15 March 2019.

47. The term "act of God" has for insurance companies a technical, that is legal, definition.

48. Sloterdijk, *Terror from the Air,* p. 88.

49. Ibid., p. 89.

50. Ibid., p. 51.

BIBLIOGRAPHY

Abbas, Ackbar. "Adorno and the Weather: Critical Theory in an Era of Climate Change." *Radical Philosophy* 174 (2012): 7–13.

Adorno, Theodor. *Minima Moralia. Reflexionen aus dem beschädigten Leben.* Frankfurt am Main: Suhrkamp, 1969.

Babich, Babette. "Constellating Technology: Heidegger's *Die Gefahr* / The Danger." In Dimitri Ginev and Babette Babich, eds. *The Multidimensionality of Hermeneutic Phenomenology.* Frankfurt am Main: Springer, 2014, 153–182.

Babich, Babette. "Heidegger and Hölderlin on Aether and Life." *Études Phénoménologique,* in *Phenomenological Studies* 2 (2018): 111–133.

Babich, Babette. "Hermeneutics and Its Discontents in Philosophy of Science: On Bruno Latour, the 'Science Wars', Mockery, and Immortal Models." In *Hermeneutic Philosophies of Social Science.* Berlin: de Gruyter, 2017: 163–188.

Babich, Babette. "Ivan Illich's *Medical Nemesis* and the 'Age of the Show': On the Expropriation of Death." *Nursing Philosophy* (2018): 1–113.

Babich, Babette. "La violenza della violenza." In Michaela Latini, Alessandra Sannella, and Alfredo Morelli, eds., *La grammatica della violenza Un'indagine a più
voci*. Milan: Mimesis Editioni, 2017: 83–98.

Babich, Babette. *Nietzsches Wissenschaftsphilosophie*. Oxford: Peter Lang, 2010.

Babich, Babette. "On Heidegger on Education and Questioning." In Michael A.
Peters, ed., *Encyclopedia of Educational Philosophy and Theory*. Singapore:
Springer, 2017: 1641–1652.

Babich, Babette. "Towards a Critical Philosophy of Science: Continental Beginnings
and Bugbears, Whigs and Waterbears." *International Journal of the Philosophy of
Science* 24, no. 4 (2010): 343–391.

Baudrillard, Jean. *Intelligence of Evil or, The Lucidity Pact*. London: Bloomsbury,
2013.

Baudrillard, Jean. *La guerre du Golfe n'a pas eu lieu*. Paris: Editions Galilée, 1991.

Bertolotti, David S. *Culture and Technology*. Bowling Green, OH: Bowling Green
State University Press, 1984.

Bostrom, Nick. "In Defense of Posthuman Dignity." *Bioethics*, 19, no. 3 (Jun 2005):
202–214.

Crawford, Ryan and Erik M. Vogt, eds. *Adorno and the Concept of Genocide*.
Amsterdam: Brill, 2006.

Fleck, Ludwik. *The Genesis and Development of a Scientific Fact*. Chicago: University of Chicago Press, 1981.

Fuller, Steve and Veronika Lipinska. *The Proactionary Imperative*. Frankfurt am
Main: Springer, 2014.

Griffin, David Ray. *The New Pearl Harbor Revisited: 9/11, the Cover-Up, and the
Exposé*. Northampton: Olive Branch (Interlink Books), 2008.

Heidegger, Martin. *Hölderlin's Hymn: The Ister*. Translated by William MacNeill
and Julia Davis. Bloomington: Indiana University Press, 1996 [1984].

Irigaray, Luce. *Between East and West: From Singularity to Community*. Translated
by Stephen Pluhácek. New York: Columbia University Press, 2002.

Irigaray, Luce. *The Forgetting of Air in Martin Heidegger*. Translated by Mary Beth
Mader. Austen: University of Texas Press, 1999.

Chapter 5

Water and Oil

Global Struggles in Sustainability

Trish Glazebrook

Heidegger's critique of technology defines a special but underdeveloped place for energy. It is underdeveloped in the literature, but also in Heidegger's writing where it appears sporadically with no systematic or consistently thematic treatment. This chapter intends to address that lacuna in a preliminary way in the hope of opening further discussion of the ontology of environmental crises that have recently quickly evolved into global environmental catastrophes, including climate change but also mass extinction and mass suffering of human and other species from food security loss, megafires, and extreme weather events. I intend to show that human inability to respond to contemporary climate catastrophe is in essence not caused simply by a desire to get maximum return on the massive investments that have been made in energy industries, but by an *ontological will to power* that sustains the essence of technology in a world that "appears as object open to the attacks of calculative thought, attacks that nothing is believed able any longer to resist."[1]

First, I examine risk blindness in the nuclear industry as both other-deception and self-deception to conclude that reinsertion of the nuclear option into United Nations Framework Convention on Climate Change (UNFCCC) (1992–present) discourse at recent Conferences of Parties (yearly meetings of the UNFCCC) displaces climate denial into a deeper blind oblivion in the essence of capital. Secondly, I turn to Heidegger's discussion of the hydro-electric power plant on the Rhine in his technology essay to show that what is at issue in that discussion is an ontology of energy. I connect that ontology to the *Gestell* of capital with particular focus on Heidegger's lesser discussed epistemological insight that *Gestell* excludes other knowledge systems such that capital self-assertively embeds value only in the Nietzschean nihilism of the technoscientific knowledge system that enables capital. Against that bleak picture, in the subsequent section, I identify a hydrontology in the praxes of indigenous peoples' knowledge systems that preserve water in its essentiality for global climate systems. In short, by reducing water to resource, technoscience dehydrates knowledge; indigenous knowledge systems harbor a saving power that immerses human understanding in the life value of water. The challenge to my reader is not to reduce "value" in "life value" immediately to the *Gestell* of capital.

THE RESURGENCE OF NUCLEAR ENERGY

In *Gelassenheit*, in the 1955 Memorial Address for Conradin Kreutzer, Heidegger asks, "In what way can we tame and direct the unimaginable vast amounts of atomic energies, and so secure mankind against the danger that these gigantic energies suddenly—even without military actions—break out somewhere, 'run away' and destroy everything?"[2] In this section, I first look at the "danger" of cascade and meltdown of which Heidegger warns. Secondly, I address his qualification, "even without military action," through the embeddedness of nuclear weaponry capacity in energy production.

The partial meltdown at Three Mile Island in the United States in 1979[3] provided a clear example of the destructive potential of nuclear power, while the meltdown at Chernobyl in the Ukraine in 1986[4] demonstrated its actual capacity for long-lasting catastrophic impacts. The disaster at Fukushima Daiichi nuclear power plant in Japan in 2011, in which an earthquake-caused tsunami flooded the facility, moreover evidenced a human capacity for risk blindness and inertia with respect to identified threat. In the 1960s, when the plant was built, tsunami countermeasures were considered acceptable because low water run-up heights had been recorded for the local coastline. By 1993, however, likelihood was established of a run-up as high as 15.7 meters (51.5 feet); despite ongoing discussion, minimal action was taken to secure against this threat in the eighteen years between the updated risk assessment and the disaster.[5] The first but lesser known nuclear accident actually occurred in northern England at Windscale in 1957, when a fire at the facility exposed employees to radioactivity that was a hundred and fifty times more than the safe-dose limit. Not long thereafter, officials attempted to cover up a massive unintended release of radioactive particles in Scotland.[6] Two years before Windscale, Heidegger warned, in *Gelassenheit*, of the danger of trying to control such "vast amounts of atomic energies."

Heidegger noted that this risk of nuclear catastrophe exists "even without military actions." Military use of nuclear weapons is not just an add-on danger, however, but entangled with energy production. The most common reactor design in the United States and elsewhere is the light-water reactor that burns enriched uranium. Uranium is "enriched" when its natural uranium-235

(U^{235}) isotope content is more fully concentrated from 0.7 to 3.5 percent.[7] Reactors capture the energy created through fission—that is, when the U^{235} is heated until its atomic structure explodes apart. "Cascade" is when the explosion cannot be controlled: the explosion cascades through the U^{235} store in a meltdown.

The explosion of a nuclear bomb is likewise a fission process. Weapons-grade, "highly enriched" uranium (HEU) that will generate an optimal explosion has minimally 20 percent but usually about 90 percent U^{235} content. When uranium is being enriched, it is impossible, without actually examining the process or product, to know whether the product is intended for energy generation or whether HEU is being produced. When the Soviet Union broke up and the Cold War ended, the US and former USSR countries signed disarmament treaties to reduce nuclear arsenals by 80 percent, and the ensuing surplus of HEU was used to displace 8,850 tons of mine production by meeting world reactor requirements through to 2013.[8] More recently, however, the Obama administration insisted on plant inspection in Iran to ensure HEU was not covertly in production, though the subsequent administration rejected this "Iran Deal" on grounds of inadequacy; and North Korea has clearly been developing its nuclear weapons program. The nuclear industry is accordingly closely related, as potentially both supplier and consumer of HEU, to a global weapons industry.

This industry puts not just populations of enemy-nations at risk, but home populations. Rabl[9] details how, also in 1957, the Kyshtym disaster at the Mayak bomb-making nuclear facility in the Soviet Union obliged locals to slaughter livestock, bury crops, and plow over fields, and over 11,000 people were evacuated from 20 villages that were then demolished. The CIA in the United States learned of the event and other issues in unsafe waste disposal and employee exposure as early as 1960, and Zhores Medvedev, a Soviet immigrant, reported further details to authorities in the West in 1976. The CIA, allegedly to the delight of Soviet leadership, downplayed Medvedev's intelligence, even going so far as to issue statements to this effect, in order to avoid the public question of safety that would put its emerging nuclear industry at risk. The general public in the United States did not become aware of the events at the Mayak facility until 1989 as the CIA in effect assisted the Soviet Union to keep its nuclear disaster a secret. Neither just war principles of necessity, distinction, proportionality, and humanity nor international humanitarian law can justify nuclear weapon deployment because of the scale of its indiscriminate impacts and long-lasting consequences. Nuclear power is accordingly entangled with a weapons industry that is immersed in the secrecies and deceptions of national security programs.

The industry itself has demonstrated remarkable lack of transparency since its inception. A mass of whistle-blowing, in the United States, for

example, concerning poor safety practices in construction and operation of
nuclear plants, has uncovered a historical tradition of public deception in a
weak regulatory context. The United Nations Atomic Energy Commission
was established in 1946 quickly followed by the Atomic Energy Act in the
United States that established the US Atomic Energy Commission (AEC). By
2003, nuclear plants in thirty countries were displacing roughly six million
barrels of oil daily to provide 17 percent of the world's energy supply; the
first electric power in the United States from nuclear energy was produced at
Experimental Breeder Reactor I at Arco, Idaho, in 1951.[10] The first accident
was at Detroit that same year, and between 1951 and 1986 the United States
had at least twelve major nuclear accidents while the Soviet Union had at
least nine.[11] In November 1974, Karen Silkwood, a technician and activist
at the Kerr-McGee Cimarron Fuel Fabrication Site in Crescent, Oklahoma,
found plutonium contamination in her home and on her body a few months
after testifying to the AEC about her health and safety concerns; she died
later in November in an unexplained automobile accident on her way to meet
with a union representative and a reporter.[12] The AEC became subject to such
strong criticism over insufficient regulatory rigor concerning radiation protection standards, reactor safety, plant siting, and environmental protection
that it was shut down and the Nuclear Regulatory Commission (NRC) was
instituted in its place in 1975.[13]

The NRC was, however, no more to be trusted. Uranium fuel-rods are
typically removed from a reactor and replaced every eighteen months. Used
rods are stored in spent-fuel pools to keep them cool so they do not fill the
plant with radioactive steam. If the water were removed from all the rods
at once, multiple core meltdown would release massive amounts of radiation and make hundreds of square miles uninhabitable. Federal guidelines
in the United States require older plants to exchange only a third of the rods
at once to minimize risk.[14] Eric Pooley documents how George Galatis, a
senior engineer at Northeast Utilities, discovered in 1992 that the Millstone
Unit 1 plant in Connecticut was routinely performing full-core offloads. This
had been going on since the 1970s, and the plant was moreover ignoring a
250-hour mandated cool-down period after reactor shutdown and before
offload that would have cost Northeast Utilities US$500,000 a day for
replacement power. A safety report submitted to the NRC to show that the
plant's network of cooling systems could function even if its main system
failed actually only provided information on loss of another, much less critical system. After eighteen months of attempting to get Northeast Utilities to
rectify these problems, Galatis went to the NRC—where he found officials
had been aware of the issues for a decade and done nothing.[15] Pooley goes
on to document harassment and persecution, including firing, throughout the
industry of employees who raise safety concerns.

This history *does not* foster trust of the nuclear power industry in the United States and *does* foster concern with regard to capacity for covert arms production of any state producing nuclear energy. The industry has also failed to work out how to dispose safely of the massive volumes of waste it has produced. This is not necessarily attributable to negligence or lack of trying—there is simply nowhere on the planet sufficiently geologically stable to guarantee no rupture and leakage, and locals, naturally, tend to mount resistance wherever storage is proposed. Yet nuclear power remains a significant energy source. The 99 reactors in the United States alone produced 805 billion kilowatt-hours of electricity in 2017.[16] Currently, there are approximately 450 reactors operating in 30 countries to provide over 2,500 billion kilowatt hours of energy (about 11 percent of the world's electricity), and globally, 50 new plants are under construction, mostly in Asia.[17]

The Millstone plant cut corners to reduce the US$500,000 per day cost of a regular shutdown. But I have come to the conclusion that the once-again growing popularity of nuclear power is attributable to more than a profit-centered desire to maximize returns from the massive investment that has already been made in nuclear infrastructure. Public protest against nuclear energy and problems indicated above reduced the popularity of nuclear power in the 1970s in Britain and the United States. For a period of time in the 1990s, nuclear was especially promoted as a bridge technology connecting the phase-out of fossil fuels to adequate carbon-free energy production. Today, however, it is not just being touted as a bridge but rather is increasingly being promoted as a long-term solution to climate change. In 2017, at the UNFCCC annual Conference of Parties in Bonn, Germany, the Women and Gender Constituency submitted a letter to the UNFCCC Secretariat protesting the prominent place given to the nuclear power industry at the entrance of the area designated for civil society organizations. In 2018, in Katowice, Poland (December 3 to December 16), the US Department of Energy's Office of Nuclear Energy lead a "NICE Future Event." The US Office of Nuclear Energy reports that New York state and Illinois have included nuclear in their clean energy policies,[18] presumably because nuclear power does not contribute atmospheric greenhouse gases that are driving climate change.

For Heidegger, the *Gestell* of technology, *Bestand*, is at work in nuclear energy. "*Bestand*"[19] is translated by William Lovitt as "standing-reserve."[20] I prefer to translate "*Bestand*" as "*resource*" because the *Gestell* of technology is a revealing that challenges and sets upon nature as something that can be exploited: "uranium is set upon to yield atomic energy."[21] I argue that the assertion of nuclear power as "clean energy" is more than just denial of the waste issue and the risk of catastrophic ecosystem contamination from radioactive emissions of a meltdown. Rather it is a blindness, an oblivion, and a deeply unconscious self-deception made possible by a globally dominant, technoscientific knowledge system that Heidegger identifies with the essence of technology. I argue, however, that technology has at its essence the *Gestell* of capital.

THE *GESTELL* OF CAPITAL

This section examines the *Gestell* of capital beginning with Heidegger's discussion of the hydroelectric power plant on the Rhine in his technology essay to show that what is at issue in that discussion is an ontology of energy. I expand that ontology as symptomatic of the *Gestell* of capital using Heidegger's lesser discussed epistemological insight that *Gestell* excludes other knowledge systems. On this basis, I argue that capital self-assertively embeds value only in the Nietzschean nihilism of the technoscientific knowledge system that enables capital. In the truth essay, Heidegger names truth using the Greek *alêtheia*, unconcealment, to argue that *lethe*, concealment, untruth as a kind of forgottenness, is "most proper to the essence of truth."[22] *Gestell* is for Heidegger a truth in that it is a way of revealing what things are in human understanding—that is, the meaning of being. I argue that the blind spot, *lethe*, in Heidegger's account of the essence of technology is the *Gestell* of capital, and that the *lethe*, the concealment most proper to the unconcealment of capital, *alêtheia*, is an ontological blindness to the very essence of life.

In the technology essay,[23] Heidegger argues that the *Gestell* of technology makes the "unreasonable demand that [nature] supply energy that can be extracted and stored" by the coal, nuclear, and hydroelectric power industries. That is, the essence of technology, in its assertion of human challenging of and control over nature, is a practice of reckoning and stockpiling energy. This challenging does not "hold true for the old windmill," unlike contemporary wind turbines. Though the old windmill's sails "do indeed turn in the wind . . . the windmill does not unlock energy from the air currents in order to store it." Heidegger contrasts this against extraction industries in which "a tract of land is challenged into the putting out of coal and ore," so that the earth "now reveals itself as a coal mining district, the soil as a mineral deposit." Likewise, in industrial agriculture as a "mechanized food industry . . . the cultivation of the field has come under the grip of [a] kind of setting-in-order, which *sets* upon nature. . . . Air is now set upon to yield nitrogen, the earth to yield ore."[24] This setting-upon, says Heidegger, challenges forth nature as an expediting both insofar as it "unlocks and exposes" but also as "directed from the beginning toward the furthering of something else, i.e., toward driving on to the maximum yield at the minimum expense." Coal is accordingly standing by so it can be burned to release the sun's warmth stored in it, which is "challenged forth for heat, which in turn is ordered to deliver steam whose pressure turns the wheels that keep a factory running."[25]

Heidegger's most well-known and well-discussed example of such stock-piling in the energy sector is the building of a hydroelectric dam on the Rhine. As the plant impedes the flow of the Rhine, the river provides hydraulic pressure to turn turbines that convert that pressure into an electric current for which "a long-distance power station and its network of cables are set up to dispatch electricity."[26] The plant is not built in the river in the same way as the bridge that for centuries has connected the river's banks. Rather, the river now appears as subject to human command and "what the river is now, namely, a water power supplier, derives from out of the essence of the power station."[27] In Heidegger's analysis, this description of the reduction of the river to its exploitability is a description of a "monstrousness that reigns." It is here that he first calls this monstrousness *Bestand*—standing-reserve, resource; then argues that this way of revealing, this truth that brings meaning to being, also reduces human being to an exploitable resource. Human being has always been vulnerable to exploitation as a labor resource—that is, the self as an energy stockpile. More importantly for Heidegger here, *Bestand*, beyond reducing everything that is to its value as resource, reduces human being to the one that is "ordering the real as standing-reserve"—this is the *Gestell* of technology.[28]

Heidegger argues that the "modern physical theory of nature prepares the way first not simply for technology but for the essence of technology" and that "the essence of modern technology has for a long time been conceal-ing itself, even where power machinery has been invented, where electri-cal technology is in full swing, and where atomic technology is well under way."[29] Modern science may have begun in the seventeenth century before technology in the eighteenth, but with respect to essence, technology began historically earlier. That is, Heidegger poses the in the last thing he wrote, an address to be read at the Heidegger Conference at DePaul University in Chicago in April 1976, "Is modern natural science the foundation of modern technology—as is supposed—or is it, for its part, already the basic form of technological thinking, the determining fore-conception and incessant incur-sion of technological representation into the realized and organized machina-tions of modern technology?"[30] His answer is clearly that modern science is not the former, the foundation and origin of modern technology, but the latter: the essence of technology is already present in the representational thinking of the sciences. I have shown elsewhere that the reckoning that is definitive of the essence of technology is an appropriation of the calculative thinking at work in the mathematical projection of nature that determines modern sci-ence since Galileo wrote in *The Assayer* in 1623 that "the universe is a book written in the language of mathematics."[31] It is as if the essence of technology is already in and thus can be born from the essence of post-Galilean science; and I argue further that the essence of capital is likewise already in and subsequently born from the essence of technology. That is to say, Galilean *quantification of nature* plays out as the *Gestell* of capital, the appropriation of nature to monetary value. Nature's mathematization affords its reduction to instrumental exchange value.

In the current iteration of the calculability of natural entities—the *Gestell* of capital—fossil fuels play a special role, especially oil that has come to dominate the fossil fuel market as well as underwrite the global economy. The significant role of oil in the post-Eurodollar global market was made starkly evident, for example, when the US shale oil boom that began in 2012 affected the capacity of Organization of the Petroleum Exporting Countries (OPEC) to control oil prices that in turn strongly influenced the global economy. Oil has leveraged massive infrastructure and other investments that are deeply embedded in global energy, transportation, and agriculture systems that determine regional standards of living and food security. At the end of the twentieth century, oil reserves were predicted to last well till the twenty-second century—production would not be constrained by the availability of hydrocarbons so much as by the price of other energy sources and the "political will of humankind."[32] It seemed clear that "tectonic shifts in the world's economies, technologies, and consumers are changing the global energy map,"[33] and that the energy sector was evolving from the domination of fossil fuels to a more balanced portfolio of multiple energy sources.[34] Yet new infrastructure to support these emerging energy sources is costly, and it is clear now, some two decades after Schollnberger and Walesh wrote about "political will" and a "balanced portfolio," that oil and gas industry leaders are "not eager to see their investments underutilized."[35] The consequence is, as Heidegger suggested in 1957, that "nature becomes a gigantic gasoline station, an energy source for modern technology and industry."[36]

I have argued above, however, that what sustains the domination of unsustainable energy sources is not just economics but an *ontology of economics*—that is, the *Gestell* of capital. What that *Gestell* is most blind to in its *abendländishe* oblivion is what it makes into an "other" as "externalities." "Externalities" in the logic of capital are costs that need not be borne by the exploiter of resources. They are generally unquantifiable in capital systems of reckoning—for example, the value of the forest as habitat for the squirrel. How the forest is an open space in which the squirrel has life is simply not visible to the capitalist precisely because it cannot be reckoned in a capital system of exchange value. The Serengeti is quantifiable as a habitat insofar as it is the exploitable home of giraffes and elephants commodifiable as a resource for the tourist industry that people pay to see in their natural habitat. In short, externalities are abject (from the Latin *iacio, iacere, ieci, iactum*, to throw, and *ab*, away), that is disposable, because they are *not exchangeable* in the capital order and accordingly do not really exist in the *Gestell* of capital. Because the value of externalities for enabling life—rather than profit—has no ontological weight in capital's *Gestell*, it is invisible.

Heidegger argues that the Greek *physis* cannot be translated as "nature" (*das Natur*) because the words do not mean the same thing. Nature in the *Gestell* of capital is resource, or to give it Marxist phrasing, the material forces of production. *Physis* is for Aristotle what moves of its own accord— that is, what drives its own growth and development.[37] That is to say, it is life. Blindness to externalities is accordingly a forgetting of life. The next section looks into other knowledge systems to unconceal life as the end beyond which there are no further ends such that life is not reducible to either resources or the already invisible and thus disposable externalities in the technoscientific exploitation of resources.

HYDRONTOLOGY

Blindness to the destructive capacity of oil in the *Gestell* of capital is especially egregious. Discovery of oil is considered as much a curse as a blessing in Africa, where it has led in Nigeria to mass, pervasive corruption, widespread environmental degradation, including air, water and land toxicity, and livelihood destruction, as well as half a century of violent conflict that has generated a male youth culture of local militarization and opportunistic profiteering.[38] In the Sudan, oil revenues financed genocide.[39] Oil is especially significant in contemporary struggle against the *Gestell* of capital because of its part in generating the greenhouse gases that are changing the planet's climate and thereby increasingly causing high impact, catastrophic events around the globe. Climate denial among national leaders is fueled by addiction to oil, especially in a wealthy nation like the United States that is, under the Trump administration, withdrawing from the Paris Agreement that was so long in the making and that is publicly rejecting Assessment Reports from the Intergovernmental Panel on Climate Change and from its own advisory institutions. To understand this, we must see that it is not just an issue of profit and greed but of the *ontology* of capital. As I have shown elsewhere, capital, not just as money but as world-opening *Gestell* that reveals everything that is as nothing more than its exchange value, drives the collusion of extraction industries, governments, and military, ex-military or paramilitary in oppression, persecution, and far too often murder of land and environment protectors who defend life from the ontology of capital.[40]

In contrast to the pessimistic assessment of the contemporary *Gestell* of technology—that he seems to be suggesting as noted above is primarily an issue of energy as technology's enabler—Heidegger is nostalgic for a pretechnological relationship to nature. In industrial agriculture, for example, "the field that the peasant formerly cultivated and set in order appears differently than it did when to set in order still meant to take care of and to maintain."[41] The peasant does not challenge the soil, but when planting, "places the seed in the keeping of the forces of growth and watches over its increase."[42] I have argued elsewhere that women's farming in the global South provides a sustainable alternative to the industrial model for growing food,[43] and that indigenous people who have lived on land for millennia are adapted to their ecosystem that is also adapted to them—human ecosystem fit in traditional communities entails responsible management, even when surrounded and regularly threatened by neocolonial systems of *Gestell*.[44] These discussions are not idealizations but respectful listening to ways of life that are alternatives to the blindness of the essences of technosciene and capital in which I grew up, and that envision a different ontology from the toxic, destructive culture of the *Gestell* of capital.

In the United States, the vision of Standing Rock has far outlived the dissolution of the Oceti Sakowin camp in February 2017 when it was cleared by security forces driving tanks and armed with machine guns. This peaceful movement of water protectors, initiated by the Lakota Sioux to protect their water supply from the Dakota Access Pipeline (DAPL), is based around the phrase *Mni Wiconi* that means "water is life," but also "water is sacred." Water is "the first medicine" that, in the words of Bobbi Jean Three Legs, "goes back to being a mother. Your baby is first coming from water, so it's very sacred. And your babies are in water for nine months before they even breathe their first breath of air."[45] Dr. Cheryl Crazy Bull also explains water as medicine: "the blood of First Creation, *Inyan*, covers *Unci Maka*, our grandmother earth, and this blood, which is blue is *mni*, water, and *mahpiya*, the sky. *Mni Wiconi*, water is life."[46]

Water is not an exploitable resource in this knowledge system, in contrast with the reductive ontology of the *Gestell* of capital, but the origin and sustaining of life. Water is the essence of a hydrontology that reveals all that is in a sacredness of place that is experiential cosmology. Tim Mentz, an archaeologist and tribal historian, describes that cosmology, its meaning to the Lakota, and the obliviousness of the DAPL representatives and archeologists sent by the US Army Corps of Engineers (ACE) to inspect the area before granting the easement that allowed DAPL to route the pipeline there.[47] In a small portion of the DAPL corridor, there are several ancestral gathering spots. This is where *Mni Wiconi* comes to earth and brings a spiritual effigy to life out of the pouring cup, where a chief might come to fast in dedication and commitment to leadership of the people, where pledges can be made and gifts exchanged, always at the meeting point of water—the first medicine. Tradition, ritual, and geography are connected. These sites are not sacred because of what happened there; rituals and meetings happen at these sites because they are sacred in this hydrontology of being-in-the-world. Events and participants are placed, in place, connected to the land of that sacrality, both honoring and being honored. Two stone rings and three half rings, called arches or crescent moons, located in relation to the handle of Ursa Major, mark where water would pour onto the land from the stars. Sites are marked by collections of small stones, but DAPL officials and ACE archeologists simply could not see the stones' specific, precise placement within the contours of the land, and their mapping to where water drains off the Great Plains.

Similarly, in India, I was shown a land reclamation project where, over a period of twenty-five years, a local community dug troughs to collect rainwater to remediate the land and built rills that would likewise retain water and soil for plants to take root. They greened a brown landscape that enabled the return of long unseen species, including a black buck I was lucky enough to see, and enabled pasturing of several thousand goats and sheep on the hills' slopes. A large-scale Enercon wind power project came to install hill-top turbines. This meant building a road into each hill that would wend its way to the top. Locals asked that just one hill be saved from this devastation and left for them. An Enron representative came to view the site. He looked down at their quarter-century's labor that had built community in the village while providing livelihoods and improving lives through purpose and better living conditions. "I don't see anything here," he simply said, and the road soon displaced their work and broke apart the community.

Such blindness means, as Vandana Shiva notes, that the globally dominant Eurocentric, technoscientific knowledge system of the global North has no respect for other knowledge systems.[48] Heidegger argues more strongly that the *Gestell* of technology "drives out every other possibility of revealing"—that is, any other understanding of nature.[49] Traditional knowledge systems built on place-based, local experience developed over generations are dismissed, ignored, or trivialized as superstition, myth, or—because the Gestell of capital is also patriarchal and misogynist—"old wives' tales." The *Gestell* of capital can see only the technoscientific knowledge system that enables global exploitation of ecosystems and people for the sake of individual accumulation of private wealth. Environmental defenders have themselves become abject. In 2016 and 2017, they were murdered around the globe at a rate of four each week.[50]

Indigenous protectors of environment, land, and water are agents of change in the face of the *Gestell* of capital. If oil is the quintessential problem of the ontology of capital that is oblivious to life, and the threat to life of climate change in the blindness of climate deniers, then water, because of its role in life, is the quintessential alternative. Standing Rock is accordingly a crucial event in envisioning a therapeutic alternative to the *Gestell* of capital. Water is the origin of every human life that spends, as noted above, nine months in the water of the womb, but also the source of life on land that emerged out of the sea. It seems water is likely the difference between life on Earth and the Martian wasteland.

The Earth is in fact fundamentally a water-management system. Oil disrupts that cyclic system through hydrotoxicity from spills during production and transport and climate change impacts caused by greenhouse gases pouring into the atmosphere when oil is burned as an energy source. Climate impacts on water include droughts, floods, hurricanes, rising sea levels, and changing rainfall patterns, including change in monsoons. Water is a circle from sea to air to land to sea that enables life in contrast to rectilinear profit extraction—a straight line of oil from ground to bank account—that is oblivious to life.

Capital appears in its *Gestell* as an ordering of nature, but it actually is an ontological entropy that is moving the planet's ecosystems to chaos and catastrophe. Its ontology denies nature's openness to the ordering structure of ecosystem management, whether human or nonhuman, and whether intended like birds' nests and beavers' dams, or unintended like seed defecation and predator population impacts. The current global struggle is accordingly an ontological battle between oil that structures and enables profit in the *Gestell* of capital, and water that structures and enables life.

CONCLUSION

In the global North, Kinder Morgan in Canada and DAPL at Standing Rock in the United States, and in the global South, Shell in the Niger Delta and Talisman in the Sudan, are finding or have found their activities interrupted and put into question by environmental defenders. When Heidegger was writing, Big Oil was just beginning to emerge as the immense global threat to sustainability that it poses today. Water protectors provide a "saving power"—that is, an alternative logic to the destructive *Gestell* of capital economies fueled by oil. Protectors are accordingly a threat to global power structures driven by the essence of technology that enables the "organized global conquest of the earth"[51] through the essence of capital. Indigenous protectors that I meet each year at the UNFCCC annual Conference of Parties aim *not just at transition* from fossil fuels, hydroelectric, and nuclear power to actually green renewable energy sources, but *at just transition* from the exploitative, destructive essence of technology to sustainable ontologies of building, dwelling, and thinking. In short, they aim at global shift from the *Gestell* of capital that both enables and is enabled by the reductive, exploitative essence of technoscience. It is thus crucial that more people are "woke" to the *Gestell* of capital into a hydrontology that values life as an end in itself. And it is crucial to support and protect indigenous protectors so the *Gestell* of capital does not engulf other knowledge systems on the planet that value and see life over capital.

NOTES

1. Martin Heidegger, *Gelassenheit* (Pfullingen: Verlag Günther Neske, 1966), 18; Martin Heidegger, *Discourse on Thinking*, trans. Anderson and Freund (New York: Harper and Row, 1966), 50.
2. Heidegger, *Gelassenheit,* 18–19; *Discourse on Thinking*, 51.
3. USNRC, 2018.
4. "Chernobyl Accident 1986." (April 2018). World Nuclear Association 2018.
5. "Fukushima Daiichi Accident." (October 2018). World Nuclear Association 2018.
6. Reese Walters, "Crime, Regulation and Radioactive Waste in the United Kingdom," in *Issues in Green Criminology*, eds. Piers Beirne and Nigel South (New York: Routledge, 2013).
7. "Uranium Enrichment." (August 2, 2017). U.S.NRC.
8. "Military Warheads as a Source of Nuclear Fuel." (February 2017). World Nuclear Association.
9. Thomas Rabl, "The Nuclear Disaster of Kyshtym and the Politics of the Cold War," *Arcadia* 20 (2012).
10. Ahmed Kahn and Barbara Eichler, "The Immortal Waste," in *Technology and Society*, eds. Horth, et al. (Upper Saddle River, NJ: PrenticeHall, 2003), 90–91.
11. Ibid., 96.
12. Richard Rashke, *The Killing of Karen Silkwood* (New York: Delphinium Books, 2014).
13. "History." (September 25, 2017). U.S.NRC.
14. Eric Pooley, "Case Study: Nuclear Warriors," in *Technology and Society*, eds. Horth, et al. (Upper Saddle River, NJ: PrenticeHall, 2003), 101.
15. Ibid., 102.
16. Energy.gov, "Operating Fleet Status. Nuclear Power Summary—August 2018," Office of Nuclear Energy, https://www.energy.gov/ne/nuclear-power-summary-august-2018.
17. World Nuclear Association, "Fukushima Daiichi Accident."
18. Energy.gov, "Operating Fleet Status."
19. Martin Heidegger, *Vorträge und Aufsätze* (Stuttgart: Verlag Günther Neske, 1997), 20.
20. Martin Heidegger, *The Question Concerning Technology and Other Essays*, edited by William Lovitt (New York: Harper and Row, 1977), 17.
21. Martin Heidegger, "Neuzeitliche Naturwissenschaft und modern Technik"/"Modern Natural Science and Technology," trans. John Sallis, *Research in Phenomenology* 7, nos. 1–4 (1977): 18/15.
22. Martin Heidegger, "Vom Wesen der Wahrheit," in *Wegmarken, Gesamtausgabe Band 9*. 3. Auflage (Frankfurt am Main: Vittorio Klostermann, 1996), 193;

Martin Heidegger, "On the Essence of Truth," in *Basic Writings*, ed. David Farrell Krell (New York: HarperCollins, 1993), 130.

23. Heidegger, *Vorträge und Aufsätze*, 18; *The Question Concerning Technology*, 14.

24. Ibid., 18/15.

25. Ibid., 19/15.

26. Ibid., 19/16.

27. Ibid.

28. Ibid., 23/19.

29. Ibid., 25–26/22.

30. Heidegger, "Neuzeitliche Naturwissenschaft," 2/3.

31. Stillman Drake, *Discoveries and Opinions of Galileo* (London: Anchor Books, 1957), 238; Trish Glazebrook and Matt Story, "The Community Obligations of Canadian Oil Companies," in *Corporate Social Irresponsibility*, eds. Tench, Sun, and Jones (Bingley, UK: Emerald Group Publishing, 2012), 131–132.

32. Wolfgang E. Schollnberger, "Projections of the World's Hydrocarbon Resources and Reserve Depletion in the 21st Century," *Houston Geological Society Bulletin* (1998).

33. OGJ, "Petroleum Industry Faces Tectonic Shifts Changing Global Energy Map," *Oil and Gas Journal* 97, no. 50 (1999).

34. S. G. Walesh, *Engineering Your Future* (Englewood Cliffs, NJ: Prentice Hall, 1995), 395.

35. Russell Gold and Michael E. Webber, *Energy 101: Energy Technology and Policy* (Austin: University of Texas, 2014).

36. Heidegger, *Gelassenheit*, 18; *Discourse on Thinking*, 50.

37. Aristotle, *Physics, Books I-IV*, trans. P. H. Wicksteed and F. M. Cornford (Cambridge, MA: Harvard University Press, 1929), 192b14.

38. Trish Glazebrook and Anthony Kola-Olusanya, "Justice, Conflict, Capital, and Care: Oil in the Niger Delta," *Environmental Ethics* 33, no. 2 (2011).

39. Glazebrook and Story, "The Community Obligations of Canadian Oil Companies."

40. Trish Glazebrook and Emmanuela Opoku, "Defending the Defenders: Environmental Protectors, Climate Change and Human Rights," *Ethics and the Environment* 23, no. 2 (2018).

41. Heidegger, *Vorträge und Aufsätze*, QCT, 18/14–15.

42. Ibid.

43. Trish Glazebrook and Matt Story, "Heidegger and International Development," in *Heidegger in the Twenty-First Century*, eds. Georgakis and Ennis (Dordrecht: Springer Science+Business Media, 2015).

44. Trish Glazebrook, "This is Not a Love Story: Robot Girl and *das Rettende* after Heidegger," in *After Heidegger*, eds. Polt and Fried (New York: Rowman & Littlefield, 2017).

45. Bobbi Jean Three Legs, "Water is Life. Water is Sacred. Standing Rock's Bobby Jean Three Legs Speaks Out against Trump," *Democracy Now!* 2017.

46. Cheryl Crazy Bull, "Woonspe—Education Gives Meaning to Mni Wiconi—Water Is Life," *Indian Country Today,* 2016.

47. KOLC-TV, Tim Mentz: Updated, YouTube.

48. Vandana Shiva, *Ecology and the Politics of Survival* (Thousand Oaks, CA: Sage Publications, 1991), 34–35.

49. Heidegger, *Vorträge und Aufsätze/QCT*, 31/27.

50. Jonathan Watts, "Almost Four Environmental Defenders a Week Killed in 2017," *The Guardian*, February 2, 2018, https://www.theguardian.com/environment/2018/feb/02/almost-four-environmental-defenders-a-week-killed-in-2017?CMP=share_btn_tw.

51. Martin Heidegger, *Nietzsche II, Gesamtausgabe, Band 6.2* (Frankfurt am Main: Vittorio Klostermann, 1997), 358; *Nietzsche, Volume IV: Nihilism*, trans. Frank A. Capuzzi (Harper and Row, 1982), 248.

BIBLIOGRAPHY

Aristotle. *Physics, Books I-IV*. Translated by P. H. Wicksteed and F. M. Cornford. Cambridge, MA: Harvard University Press, 1929.

Crazy Bull, Cheryl. "Woonspe—Education Gives Meaning to Mni Wiconi—Water Is Life." *Indian Country Today,* 2016. https://indiancountrymedianetwork.com/education/native-education/woonspeeducation-gives-meaning-to-mni-wiconi water-is-life/.

Drake, Stillman. *Discoveries and Opinions of Galileo*. London: Anchor Books, 1957.

Energy.gov. "Operating Fleet Status. Nuclear Power Summary—August 2018." Office of Nuclear Energy. https://www.energy.gov/ne/nuclear-power-summary-august-2018.

Glazebrook, Trish. "This is Not a Love Story: Robot Girl and *das Rettende* after Heidegger." In *After Heidegger,* edited by Richard Polt and Gregory Fried, 347–356. Lanham, MD: Rowman & Littlefield, 2017.

Glazebrook, T. and Anthony Kola-Olusanyu. "Justice, Conflict, Capital, and Care: Oil in the Niger Delta." *Environmental Ethics* 33, no. 2 (2011): 163–184.

Glazebrook, Trish and Matt Story. "Heidegger and International Development." In *Heidegger in the Twenty-First Century, Contributions to Phenomenology,* edited by Tziovanis Georgakis and Paul J. Ennis, 121–139. Dordrecht: Springer Science+Business Media, 2015.

Glazebrook, Trish and Matt Story. "The Community Obligations of Canadian Oil Companies: A Case Study of Talisman in the Sudan." In *Corporate Social Irresponsibility: A Challenging Concept*, edited by Ralph Tench, William Sun, and Brian Jones, 231–261. Bingley, UK: Emerald Group Publishing, 2012.

Gold, Russell and Michael E. Webber. *Energy 101: Energy Technology and Policy*. Austin: University of Texas at Austin/Disco Learning, 2014. http://www.webberenergygroup.com/test/html/foreword.html.

Heidegger, Martin. *Discourse on Thinking*. Translated by John M. Anderson and E. Hans Freund. New York: Harper and Row, 1966.

Heidegger, Martin. *Gelassenheit*. Pfullingen: Verlag Günther Neske, 1992.

Heidegger, Martin. "Neuzeitliche Naturwissenschaft und modern Technik"/"Modern Natural Science and Technology." Translated by John Sallis. *Research in Phenomenology* 7, nos. 1–4 (1977): 1–4.

Heidegger, Martin. *Nietzsche, Volume IV: Nihilism*. Translated by Frank A. Capuzzi. San Francisco: Harper and Row, 1982.

Heidegger, Martin. *Nietzsche II, Gesamtausgabe, Band 6.2*. Frankfurt am Main: Vittorio Klostermann, 1997.

Heidegger, Martin. "On the Essence of Truth." In *Basic Writings*, edited by David Farrell Krell, 115–138. New York: HarperCollins, 1993.

Heidegger, Martin. *The Question Concerning Technology and Other Essays*, edited by William Lovitt. New York: Harper and Row, 1977.

Heidegger, Martin. "Vom Wesen der Wahrheit." In *Wegmarken, Gesamtausgabe Band 9*. 3. Auflage. Frankfurt am Main: Vittorio Klostermann, 1996.

Heidegger, Martin. *Vorträge und Aufsätze*, 8te Auflage. Stuttgart: Verlag Günther Neske, 1997.

Kahn, Ahmed S. and Barbara A. Eichler. "The Immortal Waste." In *Technology and Society*, edited by Linda S. Horth, Barbara A. Eichler, Ahmed S. Khan, and John A. Morello, 90–100. Upper Saddle River, NJ: PrenticeHall, 2003.

KOLC-TV. Tim Mentz: Updated. YouTube (9:26 mins). Filmed 09/03/2016. Posted 09/17/2016. https://www.youtube.com/watch?v=w6NapCXUjU0.

OGJ. "Petroleum Industry Faces Tectonic Shifts Changing Global Energy Map." *Oil and Gas Journal* 97, no. 50 (1999). https://www.ogj.com/articles/print/volume-97/issue-50/petroleum-in-the-21st-century/oils-changing-role-in-the-world/petroleum-industry-faces-tectonic-shifts-changing-global-energy-map.html.

Pooley, Eric. "Case Study: Nuclear Warriors." In *Technology and Society*, edited by Horth, Eichler, Khan and Morello, 101–110. Upper Saddle River, NJ: PrenticeHall, 2003.

Rabl, Thomas. "The Nuclear Disaster of Kyshtym and the Politics of the Cold War." *Arcadia* 20 (2012). Environment & Society Portal. https://doi.org/10.5282/rcc/4967.

Rashke, Richard. *The Killing of Karen Silkwood*. New York: Delphinium Books, 2014.

Schollnberger, Wolfgang E. "Projections of the World's Hydrocarbon Resources and Reserve Depletion in the 21st Century." *Houston Geological Society Bulletin* 52–53 (1998). http://archives.datapages.com/data/hgssp/data/036/036001/52_hgs0360052.htm.

Shiva, Vandana. *Ecology and the Politics of Survival: Conflicts Over Natural Resources in India*. Thousand Oaks, CA: Sage Publications, 1991.

Three Legs, Bobbi Jean. "Water is Life. Water is Sacred. Standing Rock's Bobby Jean Three Legs Speaks Out against Trump." *Democracy Now!* 2017. https://www.democracynow.org/2017/1/25/water_is_life_water_is_sacred.

U.N.NRC. "Uranium Enrichment." (August 2, 2017). https://www.nrc.gov/materials/fuel-cycle-fac/ur-enrichment.html.

U.N.NRC. "History." (September 25, 2017). https://www.nrc.gov/about-nrc/history.html.

U.N.NRC. "Backgrounder on the Three Mile Island Accident." (June 21, 2018). https://www.nrc.gov/reading-rm/doc-collections/fact-sheets/3mile-isle.html.

Walesh, S. G. *Engineering Your Future*. Englewood Cliffs, NJ: Prentice Hall, 1995.

Walters, Reece. "Crime, Regulation and Radioactive Waste in the United Kingdom." In *Issues in Green Criminology: Confronting Harms against Environments, Humanity, and Other Animals*, edited by Piers Beirne and Nigel South, 186–205. New York: Routledge, 2013.

Watts, Jonathan. "Almost Four Environmental Defenders a Week Killed in 2017." *The Guardian*, February 2, 2018. https://www.theguardian.com/environment/2018/feb/02/almost-four-environmental-defenders-a-week-killed-in-2017?CMP=share_btn_tw.

World Nuclear Association. http://www.world-nuclear.org/.
"Military Warheads as a Source of Nuclear Fuel." (February 2017).
"Chernobyl Accident 1986." (April 2018).
"Fukushima Daiichi Accident: The Two Fukushima Plants and their Siting." (October 2018).
"Plans for New Reactors Worldwide." (November 2018).

Chapter 6

The Ontogenesis of Wind Turbines and the Question of Sustainability

Róisín Lally

This chapter argues that our ambiguity toward renewable technologies arises from our understanding that the nature of the machine is somehow alien and external to us. Historically, we have thought of the machine as lacking cultural signification. As a result, the machine has been relegated to mere utility rather than having any axiological or human reality. Thinking of the machine as utterly other has exercised a certain xenophobia or misoneism as well as an uncritical technophilia. This ambiguity arises from our acceptance that technology is based on the principle of conservation, a sameness underlying change that is traceable to Aristotle's theory of causality with its implicit ontological distinction between natural and human made objects.

To overcome such teleology, we need a different ontological ground on which to consider the concept of technology. Gilbert Simondon gives us such tools. His work is slowly surfacing with thinkers such as Bernard Stiegler and more recently in the English-speaking academy with thinkers such as Elizabeth Grosz and Andrew Feenberg.[1] This chapter will show how both Aristotle's phenomenology of technology and Simondon's ontogenesis can help to think though the challenges of renewable technologies associated with climate change. It will outline Aristotle's phenomenology of technology and illustrate the intersection and departure of Simondon's ontogenetic epistemology through his three-phase principle of individuation: elemental phase, individual phase, and ensemble phase. For Simondon all objects become whole (*sunolos*) though a process of individuation, which explains the coming into being and the existence of beings of all kinds. There are three phases: the elemental which is the spontaneous excess of being; individuation is the successive multistability of being where being splits becoming both the individual and the many; and finally the ensemble

83

where the being is concretized becoming more than a unity. At this stage of continuity, and in a spiraling way, the entity enters into the pre-individual stage once again. Using the principle of individuation, we can clearly see the radical rupture between ancient technology and more advanced modern technology while at the same time retaining an evolutionary tension. This tension draws out the ontological and cultural significance of renewable technologies, specifically with regard to the ontogenesis of wind energy. The final section of this chapter appeals to an aesthetic sensibility and its relation to time and space when designing renewable technologies. It argues that artists, as prenoetic creators, must take the lead in designing renewable technologies of the future, a future sensitive to the needs of the earth and human beings.

ELEMENTAL PHASE: MATTER AS PROTOMATTER

The question of genesis preoccupied philosophers in antiquity, culminating in Aristotle's prescient theory of causality explaining the origin and generation of things. And because this chapter is concerned with the emergence of new technologies designed for changes in climate, it will be instructive to revisit Aristotle's production metaphysics as the point of departure to think through the genesis of how a thing is caused or comes into being. For Aristotle, the genesis of being is a becoming, a movement that affects material things.[2] There are three ways something comes into being: through human action (*technē*), self-generation (*poiēsis*), and through chance (*efkairía*). Furthermore, under the theory of causality, beings are subject to change; that is, they undergo prior and posterior time, and because time is the universal form of change, time (or some derivative of time) must exist in the things themselves and cannot be reduced to an epistemological category. This is not apparent to us because the complex interrelatedness of Aristotle's four causes has been systematically overlooked since the late-Scholastic turn to efficient cause as the only ground for any experience whatsoever.[3] However, for Aristotle, our experience of the world first comes to us from sense perception, thereby understanding the things around us in a way in which change cannot be reduced to the invisible action of past forces.

For the most part, when we consider the elemental constitution of a thing, we say that it is made of "matter" or elements. But what does that mean? Perhaps we might say elements are composed of atoms and atoms of subatomic particles. But this is not very helpful, for modern physics does not yet know if fundamental particles even exist. Even if they do, it is not at all clear whether the thing we seek to know can be clarified or distinguished from other things, by knowing that it is composed of some ratio of these fundamental particles.

Yet this is a common way in which the material components of natural things are understood today. The relation between an Aristotelian notion of material cause and the new field of quantum mechanics is still being worked out[4] and will require a further detailed engagement between Aristotelian philosophy and the results of contemporary physics.[5] Yet Aristotle had already realized that one cannot rest content by simply pointing to some material stuff, such as wood or bronze, as the most basic material explanation of natural things. Therefore, material cause must be some sort of principle of conservation that persists or endures through all the natural changes in things. Aristotle called this principle "protomatter" and thought of it as a kind of basic potentiality for existing in various ways.[6] Thus, matter, for Aristotle, is neither some specific material stuff such as water or air nor is it empty space. Rather, it is an indefinite material substratum that embodies the possibility of actualization in some form or other. What then is the substratum of existence? Michael Tkacz, an Aristotle and Albertus Magnus scholar, interprets this as something like the modern concept of energy that is a kind of power the universe has to realize for the various states, properties, and activities of physical reality.[7] Consequently, matter need not, indeed should not, be limited to tangible material stuffs.

Therefore, the generation of an entity at this elemental stage is "potential energy" which exists prior to the being's existence. It is an energy that emerges freely from its own internal tendency, not acted upon from external forces, as a spontaneous act. This is precisely what Simondon calls the *elemental phase* of individuation. Prior to a being coming into existence it undergoes a pre-individual stage. In "The Genesis of the Individual" he describes this pre-individuation arising from a process of differentiation as a "pre-individual" that splits into an individual and a milieu. Milieu refers to an active "becoming" from relative reality to being. It can be understood as the excluded middle to use Aristotle's term. This decoupling during the elemental stage brings into existence that which does not submit to either form or principle. Simondon writes:

> The process of individuation must be considered primordial, for it is this process that at once brings the individual into being and determines all the distinguishing characteristics of its development, organization and modalities. Thus, the individual is to be understood as having a relative reality, occupying only a certain phase of the whole being in question—a phase that therefore carries the implication of a preceding pre-individual state, and that, even after individuation, does not exist in isolation, since individuation does not exhaust in the single act of its appearance all the potentialities embedded in the preindividual state. Individuation, moreover, not only brings the individual to light but also the individual—milieu dyad. In this way, the individual process is only a

relative existence in two senses: because it does not represent the totality of the being, and because it is merely the result of a phase in the being's development during which it existed neither in the form of an individual nor as the principle of individuation.[8]

So for Simondon, then, the very meaning of "matter" springs up within a complex web of potentialities: form, matter, and energy (or force).[9] Indeed in a note on the milieu dyad, Simondon explicitly points to a tension in force between the two extreme orders of magnitude where the ontogenetic development itself can be considered as *mediation* rather than matter.[10] Thus, the origin of beings cannot be characterized as matter alone. While elements are potentially compoundable in various ways such that, under the right circumstances, their potentiality for acting and reacting in the metabolic process can be effected, this is only ever *relatively* actualized.

Here the individual is always more than itself, it is *supersaturated*, constantly in a process of undergoing further changes, but not in any linear way. The individual constitutes both the individual and the potentialities of the individual. Grosz explains, "Being is at once pre-individual, individuating and individuated; it becomes something, something emerges or erupts, but it leaves in its context or milieu a residue or excess that is the condition for future becomings."[11] According to Feenberg, "The individual is not independent of the world but arises from a process of differentiation in a "pre-individual" medium that splits into individual and milieu."[12] He sees a similar process at play in Bruno Latour's actor-network theory where the social originates in the structure of the network of human and nonhumans. Social groups exist only through their connections, which are sustained by technical artifacts. The human and the nonhuman are tied together, each serving as the milieu of the other in a reciprocal process of individuation.[13] Becomings are the spontaneous potentialities of disparate forces including objects and materials forming a system that preserves many of the object's qualities while transforming them into a cohesive whole.

Thus, for both Aristotle and Simondon the material components that constitute a thing are not solely determinative of it, but merely a relative reality, arising out of a more primordial protomatter which is the result of a phase in the being's development; it is only a partial or relative resolution in a system. Latent in individuation lie potentials and incompatibilities. How do these potentialities form a whole, for Simondon? Can they ever reach their full potency in perfection like they can for Aristotle? Arguably Simondon's objects never reach teleological perfection, even theoretically.[14] Rather, the technical object, while it is finite in its possibilities, tends toward a steady state—from the abstract to a concrete mode in which the system is entirely unified. This process is not a forming as Aristotle would have it, but an unfolding or informing.[15]

INDIVIDUAL PHASE: FROM FORM TO IN-FORMATION

This "unfolding of being" of both human and object means that being is more than a stable unity with a formal structure. As we have shown, materiality in its pre-individual state is neither distinct from being nor intelligible as formed matter. Rather, it is a supersaturation of the individual and its milieu where the subject and environment entangle. Juxtaposing Marx, who argues that the production-line produces standardization, for Simondon standardization is intrinsic to the object, allowing for the production-line to exist in the first place. This entanglement of standardization within the object extends to both artisanal production and industrial production, the former corresponding to the primitive stage of the evolution of the technical object (the abstract stage to which we will return to below) and the latter corresponding to the concrete stage.[16]

One such entanglement is the technology used to harness wind. Wind turbines are used around the world to harvest the kinetic energy of the wind and convert it to electricity usable by human beings. Along with solar and hydro energy, wind is categorized as a sustainable energy source: wind is free, clean, and plentiful, thus wind energy is sustaining and renewable. While this is certainly true, harvesting wind energy requires technology that itself uses fossil fuels, is excessively expensive, is disproportionately big, and is very quickly and effectively reducing land surface.[17] At a first glance, we might think that the genesis of wind energy comes not from modern physics but from ancient sail technology. There is certainly some truth in this idea, but it is a complicated story that we must look at more closely, paying particular attention to the question of ontogenesis. Sails used in the first Polynesian settlement of the South Pacific to early shipping in the Indian Ocean and Persian expeditions on the Mediterranean often originated from the Pandanus tree. In other words, the Pandanus leaf is the prenoetic or preindividual stage of the sail and, thus, has the potentiality of being formed into a sail. For Aristotle, the leaf itself has some actual form: as living tree, as sail, as ropes, as mats, and as spice. Yet, regardless of the form, it remains the leaf with the potentialities of the leaf, one of which is actualized here and now as, say, a sail. The woven sail would have been easy to identify as something composed of the Pandanus leaf. What makes a sail intelligible as sail, however, is not the fact that it is made of woven leaf, but the fact that the potentiality of the leaf is actualized here and now as a sail. In other words, it is the form of the sail that determines the artifact as sail and not, say, a boat. In *Physics* Aristotle writes,

That which is potentially flesh or bone has not yet gained its own nature, and is not a natural object, until it has acquired the form which enable us to define what the thing is and to define it as flesh or bone.[18]

Here form provides the intelligibility of the subject, and reference to the subject's form provides the subject's definition. For natural subjects that are familiar to us from our sense perception, one can, to some extent, identify the material as a sort of stuff and the form as the shape or configuration of this material. If the tree floats on water it is because the constitution of the wood is such that wood floats on water. On the other hand, that a tree has roots is because of the form of the tree and two requirements that are imposed on the shape of the thing by this form: First, trees are tall, they are vertical, and need to be rooted so they do not blow over. Secondly, trees are living things that require water and nourishment which cannot be easily obtained in air, but can be in soil.[19] This, for Aristotle, is the subject's "substantial form," for it causes the subject to be the kind of substance it is.

This is the core of Aristotle's substance metaphysics. Phenomenologically understood, let us just say that "substance" is the considered word for thing, and one can think of formal cause as the reason for the thingness and *whatness* of the natural substance, such that the substance of a thing is what is given in its definition.[20] Forms like this can be distinguished from those accidental forms that are not only true of the natural subject, but are incidental to its being what it essentially is. Accidental forms vary in presence, absence, or degree without changing the essential character of the substantial subject and are thus directly related to Husserl's method of eidetic variation. They are either attributes or modifications of the substance, but they do not determine its species, even if they are always or normally found in that species.

When human beings intellectually apprehend and define a natural subject, it is the substantial form, *hypokeimenon*, that is apprehended. Hypokeimenon is "what always already lies present."[21] Thus, such apprehension is not the same as sensory apprehension described above, because substantial form is not necessarily immediately revealed in sense perception. Substantial form, of course, is derived from sense experience; one must have some experience of the natural subject to begin the process of learning what it is. Yet, substantial form is more universal and determinative than what is available in sense perception. The defining characteristics of an element or a tree do not just apply to this perceivable piece of each particular tree, for these are what makes them be what they are as a unified whole. Indeed, it is the very fact that substantial form is a reality, that it can disclose the *hypokeimenon* of the substantial form.[22] Aristotle understood the importance of identifying and differentiating the individual things we encounter as individuals of a kind, a process which if left to the senses would not render scientific knowledge. In other words, the fact that simply experiencing a natural subject by means of our senses does not exhaust our knowledge of the subject shows that unless knowledge is simply a function of the imposition of human categories or words onto things, then something like substantial form is a real cause of the nature and intelligibility of the natural subject.

While substantial form accounts for the unity of the natural subject as a subject of a certain species, it also is the source for the subject's various attributes and functions. It is not sufficient to identify the form of a Pandanus tree as a certain shape or size, but to indicate a tree that manifests certain distinguishing operations such as reproducing and growing in a certain way, the long narrow bayonet leaves that halfway up bend sharply at a right angle, its long, narrow spiny fibrous leaves, and so on. Thus, for Aristotle, while part of the causal explanation of the natural subject is identifying its material component, it is also necessary to articulate its formal cause. Indeed, it is the substantial form of the subject that provides its intelligibility, accounting for its species and characteristic operation.

Therefore, Aristotle's hylomorphism insists that pointing to the material cause alone will not adequately account for all that is true of the natural subject. Moreover, one cannot reduce formal cause to material cause. One cannot explain things by simply indicating what they are made of and treating their form as mere shape, configuration, or structure of the matter. This would fail to provide an account of the subject as substance, for it would treat form as simply an accident. For any natural subject to be what it is, it must have both a material cause and a formal cause; the material components with their properties must be brought together in a certain structure in such a way that a substantial unity of a specific kind functions in specific ways: a potentiality for being this kind of thing actualized as being this kind of thing.

While Simondon wants to hold onto Aristotle's refusal to allow form to be reduced to matter and his rejection of matter as inert neutral stuff, he does not accept this formal structure of stability. Being is not a stable state of equilibrium. Rather being is in a constant state of flux and can only be grasped as the activity at the very boundary of the process of formation. This is not the convergence of matter and form but a "resolution taking place in the core of a metastable system rich in potentials: form, matter and energy preexist in the system."[23] What is this resolution of the self and the other, the individual and the milieu, at the threshold of which things come into being? Simondon writes,

> The Being in which individuation comes to fruition is that in which a resolution appears by its division into stages, which implies becoming: becoming is not a framework in which the being exists; it is one of the dimensions of the being, a mode of resolving an initial incompatibility that was rife with potentials. *Individuation corresponds to the appearance of stages in the being, which are the stages of the being*. It is not a mere isolated consequence arising as a by-product of becoming, but this very process itself as it unfolds; it can be understood only by taking into account this initial supersaturation of the being, at first homogeneous and static [*sans devenir*] in which preliminary tensions are resolved but also preserved in the shape of the ensuing structure; in a certain sense, it could be said that the sole principle by which we can be guided is that of the conservation of *being through becoming*.[24]

Here the "resolution" is by no means the process of stability that is meant in the Greek sense. Rather resolution implies a thing's becoming what it was going to be, intrinsic to its being. This anti-reductionist account of causality is the becoming of the individual-milieu dyad. For Aristotle if material cause is a potentiality, then it is a potentiality *for* something. This is not the case for Simondon. Rather, individuation is made possible by the recurrence of causality within a milieu that the technical object creates around itself from out of itself. It is simultaneously a technical and natural milieu.[25] The separation of matter and form that conceives of form as an eminent and transcendent principle privileges the formal conception of being, or as Anne Sauvagnargues puts it, "to the extent that [the Greeks] only conceived of being in a state of equilibrium, they were led to privilege a formal conception of individuation by taking form and matter separately, leaving the operation of individuation itself in the dark."[26] Western philosophy, in particular our orientation toward the rationality of technological thinking, has been framed by such an interpretation. Overcoming the ancient substance metaphysics required from Simondon a transformation in ontology itself, an ontology of becoming, what he would come to call an *ontogenesis*. What are the implications for this?

In line with our modern thinking, Simondon drops the metaphysical term "substantial" reality and the inductive logic upon which it is grounded, toward "relative reality." This means that form is no longer the fundamental structure of reality; rather, it is replaced by an *in-forming*. Informing is a transitive verb, which fits into his schema of the logic of transduction: a horizontal and vertical theory of generation. Information forms the noun, which is an "act of," a "state of," or "result of." In other words, the technical being retains the essence of its evolution as *in*-formation. For example, the movement from a Pandanus leaf to a sail means the sail retains or conserves a trace of the material form of the tree. The sail, however, takes on a relative reality that transforms the Pandanus leaf to a sail. As Grosz articulates, this transformation generates "a creative leap" from the past and present to an unknown future.[27]

Unlike the spontaneity of the elemental phase, this phase expresses a successive linear character. In the case of wind energy, the sail undergoes change simultaneously with human beings as technologies become more efficient, lighter, and versatile. This process of individuation persists through the evolution of the first recorded wind-powered device in Persia (present-day Iran) in the Middle East in AD 644. The Persians used a vertical shaft with several sails built from bundled reed and straw also known as *panemone* presumably from the Pandanus tree. Sails were used to drive a mill stone for the grinding of grain, irrigation, and wood cutting from the seventh to twelfth century.[28] By AD 1000, as sails developed, wind-powered devices became more powerful. The difference between this design and earlier designs is that the sails are shaped more efficiently to capture the wind and they spin vertically. But windmill technology evolved slowly from 1300 to 1850, maintaining its function of milling grain and occasionally pumping water. The function of the sail based on the early weavings of the Pandanus tree, endured for one thousand years. The wind turbine, however, is not the same. Theoretically, it is designed to harvest enough wind energy to replace fossil fuels. Such technology is what Simondon calls industrial technology and corresponds to the *concrete stage* of production. But can such technology be said to retain a trace of the modest windmill and hence its sustaining character?

ENSEMBLE PHASE: ONTOGENESIS
OF WIND TURBINES

According to Simondon, there would be little analogy between a wind turbine and a windmill, yet the technical being retains the essence of its past evolution in the form of its technicity.[29] Windmills reached a resolution or stable state in thirteenth-century Europe, as a technology to grind grain or to irrigate the land. In Simondon's language it can be understood as an *ensemble*. The ensemble tends toward a steady state in a system that is entirely coherent within itself and entirely unified. But this is other than Aristotle's stable equilibrium. Simondon calls it a "metastable equilibrium," "*the conservation of being through becoming*."[30] This movement itself is what Simondon calls transduction. Transduction is

> characterized by the fact that the result of this process is a concrete network including all the original terms. [It] is characterized by the conservation of information, whereas induction requires a loss of information . . . transduction does not presuppose the existence of a previous time period to act as a framework in which the genesis unfolds, time itself being the solution and dimension of the discovered systematic: time comes from the preindividual just like the other dimensions that determine individuation.[31]

Here again we see that we do not have to adopt the metaphysical implications of Aristotle's notion of teleology. By embedding things or objects within an environment and assigning time as the basic structure of existence, Simondon avoids the Aristotelian problem of defining limits, which ultimately end in nonbeing, and consequently avoids the problem of teleology in the strict sense, more broadly associated with determinism. While the core idea of determinism is closely related to causality, what we find in Simondon is causality without determinism, in particular "soft causality" that allows for an event that is not predictable from prior events.

So, on what grounds should we reject the modern notion of causal determinism as we now experience it? Well, we have the outlines of a project for doing so in Aristotle and Simondon who point us to the ways certain kinds of matter can be informed in certain kinds of stable ways so that things can engage in their characteristic functionings. However, while we can learn a great deal from the Aristotelian challenge to the modern reduction of reality to efficient causality and inert materiality, we also want to avoid the temptation toward a reduction to notions of a preordained intelligibility and remember that the ontogenesis by which these things come into being can emerge as multistabilities within an open-ended process of becoming. Understanding ontogenesis as an interweaving of materiality and form gives us the ontological ground for beginning a conversation about wind turbines that is much less restrictive than the one with which we are familiar. Instead, beyond thinking of climate sustainability as an engineering problem, we need to address it in terms of a social and cultural practice which is aesthetically informed. The next section will apply pre-individuation to the prenoetic phase of humanity, which includes, paradigmatically, the artist.

In terms of the human condition, pre-individuation is the neonoetic or pre-reflective stage of humanity, characteristically revealing the work of artistic production. Artists, as creators, are the kinds of beings that are marked by an excess of reality. Artworks emerge spontaneously creating new beings. This is not a *renewal* of something bygone. Thus, the very notion of *renewable* technology is already redundant. Of course the emergence of renewable technologies is the result of a rapidly warming climate primarily caused by burning fossil fuels. The American Wind and Wildlife Institute released their White Paper, "Bats and Wind Energy: Impacts, Mitigation, and Tradeoffs" (November 15, 2018), stating that only 6 percent of energy in the United States is generated by wind, and 17 percent is generated by all renewable sources combined.[32] We know that the pace and scale of such renewable technologies needs to accelerate to keep temperature increases below 1.5 C by 2050. Thus, the need for the shift from fossil fuels to non-carbon-emitting sources is undisputable. However, I would argue our inability to think through appropriate technologies to achieve this goal is due to our reliance on engineers and technicians to "fix" the climate problem. But the weather does not need fixing; it is not an engineering problem. Ontogenetically, thinking about harvesting wind capable of powering local and urban communities must begin at the pre-reflective stage. This means that artists and not engineers are the ontogenerators capable of breathing new life into technological design. For the sake of brevity, let me point to two artists working *with* nature toward a sustainable way of living.

Sculptor Lyman Whitaker has focused on gracefully capturing the spirit of the wind through his kinetic art. Lyman dedicates his work to the wind and weather. The sculptures are made of the highest quality stainless steel and copper. Similar to the windmill, it uses wind to harness energy. Similar to the wind turbine, these are engineer-tested to winds of 90 mph and can withstand hurricane-force winds. Uniquely, Lyman's designs have perfect balance and aerospace-grade stainless steel sealed bearings, insuring little or no maintenance. Furthermore, they do as Lyman writes "inspire love for our earth's thin, moving layer of air— it warms us, gives us breath and sustains our being."[33] Titles such as "Element Air," "Double Helix Sail," and "Lotus" indicate the interweaving or entanglement of technology and nature. This spontaneous eruption and decoupling of artist and technology informs the natural environment. "Element of Air" is a 2' 6" stainless steel blade twisted into a semi-mobius. As the wind catches it, the blade moves around like a ballet dancer in tune with the wind. The artist and art work, no longer in the process of creation, individuate into the object and the milieu; phenomenologically humanity and nature come into view. Wind sculptures not only are aesthetically appealing, but are designed to utilize wind capacity to supply energy for individual homes. Furthermore, they maintain the integrity of the natural world without the disruptive power of wind turbines. For example, bats are one of the many fatalities of wind turbines. The "Bats and Wind Energy" White Paper suggests the decline in bats is due to anthropogenic activity, with wind turbines considered one of the greatest threats to bat populations in North America and Europe, citing approximately 190,000 to nearly 400,000 fatalities in the United States and Canada in 2012 alone. These numbers have increased steadily over the last six years.[34]

Ideally, it would seem that replacing wind turbines with wind sculptures would avoid the negative consequences of modern renewables, but while this technology may be feasible for suburban and rural households, it may not be adequate for high-density urban life. For proposals of a larger scale we can turn to architect and visionary, David Fisher, who conceived the "Da Vinci Tower," which is currently planned for construction in the city Dubai, UAE. Each of the sixty-eight floors will rotate independently, and there is a space between each floor for wind turbines.[35] The rotating building will use its central horizontal axis for harvesting and storing energy created by the rotating floors. Theoretically, this is a building that will produce its own energy.[36] Fisher sees architecture as "part of nature," buildings that "adjust to life, to our needs, to our moods." His buildings reflect time and motion. This is still at the conceptual or elemental stage and is not planned for production until 2020. Prenoetically informed, the rotating building has the potential to create a living space that moves with the rhythm of nature and to produce an excess of energy for the urban region. Given more time, we could investigate other ways that wind energy could be harvested using the resources already available to us. However, it is enough to point out that wind turbine technology is at the elemental stage of development. As such we should think carefully about how to integrate both inductive and deductive logic into the genesis of the entity such that the machine is not external to humanity but built into the fabric of living.

CONCLUDING REMARKS

The present chapter has shown the ontogeneis of the windmill emerging from unpredictable protomatter; from Pandanus leaf to sail, from sail to windmill. Windmill technology endured for more than a thousand years. It was, in short, sustaining. Wind turbines, on the other hand, are undergoing a process of ontogenesis in a radically new context and, as such, remain at an early stage of development. They are at the pre-individual stage. This is not a progressive linear structure of problem solving by way of which any given technology gets more efficient over time while remaining substantially the same. Indeed, thinking of technology and technical solutions as evolutionarily determined fails to account for the radically different needs of time and place.

The excess of human creativity by the artist, can individuate a thing into a quasi or metastable reality. The resulting object enters into a second phase of individuation where the world of technical and social actors informs the object socially, culturally, and politically. The more creative the process at the elemental stage, the more scope we will have for thoughtful engagement as the technology becomes concretized. Today, it seems we have no options for reflection; either we accept the massive wind farms or we reject them. Their form seems predetermined and, therefore, outside the realm of the discussion. To break free from such enframing, we need to open up the design process of harvesting natural resources to artists—they are the creative thinkers who can imagine new designs beyond the limits of technicians and engineers Artists are attuned to the elemental stage where things remain devoid of form or content.

Because wind turbines carry the trace of their evolutionary past, that does not mean they evolve naturally from the windmill. Indeed, this kind of inductive causal connection is fallacious. If wind turbines are based on the logic of transduction, as is suggested in this chapter, then the artists and designers, in their excess of technics, can create possibilities for thinking creative ways to harvest wind. But until we understand the temporal character of our technologies, we will continue to merely "improve" on older technology (a self-fulfilling prophecy of determinism), foreclosing the possibility of designing energy-harvesting technologies that are truly sustaining for our own time and place.

NOTES

1. Other writers influenced by Simondon include Jean Baudrillard, Paolo Virno, Giorgio Agamben, Alberto Toscano, Bruno Latour, and Isabelle Stengers but will not be addressed here.

2. In *Heidegger on Being and Acting*, Schürmann refers to this as the "kinetic paradigm of origin" which constitutes both an inception and domination. He argues that "once it is understood that phenomena as a whole are knowable from the viewpoint of causality, then it can be said that a true cause is only that which begins its action "and never ceases to being it," that is, a cause that also commands." 99.

3. Indeed scholars debate about whether the four causes are really causes at all. For a useful overview of some of the various contemporary approaches, see Beebee et al. (2007). On contemporary approaches to the relation between causation and explanation, see Psillos (2002). And for a discussion on the four causes see Moravscik (1974), Freeland (1991), Lewis (1991).

4. See Peter Hoenen, *Cosmologia*, 5th ed. (1956); Hoenen, *De Noetica Geometriae* (1954); Hoenen, *The Philosophy of Inorganic Compounds* (Indiana: West Baden College, 1960); S. J. Philip Soccorsi, *De Physica Quantica* (1956), William A. Wallace, *Modelling Nature: The Philosophy of Science and the Philosophy of Nature in Synthesis* (Catholic University of America Press, 1996).

5. As modern chemistry improved on the ancient Greek theory of the four elements by developing the periodic table of the basic building-blocks of the universe, modern physicists continued to investigate the notion of conservation as an even more basic characteristic of nature.

6. Aristotle, in Chapters 7–9 of the 1st Book of *Physics*, refers to matter as "underlying nature" (191a8) and form as "the natural form" (192b1).

7. Albert Magnus, *Opera Omnia*, edited by E. Dorgnet (Paris: Vives, 1890–99), Volume 6: Metaphysicorum Libri XIII. Also, Michael Tkacz's essay, "Albert the Great and the Revival of Aristotle's Zoological Research Program," *Vivarium* 45, no. 1 (2007): 30–68.

8. Gilbert Simondon, "The Genesis of the Individual," in *Incorporations*, eds. Johnathan Crary and Sandford Kwinter (New York: Zone Books, 1992), 297–319, 300.

9. Ibid., 304.

10. Ibid., Note 1, 317.

11. Elizabeth Grosz, "Identity and Individuation: Some Feminist Reflections," in *Gilbert Simondon Being and Technology*, eds., Arne De Boever, Alex Murray, Jon Roffe, and Ashley Woodward (Cheshire: Edinburgh University Press, 2013), chap. 3, doc. 840–1245, 869. Kindle.

12. Andrew Feenberg, *Technosystems: The Social Life of Reason* (Cambridge, MA, London: Harvard University Press, 2017), 73.

13. Ibid., 74.

14. This is a controversial point, as it can be said that Aristotle has three different concepts of telos, which is not identified by Simondon.

15. Gilbert Simondon, *On the Mode of Existence of Technical Objects*, trans. Cecile Malaspina and John Rogove (Minneapolis, MN: Univocal Publishing, 2017), 29.

16. Ibid., 29.

17. *Institute of Political Economy in Utah State University Report*. https://connect icuthistory.org/halladays-revolutionary--today-in-history-august-29/ Downloaded 10/15/2017. Investigators Randy T Simmons, Ray M. Yonk, and Megan E. Hansen put together a forty-page report outlining the true cost of producing electricity from wind power. The report claims that wind energy is indefensible. It outlines in detail the true cost of wind energy that is often overlooked, leading to a dramatic underestimation of the true costs of producing electricity from wind. In the interest of time let me point to two of the above: Government Subsidies and Transmission Costs.

18. Aristotle, *Physics,* trans. Robin Waterfield (New York: Oxford University Press, 1996), 193a30–b3.

19. Ibid., xxii.

20. Ibid., 239.

21. *Being and Time,* 35/30.

22. In more Husserlian language, this is why adumbrations that are not immediately present to consciousness are nonetheless co-present in the unity of intentional object.

23. Simondon, "The Genesis of the Individual," 303.

24. Ibid., 301.

25. Simondon, *On the Mode of Technical Objects*, 59.

26. Anne Sauvagnargues, "Crystals and Membranes: Individuation and Temporality," trans. Jon Roffe in *Gilbert Simondon Being and Technology,* eds., Arne De Boever, Alex Murray, Jon Roffe, and Ashley Woodward (Cheshire: Edinburgh University Press, 2013), chap. 4, doc. 1258–534, 1277. Kindle.

27. Grosz, "Identity and Individuation," 947.

28. Anindita Roy and Santanu Bandyopadhyay, *Wind Power Based Isolated Energy Systems* (Springer International Publishing, 2018), 17.

29. In a note, Simondon refers to the technical being as "analectic," that is, the barer of the technicity can be the object of adequate knowledge, "only if the latter grasps the temporal sense of tits evolution: this adequate knowledge is a culture of technics, distinct from technical knowledge, which is limited to the actuality of isolated schemas of operation." See Simondon, OMETO, Note 1, 26.

30. Simondon, "The Genesis of the Individual," 301.

31. Simondon, *Being and Technology,* 315.

32. American Wind and Wildlife Institute released their White Paper, "Bats and Wind Energy: Impacts, Mitigation, and Tradeoffs" (November 15, 2018), 3. See also IPCC, 2018: Global warming of 1.5 °C. An IPCC special report on the impacts of global warming of 1.5 °C above preindustrial levels and related global greenhouse gas emission pathways, in the context of strengthening the global response to the threat of climate change, sustainable development, and efforts to eradicate poverty (V. Masson-Delmotte, P. Zhai, H. O. Pörtner, D. Roberts, J. Skea, P. R. Shukla, A. Pirani, Y. Chen, S. Connors, M. Gomis, E. Lonnoy, J. B. R. Matthews, W. Moufouma-Okia,

C. Péan, R. Pidcock, N. Reay, M. Tignor, T. Waterfield, X. Zhou [eds.]). file:///C:/
Users/home/AppData/Local/Microsoft/Windows/INetCache/IE/PRLDWK38/AWWI
-Bats-and-Wind-Energy-White-Paper-FINAL.pdf.
    33. Lyman Whitaker, Worthington Gallery Art for Life, https://worthingtongal-
lery.com/ Downloaded 10/15/2017.
    34. American Wind Wildlife Institute (AWWI), "Bats and Wind Energy: Impacts,
Mitigation, and Tradeoffs" (Washington, DC, 2018), 11.
    35. Chad Randl, *Revolving Architecture: A History of Buildings that Rotate,
Swivel, and Pivot* (New York: Princeton Architectural Press, 2008), 188.
    36. Paul Goldberger, "Shape-Shifter," *The New Yorker*, July 21, 2008, https://www.
newyorker.com/magazine/2008/07/21/shape-shifter-paul-goldberger, Retrieved, January 21, 2019.

BIBLIOGRAPHY

Albertus Magnus. *Opera Omnia: Vol 6*. Edited by E. Borgnet. Metaphysicorum Libri
    XIII, 1890.
Aristotle. "Metaphysics." In *The Basic Works of Aristotle*, edited by Richard
    McKeon. New York: The Modern Library, 2001, 689–934.
Aristotle. *Physics*. Translated by Robin Waterfield. New York: Oxford University
    Press, 1996.
Aristotle. *The Basic Works of Aristotle*. Edited by Richard McKeon. New York:
    Random House, 1941.
Bandyopadhyay, Santanu, and Anindita Roy. *Wind Power Based Isolated Energy
    Systems*. Springer International Publishing, 2018, 17–32.
De Boever, Arne, Alex Murray, Jon Roffe, and Ashley Woodward, eds, *Gilbert
    Simondon Being and Technology*. Cheshire: Edinburgh University Press, 2013,
    chap. 3, Kindle.
Feenberg, Andrew. *Technosystems: The Social Life of Reason*. Cambridge, MA and
    London: Harvard University Press, 2017.
Hoenen, Petrus. *The Philosophy of Inorganic Compounds*. Indiana: West Baden
    Springs. Ind., West Baen College, 1960.
MacKay, David. *Sustainable Energy—Without the Hot Air*. UIT Cambridge, 2009.
    http://www.withouthotair.com.
Psillos, Stathis. *Causation & Explanation Central Problems of Philosophy*. Edited by
    Johan Shand. New York: Routledge, 2002.
Randl, Chad. *Revolving Architecture: A History of Buildings that Rotate, Swivel, and
    Pivot*. New York: Princeton Architectural Press, 2008.
Schürmann, Reiner. *Heidegger on Being and Action: From Principles of Anarchy*.
    Bloomington: Indiana University Press, 1990.
Simondon, Gilbert. *On the Mode of Existence of Technical Objects*. Translated by
    Cecile Malaspina and John Rogove. Minneapolis, MN: Univocal Publishing, 2017.
Simondon, Gilbert. "The Genesis of the Individual." In *Incorporations*, edited Johna-
    than Crary and Sandford Kwinter. New York: Zone Books, 1992, 297–3137.

Tkacz's, Michael. "Albert the Great and the Revival of Aristotle's Zoological Research Program." *Vivarium* 45, no. 1 (2007): 30–68.

Wallace, William A. *The Modelling of Nature: Philosophy of Science and Philosophy of Nature in Synthesis*. Washington, DC: Catholic University of America Press, 1996.

Whitaker, Lyman. Worthington Gallery Art for Life. https://worthingtongallery.com.

Part III

SUSTAINABILITY AND DESIGN

Chapter 7

We're in this Together

Climate Change and Reproductive Technology in the Age of Ge-stell

Dana S. Belu

Choosing to have multiple biological children, especially through the use of advanced reproductive technology (ART), is environmentally problematic in the age of the Anthropocene. According to recent research, the proliferation of ART in first world countries and for first world customers operating in third world countries increases carbon emissions and cuts against widespread efforts to promote the sustainability of the planet. While this is one of ART's overlooked externalities, there is a more concealed phenomenon closely associated with the proliferation of ART. The use of advanced in vitro fertilization (IVF)-based ART, such as cytoplasmic transfer (CT) and gestational surrogacy among others, sets up women as (extractable) resources in the service of reproductive technologies. This contributes to the instrumentalization of human relationships and it reflects the reduction of all things to mere resources, a phenomenon that underlies the wider ecological crisis.

While the discourse of freedom as autonomy emphasizes that ARTs empower women, it conceals their resource status. The inversion, women primarily serving the technology rather than the technology serving women, is not clearly visible at the individual level, but comes into full view when women in their relationship to various ARTs are framed as a group, such as in the practice of international gestational surrogacy. This reframing reveals the women and their offspring as extractable resources, their bodies serving the technologies allegedly designed to meet their needs. Each new generation of IVF children contributes to the naturalization of ARTs while at the same time helping to enroll new human beings as resources for a growing ART network.

Since the birth of the first IVF baby, Louise Brown in 1978, at least six million children have been born through IVF[1] worldwide, probably many more. Records are scarce, but since 2004, up to a few million children are born each year through transnational gestational surrogacy, the most popular IVF-based ART.[2] These millions of IVF children are adding to high carbon emissions by multiplying the carbon legacies[3] of the planet. In the global debate about how to cope with climate change, the critical focus is usually on the environmental devastation perpetrated by deforestation and the use of fossil fuels, especially coal and oil. Thus, "Climate change mitigation requires, first and foremost, that carbon emissions into the atmosphere be drastically reduced" since they "represent the number-one threat to Earth's ability to sustain life."[4] Despite the obvious fact that "as the human population on the earth increases, so does the use of fossil fuels . . . and that the two primary drivers of climate change—fossil fuel use and land alteration—are intensified by an increase in population,"[5] the environmental impact of ART on these two sources of pollution remains largely invisible. For example, in a recent study regarding the risks associated with international gestational surrogacy (the most popular of all the ARTs), seven ethical, cultural, economic, and legal risks to countries, doctors, and surrogates were evaluated.[6] The environmental risk was not even mentioned, remaining completely concealed. Unfortunately, the concealment of ART as a source of carbon pollution is further masked by the fact that, as Finis Dunaway notes, climate change itself, "like other problems associated with the Anthropocene, is a fundamentally different kind of threat: not an immediate, highly visible catastrophe but a gradually escalating, often invisible form of environmental danger."[7]

In their recent groundbreaking article, "The Climate Mitigation Gap: Education and Government Recommendation Miss the Most Effective Individual Actions," Wynes and Nicholas show that having fewer children is the most effective way for individuals to reduce carbon emissions.[8] Having one fewer child amounts to a 58 tons reduction of carbon dioxide emissions per year compared to a mere 2.4 tons yearly reduction from not driving a car. This article underscores the groundbreaking carbon legacy analysis in "Reproduction and the Carbon Legacies of Individuals" which demonstrates that the *carbon footprint* of each parent in first world countries is exceedingly high due to over consumption. Moreover, the carbon legacies of all parents are determined in relationship to their biological children and they *grow exponentially* with the birth of each child.[9] So, fewer biological children for some mean lower emission levels for all.

Currently, the ART industry is unregulated, helping to produce human beings that would not exist otherwise. This production takes place through societally funded medical procedures but without public discussion or ethical considerations. Since human beings are the biggest source of carbon emissions, it is imperative to impose regulations on the ART industry in order to reduce life threatening carbon emissions. Moreover, since ART parents are primarily from first world countries, and since first world persons are responsible for vastly greater carbon emissions than non–first world persons, ART industry regulations in first world countries are urgently needed in order to reduce carbon emissions. According to Murtaugh and Schlax, "Under the current emissions scenario, an extra child born to a woman in the United States ultimately increases her carbon legacy by an amount (9,441 metric tons) that is nearly seven times the analogous quantity of a woman in China (1384 tons) . . . [and 168 times the quantity of a woman in Bangladesh, 56 tons]."[10] Bioethicist Cristina Richie sums up several factors that support these findings and that contribute to ecocide by carbon emissions in first world countries. She writes,

It is not only the use of fossil fuels to power cars, planes and recreational vehicles, but also high calorie diets, planned technological obsolescence, and simply too much material depletion that is polluting the atmosphere, demanding deforestation for luxury items, and recklessly exhausting the world's resources without consideration for others on the planet.[11]

Furthermore,

As of 2010, the largest number of ART babies came from the U.S.A., the country the EPA listed as the number one carbon emitter in the world. In the USA, each child will use the equivalent in resources of seven children in China. This is environmentally significant, more so than just the number of ART births. . . . In America, there is nothing that a parent can do, short of moving to another country, to offset the carbon of a biological child.[12]

In view of this stark reality, first world parents ought to voluntarily cap the number of their biological children, and the ART industry ought to also enforce a regulatory cap. Ecologist William Rees can be seen to underscore this approach when he says, "Any diversion of material and energy to grow more humans and their 'furniture' . . . [and] the increased production/consumption for humans adds to the pollution load on natural ecosystems."[13]

But does the burden fall more heavily on future parents of ART babies than on parents of non-ART babies? Are ART babies more harmful to the planet than non-ART babies? Seeing the additional harm requires that we consider ART's environmental externalities, unintended consequences that end up being absorbed by society rather than by the individual who produces them.

Some of these externalities include the extended use of carbon-heavy medical buildings, medical equipment, and extensive car travel for medical purposes. According to bioethicist Cristina Richie,

> ARTs use scarce communal resources such as intellectual research, government funding for development and medical buildings. Natural procreation qua procreation does not. That is, a woman wishing to become pregnant through ARTs has to go to a clinic, visit a doctor and use the carbon-intensive resources of the medical industry. In contrast, a natural pregnancy takes no extra physical resources to achieve conception. And, considering many fertile people who could become pregnant without any extra resources use ARTs, this is an environmental waste that contributes to the bloated carbon footprint of the medical industry.[14]

Moreover, first world parents of children born through gestational surrogates in developing countries must take transatlantic flights to organize the transaction and to pick up the babies. According to Wynes and Nicholas, transatlantic flights rank third among sources of individual carbon emission, just behind having a child and driving a car.[15] Finally, the birth of unintended children, twins or triplets or more, is the most emission-heavy externality of ARTs.

Richie proposes adoption, fostering, and spiritual parenting as sustainable[16] or "green" alternatives to "brown" (i.e., fossil fuel centric) ART reproduction. She also endorses public policy that would temporarily cap ART reproduction to one child per couple and recommends that only women who are biologically infertile should receive federal funding for ART treatment.[17] As noted above, since human reproduction in first world countries is currently the heaviest individual environmental burden on the planet, Richie's advocacy of fertility control seems reasonable.

While Richie seems to have her finger on the pulse when recommending the regulation of ART, I disagree with Richie's phenomenologically naïve privileging of biological infertility over social and what she calls "functional"[18] infertility—that is, acquired infertility. Her argument does not justify this privilege. Richie recognizes that single women and women in same sex partnerships are "in a way infertile," and she does not recommend that they be "forced into an unwanted sexual relationship."[19] However, when she downgrades the significance of non-somatic infertility on the grounds that it is merely social, she abstracts the biological body from the lived body, with which it is always already intertwined. This separation is artificial because the lesbian woman or the single mother who is unwilling to enter into an "unwanted sexual relationship" has no access to her biologically fertile body without reproductive technology. While artificial insemination may work for some, it's likely to fail older women who need additional help to achieve pregnancy.

Moreover, Richie's position ignores the causal connection between social and somatic infertility, what she calls "functional" infertility. This connection is again concealed by the artificial separation between the social and the medical body. For example, women who are undernourished because of extreme poverty and/or lack of education and women who are abused can become biologically infertile even though they were born fertile. Finally, privileging biological fertility for ART funding implicitly privileges a heteronormative right to a biological child. It also privileges a classist right to a biological child, since in patriarchal societies, single women tend to be less financially stable than married women. Failing to recognize the significance of different kinds of infertility can amount to perpetuating classist and sexist stereotypes, promoting their institutionalization, however, unwittingly. Richie's claim that "the capacity to use one's fertility does not always correspond to one's sexual orientation or partner status"[20] carries descriptive value, but it is shortsighted and does not carry the normative weight that Richie attributes to it.

The growing demand for IVF and IVF-based ARTs suggests that biological parenthood is not being replaced with adoption and fostering any time soon. Financial, medical, and human resources are being poured into the reproductive market for the sole purpose of making more "carbon emitting humans" at a time when, paradoxically, the well-being and long-term survival of the human species calls for cutting carbon. Women's reproductive bodies are harnessed as resources for the reproductive market, but this (en)framing is concealed along with the resulting carbon legacies.[21] Increasingly popular IVF-dependent ARTs, such as CT and gestational surrogacy, purport to serve women's reproductive needs, yet a closer look reveals the opposite. Women's reproductive bodies show up as extractable, techno-social resources that serve ARTs, technologies that are not "flexible, resilient, sustainable and benign"[22] but an indirect source of carbon emissions. This interpretation comes into sharper focus when applying Martin Heidegger's account of the essence of the technological age—that is, enframing (*Ge-stell*).

Enframing refers to the dominant cultural legacy in the West that, beginning with the seventeenth century, views the world and nature as a heap of raw materials. Heidegger calls this ontological, rather than sociological, view a "mode of revealing." Our current mode of revealing, or *Ge-stell* describes the relationship between an attitude of imposition or "challenging forth," (*Herausforderung*) and what this attitude discloses: a world of fungible raw materials, resources or "standing-reserve" (*Bestand*)[23] awaiting optimization. The dominant value embodied by the attitude of challenging forth is a constant "driving on to the maximum yield at the minimum expense."[24] This drive places an uncritical value on the reduction of all things to resources available on demand. Resource optimization, flexibility, and storing become dominant, self-sufficient goals. Thus, a constant ordering as "continuous attack"[25] discloses a world of uniform and replaceable entities whose potential is "stored up . . . distributed . . . and switched about ever anew," without serving a fixed and final goal, without limit (*peras*).[26] In "Traditional Language, Technological Language," Heidegger underscores this idea as follows: "What is peculiar to technology resides in . . . the demand to challenge nature forth into placing it at our disposal and securing it as natural energy. This demand is more powerful than any human positing of ends."[27] The indefinite capability to do as much as we can in the future with whatever energies we are able to extract from nature, including human nature, becomes the overarching ambition.

Heidegger's analysis makes visible two kinds of resources: human resources who order and are ordered by the ordering, and nonhuman resources who are merely ordered. It also brings out two features of human resources: the collapse of the traditional subject-object relationship and the absence of pain or discomfort in the challenging forth of human resources. Furthermore, Heidegger divides the energies of nature into nonrenewable, extractable resources, such as coal and ore, and renewable resources, such as wind energy.[28] While the latter *give themselves away*, the former must be technologically dug out, challenged forth, and stored. The pollution of the environment through technological depletion of brown, extractable resources is the mark of the Anthropocene, and this can be seen to concretize the consummation of the enframing.[29]

I transpose Heidegger's distinction to the technologization of women's reproductive bodies in order to show that ART solicits these bodies *as if* they were extractable resources. This solicitation makes sense against the background of enframing, a world view that naturalizes the control and mastery of nature, the transformation of people and things into available resources. As Casey Rentmeester notes in *Heidegger and the Environment*, "When the natural world is insufficient in supplying resources, human beings use their ingenuity and ambition to create resources artificially. When the world has become a repository of resources, it doesn't much matter if they are natural or *manufactured*."[30] The technological recasting of women's reproductive bodies as extractable resources for carbon emitting ARTs exacerbates the climate crisis even while this exacerbation conceals itself. In what follows I take a look at optimizing women's reproduction through CT and gestational surrogacy, in order to show how these procedures reflect the enframing while eschewing environmental responsibilities in a time of environmental crisis.

Unlike a resource, a rational subject defines herself through individual acts of reflection and autonomous choice. As such she is not interchangeable with other subjects or with objects, but an object is not necessarily fungible, either. It is not essentially interchangeable with another object and usually has its own standing and purpose. When an object is made continuously available and fungible, interchangeable with other objects, it becomes a resource. Continuous acts of self-objectification turn a subject into a resource. According to Iain Thomson, "Once modern subjects dominating an objective world begin treating *themselves* as objects, the subject/object distinction itself is undermined, and the subject is thereby put on the path toward becoming just another resource to be *optimized,* that is, '*secured and ordered for the sake of flexible use*' . . . self-objectification . . . dissolves the subject into the resource pool."[31]

I introduce the term *reproductive enframing* to reveal the ongoing transformation of women's reproductive bodies into extractable, medical resources. *Reproductive enframing* describes the separation of the potential of the womb from the woman's body with which it was traditionally regarded as forming a whole. This manipulation introduces a fragmented approach to conception, one that frames the womb as a collection of discrete and movable reproductive parts: ovaries, follicles, eggs, fallopian tubes, hormones, and so on.[32] In the last two decades, IVF-reliant CT was popularized in the United States as a fertility procedure that "refreshes" older women's eggs by combining them with younger women's eggs. The procedure relies on extracting eggs from both women by passing a fine needle through the vaginal wall to the follicles, using ultrasound guidance.

> [CT] . . . revitalizes old eggs by combining the nucleus of an older woman's egg (that is, the egg of the woman trying to become pregnant) with the cytoplasm of a younger woman's egg (that is, the donor). The resulting embryo is thought to be healthier and more likely to implant in the uterus, but it may also contain genetic material from both eggs because the mitochondria in the younger egg's cytoplasm also contain genetic material.[33]

This procedure reveals the fungibility of the participating women, since each is reduced to her egg bearing function and all eggs are framed as "extractable resources"[34] enrolled in reproductive networks that multiply the carbon legacies of the planet. Since the viability of women's eggs is limited by age and by other health factors and since egg donation is associated with serious health risks for women, risks that are often withheld by medical staff and doctors,[35] the development of this technology inherently relies on new flows of women enrolling in these experimental processes.

While IVF enables reproduction with two living genetic mothers, as in CT, it also enables the production of offspring with no living genetic mothers at all. This process aims to produce biologically motherless babies, babies whose mothers were never born, "unborn mothers." In this procedure "Viable eggs [are] collected from the ovarian tissue of aborted fetuses for use in fertility treatments such as IVF. Success with this procedure has been limited; by stimulating the tissue with hormones, researchers are able to develop primary and secondary egg follicles about halfway to the point of maturity."[36] We see how the potential reproductive energy contained in this stock—that is, in the ovarian tissue of the dead fetus—is extracted, challenged forth so that, as Heidegger stated, "the energy concealed in [its] nature is unlocked, what is unlocked is transformed, what is transformed is stored up, what is stored up is, in turn, distributed, and what is distributed is switched about ever anew."[37] The procedure dispenses with the woman as subject and with the egg as object so that they both "disappear into the objectlessness of standing-reserve."[38] Here, reproductive "waste" is repurposed as renewable stock for the technological (re)production of new human life.

In this medical scenario, the thorny issue of informed consent is bypassed altogether since the content of the abortion becomes the property of the medical institution. There is no woman to consult. The process dispenses with the need for the female person as biological mother and woman because the so-called unborn mother is nothing but "a body part without a body, an egg donor but not a person."[39] In fact, there is no "donor" at all and no activity of gift-giving. Rather, the phenomenon is one of extraction, or what Heidegger calls a "plundering" (*Geraff*).[40] The medical production of "unborn mothers" redefines the meaning of human stock in terms that even Heidegger could not foresee. It introduces a kind of fungibility predicated on fragmentation that was merely implicit in artificial insemination and traditional IVF procedures that still presupposed the presence and cooperation of the woman. Here, the woman is a viable ovarian tissue, merely an egg *in potentia*, a storehouse of reproductive energy or an extracted, (fungible) resource serving the development of experimental reproductive techniques.

Since 2004, IVF has been the gateway technology to a billion dollar international gestational surrogacy market, also known as reproductive tourism or "cross border reproductive care." Since it generates up to a few million new "carbon emitting humans" each year, this market presents a real hindrance to reducing carbon pollution. Furthermore, the (en)framing of gestational surrogates as techno-social resources normalizes the practice, suspends responsibility, and ignores the environmental harm.

Gestational surrogacy can involve up to four different women: two genetic donors whose egg contents are combined with each other via CT, the gestational surrogate who carries the fetus but has no genetic tie to the fetus, and the social "mother" who provides the care.[41] Each gestational surrogate agrees to be implanted with the embryo of a couple she does not know and who will claim the baby at birth. Since the surrogate is a resource she is spared pain and discomfort as much as possible, but she is not consulted about decisions that impact her individually. Indian clinics, for instance, require that surrogates relocate to dormitories near or in the clinic for optimal surveillance. They take every precaution to keep the working surrogates qua workers comfortable, healthy, well fed, well rested, entertained, and well paid.[42] But this care comes at a price. Surrogates are prohibited from having sexual intercourse with their husbands. Clinics advertise this requirement under the euphemism "dedication." Moreover, surrogates are subjected to intense hormone therapy, embryo implantation procedures, and close food and drug monitoring. Their lives are medically regimented to serve the fetus, and since the fetus is a direct product of reproductive technology whose live birth consolidates the grip of the technology on the market, surrogates serve the expansion of the reproductive market.

A part of the regiment is the requirement to sign away all rights to the child and to give permission for cesarean delivery, what Indian surrogates call "the scissors." Illiterate surrogates sign with a thumbprint.[43] Moreover, a surrogate is not consulted whether or not she agrees to have a multiple pregnancy. In fact, "The surrogate is mandated to comply with all decisions made about her body."[44] Viewed through this lens of subtle coercion, including deliberate withholding of information, the surrogate can be seen as serving the reproductive technology, the collection of medical data and medical results, none of which will benefit her. Of course, she is also serving the fetus, the direct product of the medical technology. A healthy baby is expected by first world parents waiting on the other side of the ocean. Good surrogates comply with the demands knowing that they can make more money in ten months (up to $10,000) than they would otherwise make working for many years crushing glass or cleaning houses.

The burgeoning feminist and ethnographic literature regarding the practice of gestational surrogacy in developing nations leave little doubt that many of the surrogates are exploited,[45] their human rights violated as objects of wrongful instrumentalization and wrongful fungibilization,[46] treated *merely* as a *means* to an end and as interchangeable by the clinics, the commissioning couples, and often by their husbands.[47] Liberal feminists who argue that gestational surrogacy is a woman's free choice and should be respected as such still carry the burden of proof to rescue this "choice" from the constraints of dire poverty and systemic social oppression, including lack of adequate food, lack of housing and education, the unbearable burden of drunk and unemployed husbands, and organized "sterilization programs."[48]

Once she joins the transnational surrogate market, the gestational surrogate learns to see herself as neither subject nor object but as a reproductive resource, a "rented womb," "empty space,"[49] or the "spare space"[50] for "housing" another woman's embryo.[51] In order to see herself as a resource, the gestational surrogate first learns how to disassociate from the fetus and to see herself as an object, a vessel. Her object-body is even more abstract than a vessel, however, since a vessel might be perceived as the appropriate *place* for a thing, "a mold that embraces the thing" and gives the thing its being[52]—whereas the language of "spare space" directed at the surrogate reminds her that she is inessential to the fetus. She is an "I" who is neither mother (the baby has someone else's DNA) nor whore (she is not stigmatized by sexual relations outside of marriage) nor worker (she is not acquiring any skill). According to one doctor, clinics ensure that "no feelings" develop in the surrogate for the child or in the child for the surrogate.[53]

Seeing herself as a resource, the surrogate eventually tries to network directly with the commissioning couples. Many surrogates enter these arrangements hoping to get rehired and to "potentialize their relationships with commissioning couples" for years to come.[54] In fact, in India, gestational surrogacy is beginning to "displace the narrative of exploitation with the discourse of fulfilling unrealized potential."[55] Increasingly surrogates see their choice as a way out of poverty, and the renting out of the "empty space" in their body makes good sense. Local narratives are organized around commercial abstractions such as available space and potential. But a self-identification with empty space and/or potential is an identification with *nothing* at all, and this undermines her sense of subjectivity and her place in the world. Further, it is an identification with vital energy that can be extracted for a limited time only since each successful surrogate is allowed no more than three commissioned pregnancies.

Learning to psychologically separate from the fetuses inside of them, seeing them as mere objects, a "not-me" temporarily housed within, enables some Israeli gestational surrogates to see themselves as free subjects, subverting the surrogacy system and helping doctors and their technologies to fool nature. According to ethnographer Elly Teman, the belief that genetic kinship is necessary for motherhood runs so deep with Israeli gestational surrogates that they readily cut off any relationship with the fetus whose genetic makeup they do not share.[56] These surrogates enforce a double subject-object separation between themselves and the fetuses and between their "natural bodies" and their "artificial bodies"—that is, the pregnant bodies—the result of medical technique alone, which are not natural and do not belong to them. According to Teman's ethnography, the surrogates' welcoming of medical technology is an act of their *subversive agency*, "willingly relinquishing control of their bodies."[57] But this relinquishment is a strange splitting[58] which looks much more like self-objectification than subversion. In this splitting the surrogate turns the objectifying gaze—initially directed at the fetus—against herself, reordering her entire body as "artificial," seeing it as separate and other. In this act of heightened self-objectification she shows up as a resource, asking to be optimized for the express purpose of making more "carbon emitting humans" while failing to acknowledge her connection to the fetus and her responsibility to the earth. Instead, she unwittingly participates in challenging forth the earth to support ever bigger human systems instead of learning to respect the "limits of the Earth's carrying capacity."[59]

Finally, the surrogate's splitting also reaffirms harmful stereotypes about pregnant women (including by the women themselves) as passive vessels—or worse, "spare space"—primarily valued for their reproductive abilities. We can see harmful prejudices about pregnant women finding legitimacy in these gestational surrogacy narratives and ideology, even though they may be challenged in society at large. The script is ideological because it covers over the myriad ways, psychological, physiological, and political,[60] in which the surrogate is connected with the fetus, including environmentally through the unregulated production of new human beings, primarily "high-consuming humans with energy-intensive lifestyles that are leaving knee-deep Anthropocene footprints,"[61] and generating new carbon legacies at a time when cutting carbon emissions is urgent.

Given the high numbers of humans produced on the international gestational surrogate market, each surrogate must be viewed on a continuum with new flows of such surrogates. The new flows include new generations of surrogates and their IVF offspring, most of whom grow up in first world countries where they generate big carbon legacies. The new generations of offspring inevitably contribute to the naturalization of ARTs, and this helps to enroll new human resources into a growing ART industry that still eschews responsibility for a sustainable future. This trend contributes to the deepening sense that all things, including human beings, are orderable resources, a hallmark of the enframing that is at the heart of our environmental crisis.

NOTES

1. IVF or in vitro fertilization is a reproductive technique that requires that a woman's egg be extracted from the egg follicle and then fertilized by sperm in a petri dish. The embryo is then transferred into the uterus for implantation in the uterine wall. This step is considered to be the most difficult hurdle in the IVF process.

2. Raywat Deonandan, "Recent Studies in Reproductive Tourism and International Surrogacy," *Risk Management Health Policy* 8 (2015): 112. Dr. Deonandan emphasizes that the numbers could be anywhere from hundreds of thousands of births up to a few million every year. Poor record keeping of gestational surrogacy in the United States and abroad makes accurate data difficult to ascertain. For the purposes of this article even just a few hundred thousand new human births a year present a tremendous carbon burden.

3. My working definition of carbon footprint is the sum total of all emissions of CO_2 (carbon dioxide) and CO (carbon monoxide) that result from a person's activities over a defined period of time, usually measured each year. According to the influential 2009 article "Reproduction and the Carbon Legacies of Individuals" by Paul

A. Murtaugh and Michael G. Schlax in *Global Environmental Change* 19 (2009): 14, an individual's carbon legacy refers to "the carbon emissions of his descendants, weighted by their relatedness to him."

4. Kent E. Portney, *Sustainability* (MIT Press, 2015), 27.

5. Casey Rentmeester, *Heidegger and the Environment* (London: Rowman & Littlefield International, 2016), 13.

6. Deonandan, "Recent Studies in Reproductive Tourism and International Surrogacy," 113–117.

7. Finis Dunaway, "Picturing Planetary Peril," in *Living in the Anthropocene: Earth in the Age of Humans*, eds. Kress and Stine (Washington, DC: Smithsonian Institute, 2017), 129.

8. Seth Wynes and Kimberly A. Nicholas, "The Climate Mitigation Gap," *Environmental Research Letters* 12, no. 7 (2017): 2.

9. Paul A. Murtaugh and Michael G. Schlax, "Reproduction and the Carbon Legacy of Individuals," *Global Environmental Change* 19 (2009): 14. "Our basic premise is that a person is responsible for the carbon emissions of his descendants, weighted by their relatedness to him. For a descendant that is n generations removed from the focal individual, the weight is $\delta 1 = 2^{-n}$. So, for example, a mother and father are each responsible for one half of the emissions of their offspring, and 1/4 of the emissions of their grandchildren."

10. Ibid., 18.

11. Cristina Richie, "'Green' Reproduction, Resource Conservation, and Ecological Responsibility," *Worldviews* 18 (2014): 151.

12. Cristina Richie, "What Would an Environmentally Sustainable Reproductive Technology Look Like?" *Journal of Medical Ethics* 41 (2015): 384.

13. Cited in Portnoy's, *Sustainability*, 26.

14. Richie, "What Would an Environmentally Sustainable Reproductive Technology Look Like?" 385.

15. Wynes and Nicholas, "The Climate Mitigation Gap," 3–4.

16. My working definition of sustainability comes from Portney, *Sustainability*, 4, 25. For instance, "At its core, sustainability is a concept that focuses on the condition of Earth's biophysical environments, particularly with respect to the use and depletion of natural resources. The basic premise of sustainability is that Earth's resources cannot be used, depleted, and damaged indefinitely . . . . Their exploitation actually undermines the ability of life to persist and thrive" (4). Also, "Sustainability is . . . the search for peaceful coexistence between economic development and the environment" (25). A more demanding definition of sustainability calls for the minimizing of negative social, economical, and environmental impacts, the reversal of the gap between rich and poor and the reversing of the degradation of the ecological system. See Mashal Kaynat's, "Environmental Ethics of Renewable Energy," *Academia.edu*. (2015): 17–18, https://www.academia.edu/11200656/environmental_ethics_of_renewable_energy.

17. Richie, "What Would an Environmentally Sustainable Reproductive Technology Industry Look Like?" 385.

18. Ibid., 386.

19. Ibid., 385.

20. Ibid.

21. Drawing out the kinship between women's reproductive bodies enrolled in ART and Haraway's cyborgs, "a hybrid of organism and machine"—beings in between—can be fruitful. See "A Cyborg Manifesto" (1991), 161.

22. Robert Darrow, "Is Renewable Energy Technology Revolutionary?" in *Spaces for the Future: A Companion to the Philosophy of Technology*, eds. Joseph Pitt and Ashley Shew (New York: Routledge Press, 2017), 253.

23. Martin Heidegger, "The Question Concerning Technology," in *The Question Concerning Technology and Other Essays*, trans. W. Lovitt (New York: Harper & Row, Publishers, Inc.), 17.

24. Ibid., 15.

25. Martin Heidegger, *Bremen and Freiburg Lectures: Insight into that Which Is and Basic Principles of Thinking*, trans. Andrew Mitchell (Bloomington: Indiana University Press, 2012), 42, 62.

26. Heidegger, "The Question Concerning Technology," 16. One of the defining (and problematic) features of the resource (unlike the object) lies in its availability and flexibility, lacking in fixed limits.

27. Martin Heidegger, "Traditional Language, Technological Language," trans. W. T. Gregory, *Journal of Philosophical Research* 23 (1998): 138.

28. Heidegger, "The Question Concerning Technology," 14–15. Heidegger's famous analysis of the damming up of the Rhine river into the hydroelectric power plant reveals a hermeneutical recasting of the river as enframed, an extractable resource on call for the plant's production of electricity and for the tourist industry, 16.

29. Yet enframing is abstract enough that it could also apply to the post-Anthropocene age, as the most sustainable, efficient, and flexible deployment of all resources and renewable technologies. Maximizing control over the planet, being in charge of healing the planet can be seen as the mark of the *Ge-stell*.

30. Casey Rentmeester, *Heidegger and the Environment* (London: Rowman & Littlefield International, 2016), 51.

31. Iain Thomson, *Heidegger on Ontotheology: Technology and the Politic of Education* (New York: Cambridge University Press, 2005), 60.

32. Dana S. Belu, *Heidegger, Reproductive Technology & The Motherless Age* (New York: Palgrave Macmillan, 2017), 28.

33. Karey Harwood, *The Infertility Treadmill: Feminist Ethics, Personal Choice, and the Use of Reproductive Technologies* (Chapel Hill: University of North Carolina Press, 2007), 27.

34. By enabling fertilization in older women, CT and its counterpart, intracytoplasmic sperm injection, help detract attention from feminist concerns with racial and economic gender inequities, such as the lack of support for working mothers, the working poor, and the high demands of career life—inequities that often compel women to postpone pregnancy until well into their forties when they require IVF and IVF-based technologies.

35. Belu, *Heidegger, Reproductive Technology & The Motherless Age*, 27.

36. See Lisa Guenther's, *The Gift of the Other: Levinas and the Politics of Repro-duction* (Albany: State University of New York Press, 2006), 156.

37. Heidegger, "The Question Concerning Technology," 16.

38. Ibid., 19.

39. Guenther, *The Gift of the Other: Levinas and the Politics of Reproduction*, 156.

40. Heidegger, *Bremen and Freiburg Lectures.*

41. See Gena Corea, "Egg Snatchers," in *Test Tube Women,* eds. Rita Arditti, Renate Duelin Klein, and Shelley Minden (London: Pandora, 1984), 38.

42. Alison Bailey, "Reconceiving Surrogacy: Toward a Reproductive Justice Account of Indian Surrogacy," *Hypatia* 26, no. 4 (2011): 721.

43. Ursula Smerdon, "Crossing Bodies, Crossing Borders: International Surrogacy between the United States and India," *Cumberland Law Review* 39 (2009): 84.

44. Since they do not receive a contract, they cannot sue. For more, see Amrita Pande, "This Birth and That: Surrogacy and Stratified Motherhood in India," *phi-loSOPHIA* 4, no. 1 (2014): 51.

45. For a multifaceted ethnographic presentation of this exploitation, see Amrita Pande's, "Transnational Surrogacy in India: Gift for Global Sister," *Reproductive Biomedicine* Online 23 (2011): 618–625; Smerdon's, "Crossing Bodies, Crossing Borders," 15–85; and Kalindi Vora's, "Potential Risk and Return in Transnational Indian Surrogacy," *Current Anthropology* 54, no. 7 (2013): 97–106.

46. Sheela Saravanan, "An Ethnomethodological Approach to Examine Exploita-tion in the Context of Capacity, Trust and Experience of Commercial Surrogacy in India," *Philosophy, Ethics and Humanities in Medicine* Open Access (2013): 11.

47. Stephen Wilkinson, *Choosing Tomorrow's Children: The Ethics of Selective Reproduction* (New York: Oxford University Press, 2010), 144–145.

48. According to Alison Bailey's, "Reconceiving Surrogacy: Toward a Repro-ductive Justice Account of Indian Surrogacy," *Hypatia* 26, no. 4 (2011): 734, these sterilization programs in India, paradoxically deny women their role as mothers, one of the few social roles and sources of power and pride that they are allowed.

49. "The reformulation of the surrogates' bodies as empty spaces that can be cultivated to reproduce Western society and Western lives recapitulates the colonial epistemology of land as property, where resources, including native labor, were used to sustain the metropole" (Kalindi Vora, *S&F* Online, 5).

50. Vora, "Potential Risk and Return in Transnational Indian Surrogacy," 104.

51. So, because she is not genetically tied to the fetus she is a better resource than traditional surrogates who contribute their genes and thus are not viewed as spare space. Since the gestational surrogate makes no such contribution, she is more fungi-ble than the traditional surrogate who cannot cross racial borders. I agree with Doro-thy Robert's claim in *Killing the Black Body: Race Reproduction and The Meaning of Liberty* (Vintage, 1999), that in a racist culture "Feminist opponents of surrogacy miss an important aspect of the practice when they criticize it for treating women as fungible commodities. A Black surrogate is not exchangeable for a white one" (279). While this may be true of a traditional surrogate it does not apply to gestational sur-rogacy. A Black gestational surrogate is exchangeable for a white one and a white one for a Black one. Both are revealed as reproductive stock and both are able to optimize their reproductive bodies and to serve the reproductive market.

52. See Luce Irigaray, "Place, Interval: A Reading of Aristotle, *Physics IV*," in *An Ethics of Sexual Difference*, trans. C. Burke and G. C. Gill (Ithaca: Cornell University Press, 1993).

53. Sheela Saravanan, "An Ethnomethodological Approach to Examine Exploitation in the Context of Capacity, Trust and Experience of Commercial Surrogacy in India," *Philosophy, Ethics and Humanities* in Medicine Open Access (2013): 10.

54. Vora, "Potential Risk and Return in Transnational Indian Surrogacy," 104.

55. Ibid., 100.

56. Moreover, they would never consider traditional surrogacy, as they believe this would be tantamount to giving away or selling your own child—a horrible offense against nature and Jewish religious law. As mandated by the state of Israel, moreover, they also refuse to gestate any non-Jewish embryos, such as Arab or Christian ones, thereby patrolling political, religious, and racial borders.

57. Elly Teman, "The Medicalization of 'Nature' in the Artificial Body: Surrogate Motherhood in Israel," *Medical Anthropology Quarterly* 17, no. 1 (2003): 86.

58. This sense of splitting differs in important respects from the compelling psychoanalytical account of splitting (in pregnancy) presented by Julia Kristeva in her well-known essay "Women's Time," in *The Kristeva Reader* (New York: Columbia University Press, 1986). She writes: "Pregnancy seems to be experienced as the radical ordeal of the splitting of the subject: redoubling up of the body, separation and coexistence of the self and of an other, of nature and consciousness, of physiology and speech. This fundamental challenge to identity is then accompanied by a fantasy of totality—narcissistic completeness—a sort of instituted socialized, natural psychosis" (206).

59. Portney, *Sustainability*, 19.

60. Since 2012, over 4 percent of Israel's population is produced through traditional and gestational surrogacy.

61. Rob Nixon, "The Unequal Anthropocene," in *Living in the Anthropocene: Earth in the Age of Humans*, eds. W. John Kress and Jefffrey K. Stine (Washington, DC: Smithsonian Institute), 151.

BIBLIOGRAPHY

Bailey, Alison. "Reconceiving Surrogacy: Toward a Reproductive Justice Account of Indian Surrogacy." *Hypatia* 26, no. 4 (2011).

Belu, Dana S. *Heidegger, Reproductive Technology & The Motherless Age*. New York: Palgrave Macmillan, 2017.

Corea, Gena. "Egg Snatchers." In *Test Tube Women*, edited by Rita Arditti, Renate Duelin Klein, and Shelley Minden, 37–51. London: Pandora, 1984.

Darrow, Robert. "Is Renewable Energy Technology Revolutionary?" In *Spaces for the Future: A Companion to the Philosophy of Technology*, edited by Joseph Pitt and Ashley Shew. New York: Routledge Press, 2017.

Deonandan, Raywat. "Recent Studies in Reproductive Tourism and International Surrogacy: Ethical Considerations and Challenges for Policy." *Risk Management Health Policy* 8 (2015).

Dunaway, Finis. "Picturing Planetary Peril: Visual Media and the Environmental Crisis." In *Living in the Anthropocene: Earth in the Age of Humans*, edited by W. John Kress and Jeffrey K. Stine. Washington, DC: Smithsonian Institute, 2017.

Guenther, Lisa. *The Gift of the Other: Levinas and the Politics of Reproduction*. Albany: State University of New York Press, 2006.

Harwood, Karey. *The Infertility Treadmill: Feminist Ethics, Personal Choice, and the Use of Reproductive Technologies*. University of North Carolina Press, 2007.

Heidegger, Martin. *Bremen and Freiburg Lectures: Insight into that Which Is and Basic Principles of Thinking*. Translated by Andrew Mitchell. Indiana University Press, 2012.

Heidegger, Martin. "The Question Concerning Technology." In *The Question Concerning Technology and Other Essays*. Translated by W. Lovitt. New York: Harper & Row, Publishers, Inc., 1977.

Heidegger, Martin. "Traditional Language, Technological Language." Translated by W. T. Gregory. *Journal of Philosophical Research* 23 (1998).

Irigaray, Luce. "Place, Interval: A Reading of Aristotle, *Physics IV*." In *An Ethics of Sexual Difference*. Translated by C. Burke and G. C. Gill. Ithaca, NY: Cornell University Press, 1993.

Kaynat, Mashal. "Environmental Ethics of Renewable Energy." https://www.academia.edu/11200656/environmental_ethics_of_renewable_energy, 2015.

Kristeva, Julia. "Women's Time." In *The Kristeva Reader*. New York: Columbia University Press, 1986.

Murtaugh, Paul A. and Michael G. Schlax. "Reproduction and the Carbon Legacies of Individuals." *Global Environmental Change* 19 (2009).

Nixon, Rob. "The Unequal Anthropocene." In *Living in the Anthropocene: Earth in the Age of Humans*, edited by W. John Kress and Jefffrey K. Stine. Washington, DC: Smithsonian Institute, 2017.

Pande, Amrita. "This Birth and That: Surrogacy and Stratified Motherhood in India." *philoSOPHIA* 4, no. 1 (2014).

Pande, Amrita. "Transnational Surrogacy in India: Gift for Global Sister." *Reproductive Biomedicine* Online 23 (2011).

Portney, Kent E. *Sustainability*. Cambridge, MA: MIT University Press, 2015.

Rentmeester, Casey. *Heidegger and the Environment*. Lanham, MD and London: Rowman & Littlefield International, 2016.

Richie, Cristina. "'Green' Reproduction," Resource Conservation, and Ecological Responsibility." *Worldviews* 18 (2014).

Richie, Cristina. "What Would an Environmentally Sustainable Reproductive Technology Look Like?" *Journal of Medical Ethics* 41 (2015).

Saravanan, Sheela. "An Ethnomethodological Approach to Examine Exploitation in the Context of Capacity, Trust and Experience of Commercial Surrogacy in India." *Philosophy, Ethics and Humanities* in *Medicine* Open Access (2013).

Smerdon, Ursula. "Crossing Bodies, Crossing Borders: International Surrogacy between the United Sates and India." *Cumberland Law Review* 39 (2009).

Teman, Elly. "The Medicalization of 'Nature' in the Artificial Body: Surrogate Motherhood in Israel." *Medical Anthropology Quarterly* 17, no. 1 (2003).

Thomson, Iain. *Heidegger on Ontotheology: Technology and the Politic of Education*. New York: Cambridge University Press, 2005.

Vora, Kalindi. "Potential Risk and Return in Transnational Indian Surrogacy." *Current Anthropology* 54, no. 7 (2013).

Wilkinson, Stephen. *Choosing Tomorrow's Children: The Ethics of Selective Reproduction*. New York: Oxford University Press, 2010.

Wynes, Seth and Kimberly A. Nicholas. "The Climate Mitigation Gap: Education and Government Recommendations Miss the Most Effective Individual Actions." *Environmental Research Letters* 12, no. 7 (2017).

Chapter 8

An Alternative to Technological Instrumentalism

Considering the Aesthetic Dimension of Sustainable Energy

Brendan Mahoney

In the "First Elegy" of the modernist poet Rainer Maria Rilke, he declares with a both awed and ominous tone that "every angel is terrifying."[1] Speaking somewhat figuratively and provocatively, I will suggest that sustainable energy technology is potentially such a Rilkean terrifying angel. As an angel would appear to do, sustainable energy promises to save both human existence and the planet as a whole from—at the very least—the most destructive consequences of global climate change. Furthermore, it not only promises to save our lives and the viability of the myriad ecosystems of the globe, but also promises to save our way of life; that is, sustainable energy offers the promise that we in the industrialized global North could continue to live in highly consumerist societies, while also potentially enabling the very same lifestyle to expand across the developing world. Like the speaker of Rilke's poem, we stand in awe of this technological angel, ready to put our faith in its promises. However, we should not overlook the fact that sustainable energy is an offspring of a much older and more expansive angel: modern technology. At its core, anthropogenic climate change was precipitated by the rapid and widespread deployment of fossil fuel technologies. Despite our current knowledge of the deleterious effects of fossil fuels, the advent of this technology also appeared as a saving angel: it, too, promised to dramatically improve the quality of human life and to advance the goals of civilization.

Faced with the mounting scientific evidence about the potentially dire consequences of climate change, the rational course of action would seem to be to accept the promise of sustainable energy technology, taking the risk that it will turn out to be a far less terrifying angel than fossil fuel technology has proven to be. Humans, however, do not always act rationally, as evinced by the various strains of opposition that have emerged over the past few decades in the United States to sustainable energy technologies and to other climate mitigation proposals. Setting aside the opposition of those who are outwardly hostile to and ignorant of science and those who have a vested interest in the continuance of extracting and burning fossil fuels, one of the more interesting objections to sustainable energy technology is aesthetic. An example of this is the resistance to the Cape Wind Project: an offshore wind farm that was proposed to be built in Nantucket Sound off Cape Cod, but was recently rejected in favor of a different offshore project that will be located off Martha's Vineyard.[2] In fairness to the opponents of this project, most of them are not in principle opposed to sustainable energy; indeed, many of them are strong advocates of it, but in the case of Cape Wind, their objections are grounded in a "NIMBY" mind-set. While their stated objections are varied (including economic, historical, tribal, and safety concerns), one of their driving concerns is aesthetic; that is, they oppose the construction of the Cape Wind Project because of the potential that it would ruin the scenic beauty of the sound, even if that was the most logical, efficient, and equitable site for the project.[3]

It is easy to portray this aesthetic objection as the superficial concern of a wealthy minority who are opposed to the installation of 1,500 GWh per year of clean energy because it might disrupt the scenic view from their mansions and yachts. While seemingly superficial, I would argue that aesthetic objections can point to a valid and much deeper concern regarding sustainable energy technology—especially if one examines this issue within the framework of Martin Heidegger's critique of modern technology. Andrew Mitchell provides a lucid and concise overview of that critique: "Heidegger understands technology as a drive toward replaceability and 'commodification' . . . whereby all that is becomes replaceable 'standing reserve.' Technology thus poses a threat to the singularity and uniqueness of things."[4] Understood in this manner, one could offer a more sympathetic reading of the opposition to the Cape Wind Project. Instead of being an objection to the disruption of their scenic views, the opponents of the project object to the potential loss of the singularity and uniqueness of Nantucket Sound. The threat of the Cape Wind Project is that it will reduce the sound to one more industrial landscape, indistinct from and wholly replaceable by any other industrial landscape; in brief, the sound would become merely a power plant.

What I will argue in this chapter is that considering the aesthetic dimension of sustainable energy can potentially help us design and implement technologies that not only are far less ecologically destructive than fossil fuels, but that also disrupt the exploitative and reductive logic of modern

[handwritten margin note: Aesthetic's keeps Nature's beauty and does not make it the same / Not make it do everything]

technology. In order to develop my argument, I will first summarize the principal components of Heidegger's critique of modern technology. I will then show how sustainable energy technology—as we currently conceive of it—risks furthering the exploitative logic of modern technology. From there, I will analyze Heidegger's claims about art's potential to foster the "saving power" against the danger of modern technology. Finally, I will examine the relevance of these concepts for designing nonexploitative sustainable energy technology.

HEIDEGGER'S CRITIQUE OF MODERN TECHNOLOGY

Heidegger's fullest articulation of his critique of modern technology appears in his seminal essay "The Question Concerning Technology," first published in 1954.[5] While the essay does examine specific technological things, Heidegger is concerned primarily with inquiring into the *essence* of technology, which, he asserts, "is by no means anything technological."[6] At the outset of his investigation, he summarizes the common understanding of technology, which he labels as the anthropological and instrumental definition of technology: the definition is anthropological because technology is understood as a human activity and it is instrumental because it is conceived as a means to an end.[7] Despite the fact that this seems like an obvious definition of technology, Heidegger charges that the instrumental definition of technology does not show us its essence. In support of his claim, he situates the instrumental definition within its historical context, arguing that it is grounded in a specific modern understanding of causality as means and ends: "A means is that whereby something is effected and thus attained. Whatever has an effect as its consequence is called a cause. . . . The end that determines the kind of means to be used may also be considered a cause."[8] Understood in this manner, causality is instrumental—that is, that which effects something, brings it about, or obtains results. However, Heidegger contends that the instrumental concept of technology is grounded in a misinterpretation of Aristotle's doctrine of the four causes that privileges the efficient cause.[9] He attributes this misinterpretation to the Roman's translation of the Greek word for "cause" (*aition*) into the Latin word *causa*. To counter this misinterpretation, he offers an alternative "translation" of *aition*: "that to which something else is indebted [*das, was ein anderes verschuldet*]. The four causes are the ways, all belonging at once to each other, of being responsible for something else."[10] He clarifies that "being responsible" does not have a moral connotation in the Greek, but means what enables something to appear, to come forth into what it is: "being responsible is this starting something on its way into arrival."[11]

Building on this explication of the ancient Greek concept of causality, Heidegger argues that the Greek notion of *technē*, properly understood, belongs to *poiēsis*—that is, "bringing forth." Working with this interpretation, he challenges the instrumental definition of technology by positing, "Technology is therefore no mere means. Technology is a way of revealing."[12] That is, instead of merely being a tool or a skill, technology is a specific way of disclosing beings, of bringing them forth. In the case of modern technology, Heidegger describes its distinct way of revealing beings as "a challenging [*Herausfordern*], which puts to nature the unreasonable demand that it supply energy which can be extracted and stored as such."[13] Modern technology imposes a specific and reductive mode of being on things: it challenges them only to reveal themselves as energy that can be unlocked, calculated, transformed, stored, and indefinitely exchanged and replaced. Once reduced to mere energy, "everything is ordered to stand by, to be immediately on hand, indeed to stand there just so that it may be on call for a further ordering."[14] The name Heidegger selects for the way that things are challenged to reveal themselves by modern technology is "standing-reserve" (*der Bestand*). As examples of standing-reserve, he lists the extraction of coal and ore from the earth, the production of nitrogen fertilizers, the mechanization of agriculture, the release of nuclear energy from uranium, the installation of hydroelectric dams, the production of cellulose from wood, and even the manufacturing and dissemination of public opinion through mass media.[15]

Since Heidegger is also critiquing the anthropological definition of technology, it is important to note that challenging things to reveal themselves solely as standing-reserve is not purely a human activity that we intentionally undertake; instead, he argues that we too are challenged "to reveal the actual, in the mode of ordering, as standing-reserve."[16] He calls this challenging that is imposed on us to reveal things as standing-reserve, "Enframing" (*das Ge-Stell*).[17] To be clear, Enframing is not a thing or the totality of technological things, but what *enables* beings to appear as standing-reserve. It is the essential way in which all things reveal themselves intelligibly to us in the modern epoch—that is, as calculable, orderable, manipulable, exchangeable, and disposable.[18] While it is true, as Julian Young observes, that "it is not merely modern but rather *any* technological practice that requires the disclosure of the world as resource," Heidegger argues that the crucial difference between the modern era and previous eras is that "where [Enframing] holds sway, it drives out every other possibility of revealing" so that everything is revealed *only* as standing-reserve.[19] In earlier epochs, one way things could appear was as resources, but that was not their essential or sole mode of being; in the modern epoch, Heidegger claims this is no longer the case. To illustrate this point, he provides a striking image: "Nature becomes a gigantic gasoline station, an energy source for modern technology and industry."[20]

THE "DANGER" OF SUSTAINABLE
ENERGY TECHNOLOGY

Given the contrast that Heidegger draws between a windmill and the extraction and burning of coal, one might assume that sustainable energy technologies would escape or run counter to Enframing. If designed and implemented properly, they have minimal to no destructive impact on the environment and the climate, and they do not exploit and exhaust natural resources in the manner that fossil fuel extraction does. However, the primary focus of Heidegger's critique of modern technology is not environmental, but ontological—that is, he considers the true danger of modern technology not to be the physical destruction of the natural environment, but the reductive manner in which beings are able to reveal themselves.[21] Furthermore, I would argue that our current thinking about sustainable energy technology operates squarely within the logic of Enframing. Although Heidegger contrasts a windmill with coal-generated power, he is describing an old windmill—presumably from the eighteenth or nineteenth century—which, he notes, "does not unlock energy from the air currents in order to store it."[22] This description is virtually the opposite of contemporary wind turbines. As battery and/or storage technology improves, the goal for wind turbine technology would be precisely to unlock energy from the air currents in order to store it, so that it will be on call for distribution throughout the electrical grid at any time. Additionally, his assertions about the purpose of coal mining perfectly fit the aim of photovoltaics: "It is being stored; that is, it is on call, ready to deliver the sun's warmth that is stored in it. The sun's warmth is challenged forth for heat."[23] The similarity between fossil fuels and clean energy is even more apparent by examining aerial photographs of oils fields and massive solar arrays—vast stretches of the earth are put to work solely for the extraction of energy. While sustainable energy technology does not result in the environmental destruction of fossil fuel usage, it still epitomizes standing-reserve. Within the logic of Heidegger's concept of Enframing, both forms of energy are ontologically indistinguishable; that is, they reduce phenomena to a calculable coherence of forces and challenge them forth to yield distributable and storable energy.

The degree to which sustainable energy technology reveals things as standing-reserve is further underscored by its reliance on the methods of modern science. Heidegger asserts: "Modern science's way of representing pursues and entraps nature as a calculable coherence of forces."[24] In brief, modern science too operates totally within the calculating logic of Enframing, which complicates the notion that sustainable energy technology is a nonexploitative alternative to fossil fuels in two ways. First, it is precisely because modern science represents—or entraps—nature as a "calculable coherence of forces" that it is capable of identifying and demonstrating the existence and principal causes of climate change, as well as other forms of environmental degradation. Second, the calculating nature of modern science enables scientists to determine crucial metrics (e.g., 350 ppm of CO_2) and run complex models that will be necessary for any attempt to successfully and globally respond to the threats posed by climate change.

This last statement should indicate that I am not advocating that humanity abandon efforts to develop and implement sustainable energy technologies on a large scale; however, I am proposing that the application of Heidegger's critique of modern technology to sustainable energy should make us cautious as to how we proceed with these technologies. Even if they are not environmentally destructive, they still reveal nature essentially as a resource to be exploited for its energy; consequently, these technologies risk continuing the very logic underlying fossil fuel extraction and usage that has led to global climate change. To briefly entertain a slippery slope, sustainable energy technologies potentially further the exploitative logic of fossil fuels in a subtler but more insidious manner precisely because they do *not* degrade the environment. Their widespread adoption might prompt us to praise ourselves for our morally "correct" choice of protecting the environment, which in turn could initiate a feedback loop of Enframing that is even more effective at masking this exploitative and reductive way of revealing nature. To be provocative, one might modify Heidegger's phrase and claim that all of this adds up to the supreme danger of sustainable energy technology.

[handwritten annotation: STILL SEE NATURE AS A MEANS NOT AN END]

[handwritten annotation: → WHILE BETTER FOR THE ENVIRONMENT, IS STILL SERVING HUMANS AND MAKING IT EVEN MORE OF A RESOURCE THAN IT ALREADY IS]

FOSTERING THE SAVING POWER

Despite the dire tone of this slippery slope and Heidegger's descriptions of the monstrousness and the supreme danger of modern technology, as well as his rather pastoral descriptions of preindustrial Swabian peasant life, his critique is not a call for a form of neo-Luddism.[25] He explicitly states, "What is dangerous is not technology. Technology is not demonic," and he warns against "rebel[ling] helplessly against it and curs[ing] it as the work of the devil."[26] Instead, he clarifies that the primary purpose of his analysis of modern technology is "to prepare a free relationship to it," which he describes as such: "We can use technical devices, and yet with proper use also keep ourselves so free of them, that we may let go of them at any time."[27] In "The Question Concerning Technology," Heidegger provides little insight into the details of *how* we may achieve a free relationship to technology; however, he does assert that art "may expressly foster the growth of the saving power."[28] Arriving in the closing paragraphs of the essay, there is scant development of this claim; as such, I will draw on his other writings on the nature of art in order to flesh it out. Since Heidegger wrote extensively on the topic of art and his ideas evolved over the course of his career, it would be beyond the scope of this chapter to fully address his philosophy of art; therefore, I will focus my explication on the aspects of his thinking that best clarify his claim about the saving power of art.[29] Even with this narrow focus, space constraints only permit me to provide a broad sketch of his argument.[30]

While the everyday usage of the word "art" encompasses a wide array of activities and media, Heidegger—in a manner similar to his inquiry into technology—is seeking the *essence* of art. To this end, he claims, "the nature of art is poetry."[31] However, he does not use or limit the word "poetry" to its commonly understood meaning: that is, the composition of poems, a literary genre, and/or a more fanciful usage of language.[32] While he does maintain that "the linguistic work, the poem in the narrower sense, has a privileged position in the domain of the arts," he argues for a deeper ontological meaning of poetry.[33] Taking inspiration from a line in the nineteenth-century German poet Friedrich Hölderlin's poem, "In Lovely Blue," Heidegger defines poetry as "what really lets us dwell" on the earth.[34] Initially, this might appear to be a very odd definition of poetry, especially since it would seem obvious that it is the activity of building that enables us to establish a dwelling on the earth. Heidegger anticipates this response and even affirms it; however, this prompts him to delve more deeply into the meaning of building.

On the surface, "to build" means to make something, and he connects this meaning to the Greek *poiēsis*, which can be translated as "the activity of making." Building on the etymological connection between *poiēsis* and poetry, he proposes that poetry is the "distinctive kind of building."[35] If we understand poetry not as a specifically literary creation but as *poiēsis*, then its essential meaning is to bring forth or reveal something in its essence or its truth. As an example of this, Heidegger discusses a Greek temple, which he claims reveals the Greek world: this encompasses the myriad paths of the humans who inhabit it, including their victories and disgraces, as well as the natural environment—for example, the rocky ground, the raging storms, the radiance of the sun, the expanse of the sky, the various plants and animals. Furthermore, the temple and the statue in its inner sanctum create a space for the corresponding god to reveal itself. Importantly, neither the temple nor the statue portrays anything; they do not accomplish their artistic work by furnishing us with images that we then represent to ourselves in our minds. As *poiēsis*, they bring forth or make manifest these things in the world to us.[36]

If poetry—in its essence—is *poiēsis*, how does it let us dwell? Heidegger first clarifies that by "dwelling" he does not mean the activity of residing in a building that is "merely one form of human behavior alongside many others"; instead, he uses the term "dwelling" to refer to "the basic character of human existence."[37] To flesh out what constitutes the basic character of human existence, he turns to etymology for guidance. He traces the verb "to dwell" (*wohen*) to its roots in a cluster of related Germanic words: (1) the Old Saxon word *wuon*; (2) the Gothic word *wunian*, which both mean "to be at peace" or "to remain in peace;" and (3) *das Frye* and *fry*, which mean "preserved from harm and danger, . . . safeguarded." Drawing on this cluster of meanings, he defines the fundamental character of dwelling as "sparing" and "preserving," but not merely in the negative sense of protecting something from danger; instead, he declares that there is also a positive sense: "when we leave something beforehand in its own nature, when we return it specifically to its being."[38] In short, to dwell is to stay or remain with things in such a way that one actively lets them remain in their essential way of being. Poetry, then, is what lets us dwell insofar as it brings forth or reveals the essence of things. By bringing us into dwelling, poetry or art fosters the saving power because it lets us stay with things and preserve them in their essential way of being, instead of imposing the demands of standing-reserve on them.

THE ART OF SUSTAINABLE ENERGY TECHNOLOGY

One might object that standing-reserve is not an imposition insofar as energy is one possible mode of being for things such as oil, coal, wind, water, and so on; if these things were not capable of revealing themselves as energy, then they could not be converted into sources of energy. Furthermore, one might object that creating works of art is also an imposition of a form or mode of being onto things; for example, a block of marble never naturally reveals itself as Michelangelo's *David*. While I concede that there is merit in both of these points, I would respond to these objections by clarifying that energy is *one* possible mode of being in poetic revealing, whereas it is the *only* possible mode of being within Enframing. As Richard Rojcewicz explains: "Art, in relation to technology, does not present things under an alternative essence, if 'alternative' means different but on the same level. In our epoch, art does not *replace* the understanding of things as disposables [i.e., standing-reserve] with some other understanding."[39] Art does not deny that one possible mode of being of things is to be resources; furthermore, individual art works frequently bring forth the resourceful qualities of things—for example, the durability and rigidity of stone, or the pliability of wood—but they do not attempt to block all other possible modes of being. In contrast, Enframing eradicates all modes of being except for one: to be exchangeable and replaceable energy.

I will utilize this contrast in order to examine the relevance of taking into consideration the aesthetic dimension when designing and implementing sustainable energy technologies. In the mode of standing-reserve, solar panels do not reveal the sun, wind turbines do not reveal the wind, and hydroelectric dams and tidal turbines do not reveal rivers and the seas. Each of these technologies only reveals energy, with the only distinguishing mark between them the quantity of energy revealed. How could sustainable energy technologies still bring forth the energy of these natural things, while not reducing them to resources purely for our power consumption? As a model, I will not turn to works of art, but to other natural entities—for example, a tree. Rooted to the ground but extending toward the sky, a tree reveals the wind; the sway of its branches reveals both the direction and the velocity of the wind. With current wind turbines, while their blades certainly revolve in the wind, they are designed to maximize potential power output—not to reveal the wind. As such, they tend to impose themselves on the landscape, jutting out of a ridgeline, a plain, or the sea. Although energy and efficiency indisputably need to guide much of the design and location of wind power technologies, I would argue that it is also important to consider how the turbines can be integrated aesthetically into the landscape, revealing the currents of the wind, the contours of the land, the swells of the sea, and the shifting light and weather of the sky.[40] In a similar manner, the play of sunlight on the surface of water or a mountainside could serve as a model for solar panels. As light is reflected, water surfaces and mountainsides reveal the path of the sun across the horizon, the height of its arc, its intensity, the shifting colors of the day, and the undulation of clouds. Perhaps the surface of solar panels could be designed to act in a similar manner, revealing the various dimensions of the sun and the complex play of sunlight.

What I am not proposing is that sustainable energy technologies should *mimic* natural entities—like those cellular towers camouflaged as trees, which are often *more* conspicuous than an unadorned cellular tower. Instead, what I am arguing for is the design and installation of technologies that both bring forth energy and still allow the surrounding environment to reveal itself in its essential modes of being. This undoubtedly will be more difficult with large-scale projects, which by design often must prioritize efficiency; however, if we can attain a free relationship to technology, as Heidegger suggests we should, then it should not be a concern that some of our technologies are designed with principally instrumental intentions. The danger of Enframing is not that *some* beings are revealed as resources, but that standing-reserve is the *only* mode of revealing. With that being said, there still seems to be no reason—other than purely economic considerations—why aesthetic concerns could not be one of the factors informing the design, siting, and installation of these technologies. With regard to economic considerations, Gordon G. Brittan, Jr. raises a compelling point: "Governments and utilities, and the engineers they fund, have presupposed almost from the outset the viability of a particular design, and devoted almost all of their resources to 'improving' it. In the process, they have discounted plans and ideas that might be more acceptable aesthetically."[41] Instead of assuming the feasibility of one specific design or approach and expending resources to make that acceptable to people, those same resources could be utilized to develop alternative designs that would better accord with people's aesthetic sensibilities and the unique elements of specific places.

Aesthetic considerations will likely be more viable—and I would argue more impactful—with localized and decentralized sustainable energy technologies. While efficiency and energy yield would still be principal concerns, it would presumably be much easier with localized projects to design and install technologies with much greater consideration given to the distinctive characteristics of the place, much like site-specific art works. Additionally, both the efficiency and site-disclosive power of these technologies could be augmented by incorporating them into other sustainable design practices, such as passive energy, green roofs, green walls, vertical terraces, and the construction of earth houses.[42] By attending to the specific ecological context of the project, designers can help integrate our technologies into their sites, instead of disrupting or imposing on them. These practices would not only yield energy and higher efficiency but also reveal and preserve the essential modes of being of their environments. As we integrate these technologies into their natural environments, we also further integrate our own individual and communal lives into the environment. Instead of situating power production in remote, out-of-sight locations or utilizing technology to distance us from the natural environment, more decentralized and localized energy production would reveal more directly the process by which natural phenomena are converted into energy. Furthermore, if we design and implement these technologies poetically—that is, in accordance with the Greek notion of *technē* as *poiēsis*—there is the potential that we will no longer reduce the environment to mere standing-reserve for our exploitation, but will preserve the myriad possible ways that beings disclose themselves. Integrating ourselves into the natural environment in such a manner could help us to fully practice Heidegger's concept of dwelling—that is, a "staying with things" that "brings [humans] onto the earth, making [us] belong to it."[43]

CONCLUSION: A SUSTAINABLE NARRATIVE

There is one additional aspect of Heidegger's philosophy of art that I would argue can connect the aesthetic dimension of sustainable energy technology to the ethical dimension: "To be a work means to set up a world."[44] Heidegger makes two important clarifications about his usage of the term "world": (1) "The world is not the mere collection of the countable or uncountable, familiar and unfamiliar things that are just there;" and (2) "But neither is it a merely imagined framework added by our representations to the sum of such given things."[45] That is, the world is not the totality of existing entities or a container-like space in which they exist, nor is it merely something projected by human consciousness onto external reality. Instead, to draw on Heidegger's definition of the concept in *Being and Time*, the world is the totality of significant relations.[46] Karsten Harries offers a helpful interpretation of this concept: "World here names a space of intelligibility or significance that determines the way human beings encounter persons and things."[47] Thus, when the work of art sets up a world, it brings forth and sustains the space of intelligibility of the significant relations among persons and things.

What I propose is to situate sustainable energy technology—designed and implemented as a form of *poiēsis*—within a narrative ethics framework.[48] According to Brian Treanor, "Narratives can *inspire* us (i.e., arouse in a person the desire to be virtuous) and *motivate* us (e.g., to persevere in the cultivation of virtue). In addition to this exhortative function, . . . we use narratives to *experiment* with possibilities, exploring different situations and different ethical responses."[49] With its capacity for world disclosure, art can reveal, to quote Polt, "*a system of purposes and meanings that organizes our activities and our identity, and within which entities can make sense to us.*"[50] This is particularly fruitful for narrative ethics, which often focuses on identity—that is, not "*what we do* but . . . *who we are.*"[51] Since art discloses the context of meaningfulness that underlies our identity and purposes, it can show us who we are in the world. An excellent contemporary example of this is the work of Edward Burtynsky. His photographs of manufactured landscapes show us that our world of progress and consumerism has a reciprocal effect on the same scale in the natural environment, which reveals that our identity as a society of progress also entails an identity as unrelenting transfigurers—and often destroyers—of nature.[57]

Yet, art's world-disclosive capacity need not be limited to revealing our present world; with its imaginative dimension, art can also show us *possible* worlds, thus opening a space in which we can question the values of our world, our role in it, and our own identity. In effect, art enables us to contemplate the 'as if': *as if* we lived in this world and not that one, *as if* our values were these instead of those, *as if* we were these people and not those people, and so on. What I will suggest, in closing, is that it is art's ability to disclose the possibility of the "as if" that helps us to prepare a free relationship to technology. Instead of being fatalists when confronted with the truth of Enframing and the world of modern technology, we can accept that this is *our* world, but not that this is the *only* possible world; furthermore, we can bring into question our own identity in this world and reflect deeply on which narrative we wish to guide our individual and collective lives. I would argue that sustainable energy technology undertaken as *poiēsis* can play a vital role in that process insofar as it can help us to imagine and enact a narrative in which our identity is to be inhabitants of the earth who bring forth energy while revealing and preserving the natural environment in its essential modes of being.

As a final note of caution, I would warn against binding ourselves too tightly to the narratives of apocalypse and sacrifice: i.e., staving off total environmental collapse will burden us with the need to sacrifice significant aspects of our current ways of living. While I am under no illusion that responding to climate change will necessitate alterations in our values and behaviors—particularly with regard to our level of consumption and our economic systems—I agree with Treanor that we need to frame these alterations not as burdens, but as narratives of flourishing, both for humanity and the natural environment.[53] The aesthetic dimension of technology can make a valuable contribution to that project. If aesthetic concerns can so strongly drive people to oppose clean energy initiatives, such as in the case of the Cape Wind Project, then the converse should be possible: aesthetically attuned technology could be a powerful motivator for both individuals and communities to embrace and advocate for sustainable energy technologies. Perhaps, the disclosive power of art can confront us with the terrifying angel of modern technology and provoke us to cultivate a world of environmental flourishing, while that is still a real possibility.

[handwritten margin note: GIVE A MORE POS. OUTLOOK ON TECHNOLOGY. ALTERNATIVES (MORE POSITIVITY)]

NOTES

1. Rilke, *Duino Elegies*, 5.

2. Jon Chesto, "Two Big Wind Farms."

3. The principal opposition to the Cape Wind Project is Save Our Sound. For an overview of their positions, see: saveoursound.org.

4. Mitchell, *Fourfold*, 7.

5. The earliest version of "The Question Concerning Technology" appeared as the lecture "Positionality" as part of the lecture cycle *Insight into That Which Is*, which Heidegger delivered in 1949 at the Bremen Club. He substantially revised and expanded that lecture and first delivered it under the title "The Question Concerning Technology" in 1953. For a concise history of the "Bremen Lectures" and their place in Heidegger's published works, see the "Editor's Afterward" in Heidegger, *Bremen and Freiburg Lectures*, 167–71. Abbreviated hereafter as BFL.

6. Heidegger, "Question Concerning Technology," 311. Hereafter abbreviated as QCT.

7. QCT, 313.

8. Ibid.

9. According to Aristotle, all things capable of change/motion are the result of four causes: the material cause, the formal cause, the efficient cause, and the final cause. See Aristotle, *Physics*, 194b16–195b30.

10. QCT, 314.

11. QCT, 316. Obviously, this is a highly truncated presentation of Heidegger's analysis of the connection between the instrumental definition of technology and causality. I examine these ideas in greater detail in Brendan Mahoney, "Heidegger and

the Art of Technology: A Response to Eric Katz," *Environmental Philosophy* 11, no. 2 (2014): 279–306. See pp. 284–88. For a more in-depth explication of this topic, see Rojcewicz, *Gods and Technology*, 15–66.

12. QCT, 318.

13. Ibid., 320.

14. Ibid., 322.

15. Ibid., 320–23. One of the most controversial descriptions of modern technology that Heidegger made was his comparison of modern agriculture to the Holocaust: "Agriculture is now a mechanized food industry, in essence the same as the production of corpses in the gas chambers and extermination camps" (BFL, 27). Perhaps tellingly, this statement appears in the 1949 "Positionality" lecture, but was omitted from the published version of "The Question Concerning Technology."

16. QCT, 325.

17. Since the appearance of William Lovitt's translation of "The Question Concerning Technology," "Enframing" has remained the standard translation of *Ge-Stell* within the scholarship; as such, I will adhere to that standard. However, Rojcewicz offers "all-encompassing imposition" as an alternative translation and Mitchell suggests "Positionality." Furthermore, the meaning of "Enframing" is complex and bound up with Heidegger's critique of metaphysics and his concept of the "history of Being," which would be beyond the scope of this article to fully explain. For more in-depth explications of the concept, see: Rojcewicz, *Gods and Technology*, 90–107 and Mitchell, *Fourfold*, 49–63.

18. QCT, 329.

19. Young, *Heidegger's Later Philosophy*, 46–47; QCT, 332.

20. Heidegger, *Discourse on Thinking*, 50. Abbreviated hereafter as DT.

21. QCT, 332–33. Thomas Rohrkrämer asserts, "Heidegger's main concern was not environmental pollution or degradation, and he did not mention material limits of growth, although these worries were already being voiced throughout his lifetime. Instead, he was primarily concerned about the reductionist relationship between humans and their world" ("Martin Heidegger, National Socialism," 188).

22. QCT, 320.

23. Ibid., 321.

24. Ibid., 326.

25. Heidegger, "Building Dwelling Thinking," 157–58. Abbreviated hereafter as BDT.

26. QCT, 333, 330. He elaborates in greater detail in *Discourse on Thinking*: "For all of us, the arrangements, devices, and machinery of technology are to a greater or lesser extent indispensable. It would be foolish to attack technology blindly. It would be shortsighted to condemn it as the work of the devil. We depend on technical devices; they even challenge us to ever greater advances. But suddenly and unaware we find ourselves so firmly shackled to these technical devices that we fall into bondage to them" (53–54). Both Figal ("Universality of Technology") and Lindberg ("Lost in the World of Technology") emphasize that despite Heidegger's often apocalyptic tone and misinterpretations of his thought by some of his readers, he was far from being anti-technology or calling for a return to some type of "authentic" rural living.

27. QCT, 311; DT, 54. This mode of comportment toward technology, which he claims "expresses 'yes' and at the same time 'no,'" he refers to as "*releasement [Gelassenheit] toward things*" (DT, 54). For many scholars who apply Heidegger's thought to environmental philosophy, the concept of *Gelassenheit* is central to their attempts to develop an environmental ethics out of his analysis of modern technology. I have significant reservations about the feasibility of appropriating his concept of *Gelassenheit* for environmental ethics, which I have laid out in Mahoney, "The Virtue of Burden." In the same article, I also survey the scholarship that does appropriate this concept for environmental ethics.

28. QCT, 340.

29. For more comprehensive analyses of Heidegger's philosophy of art, see: Thomson, *Heidegger, Art and Postmodernity*; Harries, *Art Matters*; Young, *Heidegger's Philosophy of Art*.

30. For a more comprehensive explication of the "saving power" fostered by art, see Rojcewicz, *Gods and Technology*, 153–207.

31. Heidegger, "Origin of the Work of Art," 72. Abbreviated hereafter as OWA.

32. Heidegger, "Language," 205; Heidegger, "Poetically Man Dwells," 211–12. Abbreviated hereafter as PMD.

33. OWA, 71.

34. PMD, 213. The specific line from Hölderlin's "In Lovely Blue" is: "Full of merit, yet poetically, man / Dwells on this earth" (qtd. in BDT, 214).

35. PMD, 213, 212.

36. OWA, 40–43.

37. PMD, 212–13.

38. BDT, 147.

39. Rojcewicz, *Gods and Technology*, 205.

40. For discussions of other ways in which aesthetic concerns factor into the design of wind turbines, see: Saito, "Machines in the Ocean" and Brittan, "Wind, Energy, Landscape." Brittan specifically discusses a wind turbine designed to look like sails (179–80).

41. Brittan, "Wind, Energy, Landscape," 181.

42. I discusses earth houses in conjunction with Heidegger's philosophy in more detail in Mahoney, "Heidegger and the Art of Technology," 300–301.

43. BDT, 149; PMD, 216.

44. OWA, 43. While I am attempting to provide a concise summary of "world," I will emphasize that the concept is quite complex in relationship to the totality of Heidegger's works. As Werner Marx notes: "The sense and significance of the concept of 'world' have altered repeatedly in the course of the development of Heidegger's thought" (*Heidegger and the Tradition*, 183). For a comprehensive overview of this topic, see pp. 183–91.

45. OWA, 43.

46. This is the conclusion of a complex phenomenological analysis that Heidegger undertakes in §§14–18 of *Being and Time*. I explain the stages of the analysis in greater detail in Mahoney, "Heidegger and the Art of Technology," 290–93. For a rigorous, yet concise explication of this concept, see: Polt, *Heidegger*, 49–54.

47. Harries, *Art Matters*, 101.

48. It is well beyond the scope of this chapter to treat the topic of narrative ethics sufficiently. For an in-depth examination of the application of narrative theory to ethics—and environmental ethics in particular—see: Treanor, *Emplotting Virtue*, especially chapters 6–8. Treanor's work is grounded in the narrative theory of Paul Ricœur, Richard Kearney, and Martha Nussbaum.

49. Treanor, *Emplotting Virtue*, 160–61. While Heidegger does not explicitly frame his ideas as such, his examples of the Greek temple and the eighteenth-century Swabian peasant farmhouse (BDT, 157–58) both present narratives of particular ways of life.

50. Polt, *Heidegger*, 54.

51. Treanor, *Emplotting Virtue*, 13.

52. For a retrospective of Burtynsky's manufactured landscape photography, which also includes commentary from and interviews with the artist, see Lori Pauli, *Manufactured Landscapes: The Photographs of Edward Burtynsky* (Ottawa, Canada: National Gallery of Canada, 2004).

53. Treanor, *Emplotting Virtue*, 375–76.

BIBLIOGRAPHY

Aristotle. *Physics*. Translated by Hippocrates G. Apostle. Grinnell, IW: Peripatetic Press, 1980.

Brittan Jr., Gordon G. "Wind, Energy, Landscape: Reconciling Nature and Technology." *Philosophy & Geography* 4, no. 2 (2001): 169–84.

Chesto, Jon. "Two Big Wind Farms to Rise off Coast of Martha's Vineyard." *Boston Globe*, May 23, 2018. https://www.bostonglobe.com/business/2018/05/23/two-big-wind-farms-rise-off-coast-martha-vineyard/vLmWsUSdLzih6M3CCZK2YL/story.html.

Figal, Günter. "The Universality of Technology and the Independence of Things: Heidegger's *Bremen Lectures* Once More." *Research in Phenomenology* 45 (2015): 358–68.

Harries, Karsten. *Art Matters: A Critical Commentary on Heidegger's 'The Origin of the Work of Art.'* Dordrecht, The Netherlands: Springer, 2009.

Heidegger, Martin. *Being and Time*. Translated by Joan Stambaugh, revised by Dennis J. Schmidt. Albany, NY: State University of New York Press, 2010.

———. *Bremen and Freiburg Lectures: Insight Into That Which Is and Basic Principles of Thinking*. Translated by Andrew J. Mitchell. Bloomington: Indiana University Press, 2012.

———. "Building Dwelling Thinking." In *Poetry, Language, Thought*. Translated by Albert Hofstadter, 141–59. New York: Perennial Classics, 2001.

———. *Discourse on Thinking*. Translated by John M. Anderson and E. Hans Freund. New York: Harper & Row Publishers, 1969.

———. "Language." In *Poetry, Language, Thought*. Translated by Albert Hofstadter, 185–208. New York: Perennial Classics, 2001.

———. "The Origin of the Work of Art." In *Poetry Language Thought*. Translated by Albert Hofstadter, 15–86. New York: HarperCollins, 2001.

————. "Poetically Man Dwells." In *Poetry, Language, Thought*. Translated by Albert Hofstadter, 209–27. New York: Perennial Classics, 2001.

————. "The Question Concerning Technology." Translated by William Lovitt. In *Basic Writings*, edited by David Farrell Krell, 307–41. New York: HarperSanFrancisco, 1993.

Lindberg, Susanna. "Lost in the World of Technology with and after Heidegger." *Epoché* 20, no. 1 (2015): 213–32.

Mahoney, Brendan. "Heidegger and the Art of Technology: A Response to Eric Katz." *Environmental Philosophy* 11, no. 2 (2014): 279–306.

Mahoney, Brendan. "The Virtue of Burden and the Limits of *Gelassenheit*: The Complex Case for Heideggerian Environmental Ethics." *Environmental Philosophy* 13, no. 2 (2016): 269–98.

Marx, Werner. *Heidegger and the Tradition*. Translated by Theodore Kisiel and Murray Greene. Evanston, IL: Northwestern University Press, 1971.

Mitchell, Andrew. *The Fourfold: Reading the Late Heidegger*. Evanston, IL: Northwestern University Press, 2015.

Polt, Richard. *Heidegger: An Introduction*. Ithaca, NY: Cornell University Press, 1999.

Rilke, Rainer Maria. *Duino Elegies*. Translated by Edward Snow. New York: North Point Press, 2000.

Rohrkrämer, Thomas. "Martin Heidegger, National Socialism, and Environmentalism." In *How Green Were the Nazis?: Nature, Environment, and Nation in the Third Reich*, edited by Franz-Josef Brüggemeier, Mark Cioc, and Thomas Zeller, 171–203. Athens: Ohio University Press, 2005.

Rojcewicz, Richard. *The Gods and Technology: A Reading of Heidegger*. Albany, NY: State University of New York Press, 2006.

Saito, Yuriko. "Machines in the Ocean: The Aesthetics of Wind Farms." *Contemporary Aesthetics* 2 (2004). Accessed August 5, 2018. https://contempaesthetics.org/newvolume/pages/article.php?articleID=247.

Thomson, Iain. *Heidegger, Art and Postmodernity*. New York: Cambridge University Press, 2011.

Treanor, Brian. *Emplotting Virtue: A Narrative Approach to Environmental Virtue Ethics*. Albany, NY: State University of New York Press, 2014.

Young, Julian. *Heidegger's Later Philosophy*. Cambridge: Cambridge University Press, 2002.

Young, Julian. *Heidegger's Philosophy of Art*. Cambridge: Cambridge University Press, 2001.

Chapter 9

Digital Cultural Sustainability

Galit Wellner

INTRODUCTION

Since the Brundtland report coined the term "sustainable development" in 1987, the word "sustainability" continues to be expanded and charged with new meanings. The expansions are frequently needed as we face a constant flow of changes in our environments, what Ulrich Beck called in his last book *The Metamorphosis of the World*. Why does he use the word "metamorphosis"? Beck explains that contemporary events

> cannot be conceptualized in terms of the notions of "change" available to social sciences—"evolution," "revolution" and "transformation." For we live in a world that is not just changing, it is metamorphosing. . . . Metamorphosis implies a much more radical transformation in which the old certainties of modern society are falling away and something quite new is emerging.[1]

For Beck, the word "revolution" is not strong enough to capture the dramatic transformations we are experiencing since the end of the twentieth century. Beck attempts to develop a framework to encompass various types of changes, such as the political changes that started with the fall of the Berlin Wall in 1989, the green revolution, and scientific and technological innovations, that have come at such a fast pace. In this chapter, I concentrate on the green and digital metamorphoses that have changed the ways in which we conceive the world. Some of the features of the green and the digital metamorphoses are strikingly similar: both are global by their nature (what Beck terms "cosmopolitan") and both offer a "mode of metamorphosis of the world" that is radically transforming our relation with technology.[2] This chapter explores some of the meeting points between these two metamorphoses.

The Brundtland report (1987) was written by the WCED chaired by Gro Harlem Brundtland and offered a conceptual framework to refer to sustainable development. The report defines sustainable development as "development that meets the needs of the present without compromising the ability of future generations to meet their own needs."[3] Thus, it suggests that our environmental goals cannot be achieved if we limit the discussion to the environment. Attention should be paid also to economic and social developments. Otherwise, "a world in which poverty and inequity are endemic will always be prone to ecological and other crises. Sustainable development requires meeting the basic needs of all and extending to all the opportunity to satisfy their aspirations for a better life."[4] The result is a call for a structure of three pillars: environment, economy, and equity (social).

Interestingly, the Brundtland report hardly mentions the digital "revolution." The only reference is limited to the ways in which digital technologies can improve data collection from the environment.[5] Digital technologies are regarded as a means to an end, and neutral informational machines at the service of policy makers. Today, thirty years later, we realize that digital technologies have a much larger role in our lives and in our environment. To which pillar should digital technologies be assigned? The Brundtland report seems to assign them to the environment. Should they be assigned to the economic one for their economic effect? Or to the social pillar, for their deep integration into everyday societal lives? In this chapter, I would like to propose assignment of digital technologies to a fourth pillar, the cultural one.

The chapter is composed of four segments. The first reviews how digital sustainability has been understood in the twenty-first century. It examines three scholarly theses each going in a very different direction—from public libraries to e-government. The following section overviews the evolution of the Bruntland Report's three-pillar structure in the direction of adding a fourth pillar, that of culture, to those of the environment, economics, and society. Most importantly for our purposes here, I will show how this pillar can accommodate digital technologies. The relations of culture to the other pillars will serve as a source of inspiration for the third section, which proposes a mapping of mobile applications intended to enhance, improve, and push the users to act in a sustainable manner. The last segment links the mapping of mobile applications and postphenomenology. It aims to expand postphenomenology by putting more emphasis on the world. However, it also helps us advance the methods of postphenomenology in important ways, by motivating an increased focus on the "world" element in the postphenomenological scheme of "I-technology-world."

DIGITAL SUSTAINABILITY

The term "digital sustainability" has been used in various contexts. It can denote digital preservation,[6] the usage of big data to assist sustainability,[7] or open e-governance.[8] A review of recent literature reveals that these meanings have still not been able to rise to the challenge of thinking the complexity of sustainability issues called for by the three-pillar structure of the Brundtland report. Even their foregrounding of digital technologies neglected by the Brundtland report does not compensate for their lack of attention to the social pillar.

In an article titled "Defining Digital Sustainability," Kevin Bradley examines the longevity of digital information and how to preserve it. The article is published in the journal *Library Trends*, hence its focus on the preservation of digital data by libraries. Bradley investigates sustainability's methodologies such as Life Cycle Assessment (LCA) to recommend how to manage digital items. This approach to data reminds me of the early efforts to preserve nature, where nature was conceived as mute and passive, contrasted against active and willing humans. Since those early days, the sustainability movement has made some progress, and today the environment is regarded as that which maintains multifaceted feedback loops with humans, among others. It is a complex system with many actors and many interrelations so that a change in one actor leads to many changes in other actors, and some of the changes are unintended and hence surprising. This change in our approach to the environment is framed by Bruno Latour as a tension between "Nature" versus "Gaia":

> When the dictionary defines "sensitive" as "something that detects or reacts rapidly to small changes, signals, or influences," the adjective applies to Gaia as well as to the Anthropos—but only if it is equipped with enough sensors to feel the retroactions. Isabelle Stengers often says of Gaia that it is a power that has become "touchy." Nature, the Nature of yesteryear, may well have been indifferent, dominating, a cruel stepmother, but She surely wasn't touchy! On the contrary, her complete lack of sensitivity was the source of thousands of poems, and it was what allowed her, in contrast, to unleash in us the sensation of the sublime: we humans were what She was not—sensitive, responsible, and highly moral. Gaia, on the other hand, seems to be excessively sensitive to our actions, and it seems to react extremely rapidly to what it feels and detects.[9]

Today we are facing Gaia, while the "Nature of yesteryear" can be hardly found. Bradley attempts to preserve a certain moment of digital data, as if to freeze it in time, like in a nature reserve in its original meaning that placed importance on the exact preservation of as many items as possible. The items are indifferent to the preservation efforts. It is a mini-cosmos of preservation.

Galit Wellner

However, contemporary sustainable development theory urges us to look not only at the environment but also at the economic and social aspects of a given act. Does the preservation of data have social aspects? Probably yes, but these are outside the scope of Bradley's analysis.

My other two examples expand digital sustainability beyond the walls of the library. Matthias Stürmer attempts to define digital sustainability as a combination of the aforementioned digital preservation and the openness movement that heralds open access to academic publishing, source code, and so on. This meaning of openness points to the social and economic pillars by referencing shared values such as the commons, intergenerational justice, regenerative capacity, economic use of resources, and risk reduction. The question Stürmer targets is how "to decide if a digital good is sustainable or not from a digital perspective"?[10] This question should be of interest to governments when managing public-private partnerships, when producing digital resources or when designing public procurement processes.

Both Bradley and Stürmer address institutions and barely refer to practices performed by people or by NGOs. Moreover, their implementation of sustainability lacks reference to the environment. Peter Seele does refer to people and environment, but as shall become evident, the people in this analysis function as "soldiers" on a "chess board"—that is, as latent actors who are subjugated to greater forces of state and corporate power. The underlying assumptions are that only governments and large corporations can decide what is good for the environment and that they should push people to behave in certain ways in order to reach sustainability goals.

Seele examines the links between big data and sustainability and the ways that the former can assist the latter. He explains that digital data tends to come in large quantities and, therefore, is frequently referred to as big data. Seele believes that big data may lead to "increased sustainability through a more efficient allocation of existing resources."[11] This efficiency can be achieved according to the author via surveillance. Here is how he builds his argument: His underlying assumption is that big data enables first and foremost surveillance en masse. It is a contemporary version of Bentham's panopticon (as depicted by Michel Foucault) in which every person can observe and at the same time be observed. Today's panopticon, also known as "dataveillance," is a central point of observation involving the collection and processing of big data. This type of panopticon is a cornerstone of Seels's concept of Digital Sustainability Panopticon (DSP).[12] Such surveillance serves governmental agencies (e.g., the American National Security Agency [NSA]) and global corporates (e.g., Google and Facebook). Seele suggests that surveillance technologies may support sustainable practices, as in the case of "Switcher (a producer of organic cotton textiles) [who] added a bar code into the product, so that the consumer may trace back the supply chain and challenges regarding sustainability and how they have been tackled."[13] If panopticon is a major feature of the digital age, then Seele attempts to examine the consequences of this situation on sustainability. He explores the meeting point between sustainability and big data and translates it into the question of how surveillance technologies (the various panopticons) "may be used to trigger and monitor sustainability on a large scale."[14] He reduces digital technologies to surveillance and attempts to show that there are not just negative sides of this set of technologies but also some positive aspects that can promote sustainability.

Seele believes that his approach is close to what is known as "computational sustainability," a theory proposing that the extraordinary challenges that the planet faces need treatment from information technology experts. Thus, surveillance operates by the same modern logic of creating imbalances between the masses on the one side and a minority of experts on the other. Needless to say, experts are sometimes blind to the effects of their acts. The early history of modern sustainability was paved by people who aimed to show how these experts lack some important knowledge, for instance, *Silent Spring* (1962) by Rachel Carson. Carson was a nonexpert in chemistry and agriculture. She was a marine biologist, yet she gained a deep understanding of the side effects of synthetic pesticides on animals and the environment as a whole that the "experts" had neglected.

Seele's positive tone toward the panopticon revives Bentham's original approach that regarded the panopticon as a practical tool as a means to an end, a solution to a problem. The unintended consequences were revealed later by Michel Foucault (1975) who showed how this structure was foundational to the unhappiness of modernity. Seele is aware of the possibility of unintended consequences (as can be evidenced from his review of the digital panopticon developments), yet he prefers to overlook them and concentrate only on the positive effects.[15] He believes that corporates and governments implementing panopticon technologies will "change their skins and spots" once they realize how these technologies can be good for the environment. This way of thinking can be conceived as a form of technological determinism that regards technology as a neutral force that may change society, or in this case—save the Earth. Seele writes, "Once implemented, the mentioned self-regulatory discipline—if and only if applied to all members—has a strong motivational force, as free riders—technologically—would be identified and sanctioned immediately."[16]

Such an optimistic technological determinism is based on the assumption that technology is always a positive influencer, so that its users—the corporates and governments in this case—will be inclined to use it for ethically good purposes. This assumption leads the author to ground his suggestions in the singularity theory. He sees forthcoming AI algorithms as the forces that will dominate in the future and will ensure that we, humans, will behave in a sustainable way. An approach that regards algorithms as superior societal powers, the deus ex machina of the digital era, cannot be accommodated into the social pillar of sustainability.

None of these three examples of contemporary thinking about sustainability made any reference to the Brundtland report and its multifaceted framework. When they refer to society, it is no more than a mechanistic approach that overlooks the need for social equity that the Brundtland report highlights. On the other hand, it is difficult to reduce digital technologies to the social pillar, either. Technologies co-shape society but they are not equal to society (unless one adheres to social determinism). The solution offered in this chapter is to look for a fourth pillar of cultural sustainability as a frame of reference to digital technologies. This will be described in the next section.

CULTURAL SUSTAINABILITY

To the three pillars of sustainability—environment, economy, and (social) equity—a fourth pillar has been added recently, termed cultural sustainability (COST Action 2011–2015). The new pillar usually includes art, literature, and other symbolic fields, sometimes leading to a confusion with the social pillar.[17] It is clear, however, that this pillar is much needed as it covers memories, identities, heritage, sense of place, creativity, and the like. In his article "Enchanting Sustainability," Hans Dieleman proposes a wider aim of this pillar as the provisioning of "a new narrative of planetary consciousness."[18] All these aims, apparatuses, institutions, and interpretations are important aspects of sustainability that can hardly fit into any of the original three pillars.

To add complexity, the relation of culture to the other pillars in the schema is subject to a lively discussion: Is it a self-standing pillar, a frame that ties together the three original pillars or a precondition functioning as a foundational structure? The COST Action maps these three possibilities with the use of three possible propositions to mark the relation between "culture" and "sustainability"—in, for, and as:

- the "in" proposition represents culture as a fourth pillar;
- the "for" proposition represents culture as mediating between the three pillars; and
- the "as" proposition represents culture as the foundation for sustainable development.

The existing definitions of digital sustainability as reviewed in the previous section hardly refer to the cultural aspects of sustainability or to the rich set of relations between culture/digital technologies and the three pillars.

In this chapter, I offer an interpretation that combines cultural and digital sustainability in a way that includes the digital domain within the cultural sustainability pillar. This structure regards digital technologies as co-existing with art and co-shaping joint cultural memories and ethics. It acknowledges that digital technologies affect people, profit, and even the planet, as they require the operation of computers that use rare materials and emit heat to the environment.[19] Like art, digital technologies mobilize people; like culture, digital technologies are conceived as that which co-constitutes the human.[20] Hence, digital cultural sustainability can function as a framework for thinking how new digital technologies participate in Dieleman's narrative and make it pertinent for the twenty-first century.

FROM CULTURAL SUSTAINABILITY TO DIGITAL SUSTAINABILITY

Browsing Apple's App Store or Google Play, one can find hundreds and even thousands of mobile apps classified with the word sustainability. These apps vary in their ambitions, the actions they enable in the world and the ways they mediate sustainability to the users. In this section, I will map some existing mobile apps that are intended to promote sustainability in various ways. The mappings principles can be applied also to applications not mentioned here. These principles may serve as a conceptual map of the sustainability apps category. The resulting map may assist developers who wish to make a difference and aim at promoting sustainability through the technologies they build.

The principles for the mapping are inspired by the three propositions framed by the COST Action for the relations between the cultural pillar and the three others of environment, economy and society, but we move beyond this to identify a spectrum on which the apps can be located in the order of their "immersiveness." This level of immersiveness will be described in the next three subsections for each category.

First Category: Digital Instructions How to Behave in a Sustainable Manner

The first category of mobile apps addresses users who want to behave in a sustainable way. It is parallel to the "culture *in* sustainability" variation because it regards technology as a stand-alone entity that assists the process of sustainability. According to the COST Action, the "in" variation shows the cultural pillar as a fourth "circle," equivalent to the other three pillars-circles of sustainability. In my mapping, the apps belonging to this category assist the user to become greener, but are not intended to shape the user's attitudes or affect the rules already in place. It is yet another type of apps.

Such apps usually developed by the local municipality, remind the user when a certain kind of garbage is being taken thereby ensuring the garbage is not piled in the street for many days. An app of this category may explain which garbage goes to which bin. This is what the mobile game "Grow Recycling" tries to teach children.[21] The recycling bins are presented as hungry creatures who want to be fed with the right garbage: the more garbage, the better.

Another way to help people behave in a green way is by recommending or rating organizations according to their commitment to the green agenda. These businesses can be hotels[22] or fashion brands.[23] "Wayaj—Earth Friendly Travel" is an eco-tourism app supporting agendas such as "eco-tourism," "sustainable tourism," and "responsible tourism."[24] The app recommends hotels, resorts, and restaurants that are sensitive to the environment and the local communities. The recommended businesses usually address tourists that have a green agenda. Eventually the app enables the user to make a reservation, probably charging a certain percentage from the total amount paid by the user to the touristic business. The app is built on an "eco-rating system" that scores destinations according to the information provided by the hotels ("eco-rating survey"[25]). Interestingly, during my visit to the website (August 2018) all the links to the eco-rating systems did not function and the FAQ on the website stated that "the rating is pending because we are currently waiting for/analyzing the answers to the questionnaire to build the eco-rating score."[26]

"Good on You—Ethical Fashion" provides information on brands related to their commitment to sustainability. For example, it allows the user to look for a brand and then it reports how the firm behind it treats its employees, how it impacts the environment, and how animals are involved in the manufacturing processes (for wool, leather, furs, etc.). The app can also recommend brands who have a green agenda and who operate accordingly. At the base, like in Wayaj, there is a rating system of major global fashion brands. Unlike Wayaj, here the app uses existing data as it integrates information from groups such as Greenpeace and from certifications such as Fair Trade and Global Organic Textile Standard (GOTS).[27]

The common denominator of these apps is that they target a user who is already aware of a green agenda and needs some guidance. The apps do not try to change habits; their aspirations are more modest. They simply try to help the user make greener choices. The gaming app can teach a kid how to use the various garbage cans but will not direct how to minimize the amount of garbage. If the user wants to buy more clothes, the fashion app would provide information on the sustainability of a given firm or direct to brands that are greener. It will not try to convince the shopper to refrain from buying more clothes. Likewise, the eco-touristic app will not try to convince the user not to fly due to the ecological footprint of airplanes but will only direct her to hotels that state they are friendly to the environment.

Second Category: Digital Tips How to Be Greener

This category also preaches to the believers, but it goes one step further. Instead of supporting existing habits, these apps urge their users to change. The apps help users discover new ways to go greener. The category is parallel to "culture *for* sustainability" where the cultural pillar is located in the middle, serving as a contact element for the three other pillars. Culture functions as a mediator that connects the planet, the people, and the profits. Correspondingly, apps of this category serve as mediators to enable the user to reach her sustainability goals, whether these be in the environmental, the economic, or the social arena. For example, the app JoulBug[28] provides sustainability tips for everyday life, such as riding bicycles, eating more vegetables and fruits, washing the laundry in cold cycle, or saving a flush. By following a tip, the user gains points and badges. This gamification is intended to encourage the users to continue using the app, and more importantly—become greener. The app developers state in the Google Play page of the app: "Save money, have fun, and be a little kinder to the planet, with JouleBug!" Interestingly saving the planet comes last while saving money is first.

Other apps of this category target specific niches to save resources and become more sustainable. For example, the app "Love Your Leftovers" provides cooking recipes according to the leftovers the user has at home, to help avoid throwing them into the garbage.[29] The intention is to reduce the amounts of food waste. Another app, "DIY recycle jeans"[30] explains that a pair of jeans is one of the most sustainable fashion artifacts because it is durable and is usually worn many times. A pair of jeans is also probably the most popular fashion item. It has a huge potential for upcycling thereby serving as an antithesis to "fast fashion" that encourages people to buy a lot of clothes even if they are worn only once. The app provides tips on how to upcycle a pair of jeans into a tote bag, an apron, or a decorative wall hanging.

The tips provided by the apps of the second category are intended to make a small difference in people's lives and consequently contribute to a slightly more sustainable environment. Like the "for" proposition, these apps mediate between the user the pillars of sustainability, though focusing mainly on the environmental pillar.

Third Category: Develop New Greener Practices

The third category of apps in my taxonomy aims at encouraging the users to develop new practices and initiate sustainability projects. It is parallel to the third positioning of the cultural pillar using the "as" proposition, where culture is drawn as a big circle that serves as a background for the three "standard" pillars-circles, that is environment, economy, and society. Apps that belong to this category are helpful for users who wish to execute a project intended to improve sustainability in the environmental, the economic, or the social sense. These apps function as a necessary background for any activity, as that which always mediates the world for us.

A prime example for this category is the "SDG in Action" app[31] that is designed to promote the seventeen sustainable development goals (SDGs) of the United Nations (UN). These goals were adopted in 2015 as part of the UN's 2030 Agenda for Sustainable Development. According to the UN's website for sustainable development, the goals are intended "to end poverty, protect the planet and ensure prosperity for all."[32] The emphasis is clearly on social and economic pillars and most of the goals are human oriented: The first five goals are: no poverty, zero hunger, good health and well-being, quality education, and gender equality. The environment can be found from the thirteenth to the fifteenth SDGs: climate action, life below water, and life on land. This is a significant change of tone, compared to the early ecology movement that attempted to preserve nature. It is also different from the Anthropocene-centered voices that put the Earth above all other considerations.

The "SDG in Action" app is an important actor in the effort to fulfill the seventeen SDGs. The app has three major modes of usage.[33] Firstly, users can learn about the goals and get updates on them through notifications. Secondly, an enthusiastic user can find a local contact person for a given SDG, join the project, and invite friends. Thirdly, an even more motivated user can initiate a project that relates to one of the SDGs and invite others to participate. Interestingly, the app was developed by the GSMA, the association of mobile operators. Together with "Project Everyone," they describe themselves as "a non-profit global campaign to spread the messaging of the SDGs."[34] Even the development of the app seems to fit into an SDG goal.

Another app that aims to make a change is "Ecosia."[35] The tactic here is different, as it does not aim to change people's behavior. Instead it tries to leverage existing environmentally neutral action. This app is a "tree-planting browser." It means that the profits generated from the browser's advertisements are directed to finance reforestation programs. The aim is "to plant one billion new trees by 2020" in order to fight climate change and to restore landscapes and communities. The operators of Ecosia explain how its servers are powered by solar panels, so the browser uses renewable energy. But the good intentions are not coherent: the browser is described as ad-free with an embedded ad blocker. If there are no ads, how does Ecosia generate revenues? The company states it uses the searches to generate profit, but given its commitment to users' privacy and the integrated ad blocker, it is not clear how revenues are generated if at all.

It is not easy to find apps in this third category. These apps target not only "the usual" environmental goals but also the economic and social, so their scope is much wider. Yet culture is not included. In addition, it requires a relatively high level of commitment to sustainability in order to develop and maintain such apps. The support of big international organizations such as the UN and the prosperous association of mobile operators seem like a necessary condition.

POSTPHENOMENOLOGY AND SUSTAINABILITY

The model developed by the COST Action for cultural sustainability served as an inspiration for the classification of the thousands of mobile apps that attempt to deal with sustainability. Like the level of involvement of the cultural pillar that intensifies from the "in" preposition through the "for" all the way to the "as," so the apps become more involved in the users' green behavior. For the first category, they just provide information; for the second, they provide tips for changing the behavior; and the third category is the most intensive one, motivating the users to engage in sustainability projects and mediating sustainability for them.

Postphenomenology can provide a coherent framework for this classification based on its scheme of "I—technology—world," But, in the process of employing this postphenomenological framework, the nature of these different apps can also help clarify recent advances in our postphenomenological method.

The first category reflects a kind of "classical postphenomenology" where the arrow of intentionality always goes from the human to the technology or to the world. In embodiment relations the arrow goes from the combo "(I—technology)" to the "world," while in hermeneutic, alterity and background relations the arrow departs directly from the "I" toward the "technology" and/or the "world."[36] In this category, human intentionality dictates the relations. Technologies and the world are relevant as long as there is a human being. This is in line with the assumption of the classical philosophical question: "If a tree falls in a forest and no one is around to hear it, does it make a sound?" As long as a forest functions, grows, and regenerates, without it ever coming to our attention, the "I" could be at the center of interest. However, with the ecological crisis we are experiencing today, the dying trees make metaphorical noises, and we should listen to them even if no one is around.

The second category follows the more complex intentionality models, what Peter-Paul Verbeek calls "cyborg intentionality."[37] These relations go beyond Ihde's influential explication of the four types discussed above and emphasize the technological intentionality that operates together with human intentionality. Cyborg intentionality comes in various forms. One of them is "composite intentionality" that refers to situations in which intentionality is distributed between humans and technologies, so that some intentionality flows from the "I" to the "technology" (as in the original permutation for hermeneutic relations), and some flows from the "technology" to the "world." In the formula for "composite intentionality," we replace the dash between "technology" and "world" with an arrow to indicate a new mode of technological intentionality:

$$I \rightarrow (technology \rightarrow world)$$

This recognizes the active role of technology in shaping users' intentions and its impact on the world. For example, the "sustainability tips" apps mentioned above try to encourage the users to become greener, to intensify the "sustainable intentionality," and to help them do more for the environment. The more intelligent the apps, the more intentionality they exhibit.[38]

The third category matches a form of intentionality that I have been studying recently,[39] where the arrow of intentionality is reversed so that it points *to* the human rather than *from* it. In the context of algorithmic writing based on artificial intelligence, where algorithms compose texts such as sports news, weather forecasts or stock market reporting, the permutation I have offered is:

$$I \leftarrow algorithm \rightarrow text \rightarrow world$$

This permutation makes sense in the case of the third category of apps where the apps aim to change the world. The browser that directs its profit to the forestation of the world is an example of technology that has an impact on the world in a very specific direction (with the support of its entrepreneurs and operators, provided that profits are eventually generated, of course). The "text" in the case of the browser is a tree that was planted in the world.

As we progress through these three categories, the role of the world slowly becomes more active. In the first category, technologies offer relatively small adjustments. If I want to put my garbage in the correct recycle bin that is located near my home, then the app would direct me what to put in each bin. It takes for granted the existence of these cans and my will to recycle. If I want to travel "green," the app will recommend sustainable hotels, but it will not directly encourage hotels to transform and reduce their ecological footprint. The second category promotes small local changes in the world such as reducing the amount of food that is wasted or the clothes that are thrown away. The third category is the most ambitious. These apps attempt to help users initiate schemes along the lines of the seventeen SDGs or contribute to large-scale initiatives such as the planting of millions of trees.

In parallel, the postphenomenological scheme of "I—technology—world" evolves to expand on the role of the world. Whereas in classical postphenomenology the world has been usually conceived as mute or simply uninteresting, the challenges of sustainable development urge us to give more attention to the role of the world in the relations between humans and technologies. The "world" can be the environment but can also be society or the economy. The principles of sustainable development demand that we revolutionize how we think. This is not the only revolution we undergo today. In parallel we experience the digital revolution that likewise transforms many aspects of our lives. The two revolutions-metamorphoses meet sporadically, mostly when the green criticizes the digital. The purpose of this chapter is to map some of the ways in which the digital participates in the green revolution. At the theoretical level, the mapping leads to an increased role of the "world" component in the analyses of the relations between humans and their technologies.

NOTES

1. Ulrich Beck, *The Metamorphosis of the World* (Cambridge and Malden, MA: Polity, 2016), 3.
2. Ibid., 61.
3. Brundtland Committee, *Report of the World Commission on Environment and Development: Our Common Future,* 1987, 41, https://sustainabledevelopment.un.org/content/documents/5987our-common-future.pdf.
4. Ibid., 41–2.
5. Ibid., 267.
6. See Kevin Bradley, "Defining Digital Sustainability," *Library Trends* 56, no. 1 (2007): 148–63.
7. See Peter Seele, "Envisioning the Digital Sustainability Panopticon," *Sustainability Science* 11, no. 5 (2016): 845–54.
8. See Matthias Stürmer, "Characteristics of Digital Sustainability," *Proceedings of the 8th International Conference on Theory and Practice of Electronic Governance* (Guimaraes, Portugal: ACM, 2014), 494–95.
9. Bruno Latour, *Facing Gaia* (Cambridge, UK: Polity Press, 2017), 123.
10. Stürmer, "Characteristics of Digital Sustainability," 495.
11. Seele, "Envisioning the Digital Sustainability Panopticon," 848.
12. Seele also refers to other modes of panopticon: A pseudo-panopticon refers to the situation in which companies attempt to "green-wash" their activities by producing "corporate social responsibility" reports that do not always contain all the relevant

facts and sometimes serve to cover and hide polluting activities; and a synopticon is a reverse panopticon where the masses watch the few—for example, actors, celebrities, and politicians. The synopticon is the basis of social media apps today. These two forms of panopticon do not participate in sustainable process, or at least such modes are not discussed.

13. Seele, "Envisioning the Digital Sustainability Panopticon," 848.

14. Ibid.

15. Seele, 2016, 849.

16. Ibid., 851–52.

17. See Galit Wellner, "From Cellphones to Machine Learning. A Shift in the Role of the User in Algorithmic Writing," in *Towards a Philosophy of Digital Media*, eds. Alberto Romele and Enrico Terrone (Cham: Palgrave MacMillan, 2018), 205–24.

18. Hans Dieleman, "Enchanting Sustainability: From Enlightened Modernity Towards Embodiment and Planetary Consciousness," in *Culture in Sustainability: Towards a Transdisciplinary Approach*, eds. Asikainen, Brites, Plebańczyk, Mijatović, and Soini, 10–21 (University of Jyväskylä: SoPhi, 2018), 11.

19. See Lorenz M. Hilty and Bernard Aebischer, "ICT for Sustainability," in *ICT Innovations for Sustainability*, eds. Hilty and Aebischer (Springer, 2015).

20. See Don Ihde, *Technology and the Lifeworld: From Garden to Earth* (Bloomington: Indiana University Press, 1990).

21. https://play.google.com/store/apps/details?id=com.groplay.grorecycling.

22. https://play.google.com/store/apps/details?id=com.wayaj.android.

23. https://play.google.com/store/apps/details?id=au.org.goodonyou.goodonyou.

24. These all are taken from the company's website and the app description in Google Play.

25. http://wayaj.com/about/.

26. http://wayaj.com/faq/.

27. https://goodonyou.eco/how-we-rate/.

28. https://play.google.com/store/apps/details?id=com.cleanbit.joulebug.

29. https://play.google.com/store/apps/details?id=au.gov.nsw.loveyourleftovers.

30. https://play.google.com/store/apps/details?id=com.RecycleOldJeans.jafsamapps (in Hebrew).

31. https://play.google.com/store/apps/details?id=org.un.sdgsinaction.app.

32. https://www.un.org/sustainabledevelopment/sustainable-development-goals/.

33. See https://sdgsinaction.com/.

34. https://sdgsinaction.com/.

35. https://play.google.com/store/apps/details?id=com.ecosia.android.

36. See Ihde, *Technology and the Lifeworld*, 1990.

37. Peter-Paul Verbeek, "Cyborg Intentionality: Rethinking the Phenomenology of Human–technology Relations," *Phenomenology and Cognitive Science* 7 (2008): 387–95.

38. See Galit Wellner, "From Cellphones to Machine Learning. A Shift in the Role of the User in Algorithmic Writing," in *Towards a Philosophy of Digital Media*, eds. Alberto Romele and Enrico Terrone (Cham: Palgrave MacMillan, 2018), 205–24.

39. Ibid.

BIBLIOGRAPHY

Beck, Ulrich. *The Metamorphosis of the World.* Cambridge and Malden: Polity, 2016.

Bradley, Kevin. "Defining Digital Sustainability." *Library Trends* 56, no. 1 (2007): 148–63.

Brundtland Committee. *Report of the World Commission on Environment and Development: Our Common Future.* 1987, https://sustainabledevelopment.un.org/content/documents/5987our-common-future.pdf (accessed December 11, 2018).

COST Action. "Investigating Cultural Sustainability." IS1007 2011–2015, http://www.culturalsustainability.eu/.

Dieleman, Hans. "Enchanting Sustainability: From Enlightened Modernity Towards Embodiment and Planetary Consciousness." In *Culture in Sustainability: Towards a Transdisciplinary Approach,* edited by Sari Asikainen, Claudia Brites, Katarzyna Plebańczyk, Ljiljana Rogač Mijatović, and Katriina Soini, 10–21. University of Jyväskylä: SoPhi, 2018.

Hilty, Lorenz M., and Bernard Aebischer. "ICT for Sustainability: An Emerging Research Field." In *ICT Innovations for Sustainability: Advances in Intelligent Systems and Computing,* edited by Lorenz and Bernard, 3–36. Springer, 2015.

Ihde, Don. "Is There a Bat Problem for Postphenomenology?" In *Technoscience and Postphenomenology: The Manhattan Papers,* edited by Jan Kyrre Berg O. Friis and Robert Crease, vii–xvi. Lanham, MD: Lexington Books, 2015.

Ihde, Don. *Technology and the Lifeworld: From Garden to Earth.* Bloomington and Indianapolis: Indiana University Press, 1990.

Latour, Bruno. *Facing Gaia.* Cambridge, UK: Polity Press, 2017.

Seele, Peter. "Envisioning the Digital Sustainability Panopticon: A Thought Experiment of How Big Data May Help Advancing Sustainability in the Digital Age." *Sustainability Science* 11, no. 5 (2016): 845–54.

Stürmer, Matthias. "Characteristics of Digital Sustainability." *Proceedings of the 8th International Conference on Theory and Practice of Electronic Governance,* 494–95. Guimaraes, Portugal: ACM, 2014.

Verbeek, Peter-Paul. "Cyborg Intentionality: Rethinking the Phenomenology of Human–technology Relations." *Phenomenology and Cognitive Science* 7 (2008): 387–95.

Wellner, Galit. "From Cellphones to Machine Learning. A Shift in the Role of the User in Algorithmic Writing." In *Towards a Philosophy of Digital Media,* edited by Alberto Romele and Enrico Terrone, 205–24. Cham: Palgrave MacMillan, 2018.

Wellner, Galit. "Social Happiness as a Cultural Value: An Analysis of Shared Values for Ecosystem Assessment." In *Cultural Sustainability: Perspectives from the Humanities and Social Sciences,* edited by Torsten Meireis and Gabriele Rippl, 101–11. Routledge, 2018.

Part IV

SUSTAINABILITY AND ETHICS

Chapter 10

Sustainable Futures

Ethico-Political Dimensions of Technology

Lars Botin

PRELUDIO

As The Amazing Chriswell, an American psychic playing himself in the movie *Plan 9 from Outer Space* (1959),[1] pronounces in a pathetic voice to his audience "*Greetings, my friend. We are all interested in the future because this is where you and I are going to spend the rest of our lives,*" we are all interested in what is going to happen in the future, because that is where our own lives, and those of our descendants, will take place.

The Amazing Chriswell, an American psychic famous for his wildly inaccurate predictions is playing himself in this low-budget film, and his character foresees the ultimate catastrophe that is going to happen in the near future as humans will develop a bomb that is going to destroy the universe. Aliens are desperately, and in vain, making plans to prevent humanity on its destructive endeavor, and this is the ninth and final attempt. Plan 9 is to resurrect the dead from their graves in order for them to stop their descendants, but paradoxically the living dead turn their anger on the aliens, who had only wanted to save humanity from its own destiny.

The alien's plan went wrong, again, as many a well-meant plan does, and we cannot help but feel with Chriswell and the aliens that our preparations for the future are hapless and a bit ridiculous. Nevertheless, we have to keep on planning, because that is the only way we can in some way confront emergent and potentially "catastrophic" events that do loom over us.

SUSTAINABILITY: REPORTS, MANIFESTOS, AND GLOBAL GOALS

We are looking into a future where we are taught that climate will change radically. Oceans will rise and temperatures will reach levels that will make it impossible for humans to thrive and live under normal conditions. We are told by climate experts (IPCC) that these changes are provoked by human activity. This is a form of activity that has been going on for the past 200 years—that is, since the beginning of the Industrial Revolution that first took place in Europe and later "emigrated" to North America and just recently, within the past fifty years, to the rest of the world. This has been a slow movement that has happened in different places at different times but with similar outcomes. Today, under the siege of globalization, we are witnessing how place and time are coming together and how the outcomes will affect us in all times and places, or perhaps, better, seem to affect us independently of place and time. Yet due to different existing conditions of geographical, demographical, economic, social, cultural, and political character, the consequences for those living in already precarious conditions in Africa, Southern Asia, and in the Pacific will be much worse, so as to threaten their very existence and thereby threaten the comfort of those in the so-called first world through uncontrolled and persistent emigration.

So, in the Western world, we make up plans in order to prevent this from happening, and we try to look into the future: 2025, 2030, 2050, but seldom longer, and globally agree on things to do in order to prevent the dramatic and death-threatening effects of climate change, poverty, and so on. We do not awake the dead from their graves in order for them to kill their self-destructive kin (us), but we certainly plan in order for humanity to be able to survive on the surface of the earth.

For the past thirty years, since the publication of the Brundtland report on *Our Common Future* (1987), there has been a focus on sustainability at all possible levels. This focus did not arise from nowhere; in looking back into the nineteenth and twentieth century, we witness how individuals and movements have raised questions and critique toward the paradigm of growth and expansion, which has characterized modern Western capitalist societies since the Industrial Revolution. We had, in a fairly naïve manner, coined this period of growth, the age of modernism, based on the opinion that here we had reached a level of thought and societal organization that was not going to be superseded by anything else or alternative. The reason for this evident *hubris*[2] was/is that everything could be accounted for by science and its constant progress, which was materialized in beautiful and wonderful machines. It is not as if modernism, as such, can be fully described in this simplistic and squared way, because modernism is revolutionary, conservatory, techno-pessimistic and optimistic, rationalist, mystic, ideal, and pragmatic at one and the same time.[3] Modernism is paradoxically multistable, and not "one dimensional"[4] or for that matter "paradigmatic"[5] as the main critique of the modern Western societal model would have it. Bruno Latour claimed that "we have never been modern,"[6] and here, in a postphenomenological stance, I claim that modernism was always "postmodern," because relational, inter-contextual, and simultaneously reaching toward dystopia and utopia, mechanical hell or heaven, through the co-construction of dream worlds where good and benevolent Messiahs would lead the way toward paradise on earth. Modernism is all of this, and even more, and this is why it is multi-stable and multiple in its essence, which means that dystopians and utopians of the modern got it equally wrong, as they constructed their imaginaries and visions of contemporary and future society and world based on an overly simple view of the modern.

Modernism is, according to the English cultural analyst Raymond Williams, "[an] internal diversity of methods and emphases: a restless and often directly competitive sequence of innovations and experiments, always more immediately recognized by what they are breaking away from than by what, in a simple way, they are breaking towards."[7] We are restlessly and constantly breaking away from something existing in ontological, epistemological, and methodological ways, even though not knowing what we are "breaking toward." In contemporary semantics of technological evolution, we are taught that we must *disrupt* in order to meet the emergent challenges of the future. In this existentially restless breaking away, we are required (again) to disrupt our mind-sets in order to meet the (unknown) challenges of the future. As Williams pointed at, there is nothing new in the concept of disruption because we have always in modern times been breaking away, but our "singularity" of focus on the actual process of disruption emphasizes the uselessness and obsoleteness of accumulated and lived experience and knowledge, might that be scientific, professional, explicit, tacit, or whatever. Humans and formations of humans are wiped from the screen as technological progression will assure the survival of those that fit into the techno-future of a transhuman condition that paradoxically ignores the imminent and emergent threats of global heating and climate change. To respond to climate change, we must come to a better understanding of this tendency toward rupture and its complex relation to modernity.

PAST, PRESENT, AND FUTURE

The German philosopher and ethicist Hans Jonas wrote in *The Imperative of Responsibility: In Search of an Ethics for the Technological Age* that we cannot think of the future without reflecting on the past and simultaneously looking into what is going on around us, in order to behave, act, and live appropriately and responsibly in the present. When the concept of "progress" is made synonymous with technology itself, we lose the ability to think coherently about our choices. In our contemporary thinking, "technology shares with its begetter-become-twin, that is, with science, the notable property that 'progress' as such is an *objective phenomenon* inherent in its autonomous motion, in the sense that every 'next' is necessarily superior to its 'before.'"[8] So, we cannot really question scientific and technological progress, because it is an *objective phenomenon* that transcends critical questioning and reasoning. If we pose these questions, then we are caught by our emotions and feelings, acting irrationally and furthermore trying to prevent scientific and technological progress that will eventually come independently of our critique and questioning. As many philosophers (of technology), in this vein, would have it,[9] progress and growth are our inevitable destiny, as technology and her begetter-twin science increase and exponentially accelerate.

On the other hand, dystopians have an equally simplistic view of technological history, seeing it as a necessary march to human diminishment. More plausibly, even critics must acknowledge the polyvalent nature of technology and, as Heidegger, Ellul, and McLuhan have done, appreciate a saving possibility in its nature. We have to recognize the Janus face of technology, reflected within the dialectical nature of our own existence. We too have Janus faces, and so we must understand the begetter twins in a dialectical way, where we see the *objective phenomenon* of technological and scientific progress under the pressure of constant economic growth as our adversary and at the same time as co-constituent of possible new ways of being together. It is not about getting rid of science and technology as an *objective phenomenon*, because their "instrumental" functioning has brought us where we are today in relation to health, wealth, and democracy. The question is whether we should continue to co-constitute with science and technology in the present purely mechanistic and instrumental way. Longer lifetimes, less disease, and more money have been the measurable outcomes of these constitutions, but it seems clear that in coping with the imminent and emergent threats of global heating and climate change, the begetter twins of science and technology are leading us toward solutions that are optimal only for the elect. We in the Western world will almost certainly be saved by scientific and technological solutions. The elected and selected will survive in a future where the begetter twins have erased death, disease, and poverty, and furthermore created technological solutions that cope with global warming and climate change. The question is whether this future is just, fair, or even appealing to humanity. Shouldn't we direct our being together with the begetter twins in a way that opens up a multiplicity of co-constitutions, where we try to converge our efforts in creative endeavors that investigate the processes that characterize the formation of both our Janus-faced technology and humanity? Martin Heidegger wrote: "It is proper to every gathering that the gatherers assemble to coordinate their efforts to the sheltering; only when they have gathered together with that end in view do they begin to gather."[10] Only in this way do we creatively destruct and disrupt the pathways made for the elected and selected and open richer possibilities for our technologically mediated relation with the world.

The American urbanist, historian, ecologist, philosopher, and activist Lewis Mumford wrote in *Technics and Civilization* that we ought to question this *objective phenomenon* of restless, endless, and all-encompassing progression of growth and expansion and think of how we could socialize and democratize modern society by gaining some sort of control of scientific and technological development. He saw this as a process constituted by *conversion, production, consumption, and creation.* "In the first two steps [conversion and production] energy is seized and prepared for the sustenance of life. In the third stage [consumption], life is supported and renewed in order that it may wind itself up, so to speak, on the higher levels of thought and culture [creation], instead of being short-circuited at once back into the preparatory functions."[11] According to this view, the *objective phenomenon* of science and technology is marked by the danger of seizing energy through conversion and production and short-circuiting this through consumption into a constant loop of conversion, production, and consumption, where creation is left out of the equation, and hence the "higher levels of thought and culture" are eliminated from human life.

Mumford tells us to *increase conversion,* which means to think of resources as anything that could support and improve our everyday living in social communities that are based on local/regional production and consumption. *Economize production* means that we transcend concepts like efficiency and optimization, in order to focus on the meaning of economy—that is, *oikos,* or what has been coined *ecological economy.*[12] In other words we should produce in order to fulfill the needs, requirements, and wishes of the household. Mumford points at contemporary (beginning of the twentieth century) economies such as Ireland, Denmark, and the state of Wisconsin, which were characterized by a "flourishing economic life depending upon an intelligent exploitation of all the regional resources."[13] Mumford's examples are agricultural economies that necessarily had to make a virtue of collaboration/cooperation in order to maximize production and hence consumption, but at the same time this increased collaborative/cooperative work on a regional basis and lead to an increase in the population's cultural and social capital. In a Danish context, this manifested in the dairy and meat cooperatives that evolved into "high school" cooperatives where peasants and workers were taught about almost everything in life: how to read, how to cook, how to mend, how to sing, and not least how to be a citizen in a democratic society. In this way conversion, production, and consumption point toward *creation,* which is a human, a social, and a cultural endeavor. As Raymond Williams has pointed out, science and technology *ought* to support and enhance in order to be truly sustainable, but if left to their own instrumental and mechanical ontology, epistemology, and methodology they will not, but instead be incessantly driven by looping conversion, production, and consumption at the behest of untamed progression, growth, and expansion.

It is striking that Mumford's original work from 1934 was republished in 1963, the year before Herbert Marcuse published *One-Dimensional Man*, Marshal McLuhan published *Understanding Media*, and, due to the efforts of Aldous Huxley, Jacques Ellul's *The Technological Society* was translated into English—all figures that had a great deal of influence on the nascent environmental movement. *The Technological Society* had a huge impact on the American academy in the mid-sixties, and Ellul himself gave guest lectures at a variety of American universities. *Understanding Media* changed forever our understanding of what the media does on a general, a universal, and a global level, and furthermore how it works in our everyday dealings with reality as such. McLuhan's conceptualization of the *global village*, which was made in a different context, becomes ever more relevant as sustainability and sustainability issues call for action on both a local and a global level. Finally, Jacques Ellul is claimed to have coined the phrase, *Think Globally; Act Locally*.

These critical and good intentions of the mid-1960s actually materialized in the youth riots of 1967 and 1968 against authority and Western capitalism and spread into alternative cultural and social communities in the 1970s and have continued to have a certain impact on how production and consumption is conceived on a general level in contemporary Western societies.

The Brundtland report (1987) on sustainable development would be unthinkable without the political, social, and cultural discussions that had been going on in the 1960s, and our conceptualizations of sustainability in that regard would be tame and mechanical if we did not bring into account what Mumford, and American pragmatism in general, taught us about how to deal with conversion, production, and consumption. We learned how to normalize, socialize, and democratize in order to be truly sustainable in our living and being together, which in Mumford's perspective could only take place in formalized regional settings—that is, conscious *economic regionalism*.[14] Mumford writes about equilibrium and balance as ways we should deal with the environment, industry, agriculture, and population. He is convinced that if we install equilibrium and balance as overall values for planning, then the "*raison d'être* of capitalism will vanish."[15] Put together in an almost prophetic (and overly optimistic) vision of what will happen the moment that we plan in order to meet the asymmetries and hierarchical structures of modern Western capitalism in a proactive way, then: "This state of balance and equilibrium—regional, industrial, agricultural, communal—will work a further change within the domain of the machine itself: a change of tempo."[16]

Mumford foresaw that a decrease in technological speed and acceleration would take place the moment that we focused on balance and equilibrium. He saw that if we rethink the technological focus on efficiency, then it would be possible to turn the concept of technology toward upholding and supporting the "maintenance and development of human life," for "efficiency, even on a lower technical level alone, means a gearing together of the various parts so that they may deliver the correct and the predictable amounts of power, goods, services and utilities."[17] In this way, the concept of *efficiency* is turned on its head in relation to how it is normally addressed in critical studies of technological development. Efficiency becomes part of the sustainability paradigm, because dealing with how "power, goods, services and utilities" are distributed in a balanced and democratic way.

Since Mumford wrote *Technics and Civilization* in the beginning of the 1930s, efficiency and speed have intensified and expanded at one and the same time, and the Western capitalist model has sovereignly ruled when it comes to technical efficiency and exponential acceleration. Mumford's *utopian* reading of our possibilities to rebuild and rethink the "machine" and make way for promises for transformation of "the nature and function of our mechanical environment and to lay wider and firmer and safer foundations for human society at large"[18] has not come to pass.

In light of this failure, Heidegger, Mumford, Jonas, Ellul, Marcuse, and McLuhan are generally considered as techno-pessimists or techno-determinists that foresee a dystopian future for mankind, seized by the uncontrollable and destructive powers of technology. It is true that the main voices coming from the social sciences and humanities that are rooted in phenomenology and critical theory have had this rather dystopian perspective on the evolution of science and technology that they understand, as Jonas did, to be inseparable "twins"—technology as the servant of science or, even worse, science as the servant of technology. Far beyond this intellectual tradition, however, there is a widespread worry that science and technology are eradicating human creativity, feelings, and emotions, such that we are left as mechanical components in the conversion, production, and consumption loop. It seems as if humans do not really fit into this mechanical construct, which explains the many efforts that are made to eliminate or minimize the human factor—that is, humans from technological systems and replace them (humans) by human-like machines (robots), or infallible and fast calculators (algorithms and AI) that even have the capacity of performing some sort of choice.

N. Katherine Hayles has written extensively on this, as I see it, rather gloomy prospect for humanity; "It is likely, however, that the evolutionary development of technical cognizers will take a different path from that of *Homo Sapiens*. Their trajectory will not run through consciousness but rather through more intensive and pervasive interconnections with other nonconscious cognizers."[19] Hayles points at the fact that we are witnessing a sort of symbiosis between humans and technical systems, and that these constitute each other in this process. Furthermore, she is convinced that "the more such symbiosis advances, the more difficult it will be for either symbiont to *flourish* without the other."[20] In order for us humans to flourish, which means to be supported and sustained in our life, we need technical systems and solutions. There is, according to Hayles and other post-human feminist thinkers, no turning back, and we should abolish retrospective romanticism. Instead, we ought to critically and constructively embrace technical systems because that is the only way we will be able to efficiently meet the challenges of an Earth that is turning its forces against us.

THE MULTISTABILITY OF SUSTAINABLE FUTURES

In this chapter, I am trying to point in a direction where values, interests, and facts are manifold, intertwined, and in a postphenomenological sense multistable.[21] This means, on the one hand, that we cannot talk of facts without thinking of norms and values, and that, on the other, values and norms must be based on facts. We live in an autopoietic system where facts are constantly produced from an origin in values and interests, and values and interests are subsequently born as a result of how facts are performed in the political arena of communication, negotiation, and power. Thus, the ethical and political dimensions of technology are multiple and multistable, and we need to take this multiplicity and multistability seriously in order to be able to foresee and engage in the political debate and discussion of sustainable futures. Taking this seriously is to think of possible outcomes of our engagement, not only on the basis of the intentionality of humans/social groups, actors, stakeholders, political parties, and so on but also on the basis of technology's intentionality,[22] for the human/technology assemblage has a will and determination that supersedes that of humans alone, if we can think of such a "thing" as humans without technology. Hayles pointed at the fact that we as humans cannot flourish as a symbiont in the assemblage without a similar and symmetrical technical flourishing.[23] This symbiotic human and technological will and determination has to be *directed* at the sites where communication, discussion, negotiation, and decisions are performed in order to fulfill ethical and political standards. The will and determination of human/technology assemblages cannot and should not be just any kind or any sort, because if so they would paradoxically be one dimensional and alienating (Marcuse), "enframing," and exploiting (Heidegger). Rather, we must include an *intentionality* that N. Hayles in her aforementioned book has called "nonconscious cognition," where machines, animals, humans, and so on act and react according to a set of values and laws that are *in* the systems—that is, in the human-technology assemblages—and that have an ethics and aesthetics that transcend classical definitions of what is right or wrong, true or false, ugly, or pretty. We have to think ethics and aesthetics anew and make way for multistable mediations of ethics and aesthetics, which means that we have to open up to the possibility of formal representations (aesthetics) that mediate situational understandings of what should or could be done. In this way, I try to expand Verbeek's notion of *Moralizing Technology* because what is needed in the performable ethical and political space of communication and negotiation in relation to sustainability is an openness toward new formal representations where the human/technological assemblages are given place, space, and time to perform according to values that critically and constructively elaborate on the nature of efficiency, growth, speed, and power.

In order to open this alternative formal approach toward the aesthetics of efficiency, growth, speed, and power, toward which Mumford gestures in *Technics and Civilization*, I think that Gilles Deleuze's and Felix Guattari's conceptualizations of becoming and process could be of relevance. What does this mean when it comes to "sustainable futures" in an ethical and political perspective? First of all, we have to accept that there actually is a "world of facts" and that this world is "given" in that it is not made up by humans or any other "maker." The world that exists is made out of processes that Deleuze and Guattari call *constant flows of becoming* where "fluid" bodies pass through the rhizome which in itself is a "fluid" body. Actors/actants, objects/things, and systems/networks cannot be concisely defined or described, because all are part of this organic and dynamic becoming of "work," practices, and actions. What we can identify, and to some extent describe, is this "working" of things that again is characterized by unpredictability and a certain degree of randomness, which means we have to "work" with serendipity and be "wise" (*phronesis*) when we move in striated spaces of apparent chaos.

Deleuze and Guattari chose to initiate their *Thousand Plateaus* with a fragment of a score by the Italian composer Sylvano Bussotti.[24] Even though some of the elements are recognizable, such as the keys and the bars, the actual musical performance of the piano piece is totally enigmatic, or at least it is not possible to play or repeat by anyone than the composer himself or the pianist David Tudor for whom it was composed. And even their interpretations of the scribbles might be very different because there is no univocal movement from a to b; classical spatio-temporal laws and rules are upheaved, and we are thrown into a universe that is totally unfamiliar. We are not told how to do and how to behave. We are in the rhizome of becoming, or as Heidegger would put it, we are walking on a wood path where only our experience can lead us the way (figure 10.1).

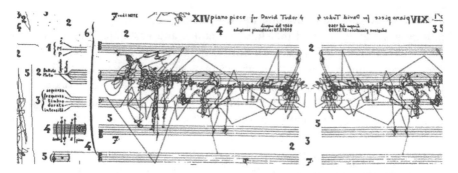

Figure 10.1   Sylvano Bussotti. 1960. *Source*: Piano Pieces for David Tudor, Music by Sylvano Bussotti, Copyright © 1958 by Casa Ricordi S.r.l., Via Benigno Crespi, 19 – 20159 Milan, Italy, *All Rights Reserved. International Copyright Secured*, Reproduced by kind permission of Hal Leonard Europe S.r.l. – Italy.

According to this reading for how to deal with sustainable futures from an ethico-political perspective when it comes to technological fore sighting, I believe that the concept of sustainability has to be qualified in the following way: in the concept of sustainability we must include that which is supporting, nurturing, caring, and cherishing of human/technology assemblages, where humans, and what it is to be human, can be identified in temporal and situational settings of becoming. When it comes to the future, then, we are not applying a blind faith in a prosperous and bright techno-future like the one we are promised by Ray Kurzweil and the "singularity" movement that foresees (prophesizes) in sermons held around the world that human suffering and death will be overcome by technological progression. On the other hand, I am not a techno-dystopian, as many have read and understood Heidegger, Mumford, Jonas, Marcuse, Ellul, and McLuhan, but am, as they actually were, open and critical toward our being with and through technology. Heidegger understood that our being human is technological, that destruction and salvation are the Janus faces of this being together, and that salvation would be in the "making" (*poiēsis*) that is art.[25] Mumford, in a much more pragmatic way, pointed toward practical solutions for this being together, where common/community-based actions toward ecological and responsible solutions were performed on a regional level. Ellul saw no escape from the technical powers of technology, but on the other hand he admitted that technology would be able to mend the gap and build the bridge to meaningful, even though technical, societal constructions. Jonas and Marcuse, both philosophers trained by Martin Heidegger and at the same time in a strong ideological and political opposition to their mentor and teacher, thought that technology should be tamed in order for human and social activity and creativity to flourish; in this reading I think that the critical and reflexive stance of Jonas and Marcuse is needed as we move in the rhizome of serendipity, randomness, and constant flux. We should play the piece on the piano and perform our version/vision of the world based on the knowledge, capacity, and skill we have at our disposal. This means that the performance is free and cannot be framed, but it is not random either, as can be seen with Bussotti's score. The framework we have set up, or the world that is constituted through it, is familiar and recognizable to us as human-technological assemblages, hence our actions and "works" are "predictable" and "forecastable," based on that framework/world wherein it is performed. The scribbles by Bussotti are clearly an indication of something that has to be played on a piano and not a "nonsense" representation of nothing. The scribbles indicate a multistability of "work" and performance that requires mastery and expertise in order for it to make sense. If not, it is just senseless and meaningless representation and indication of the opposite—that is, an expression of technological nihilism.[26]

I have moved far from the thoughts and ideas of the 1960s on sustainable and responsible action in relation to how we treat the earth and the environment, but I have done so on purpose because I think that the critique made by environmentalists and ecologists, as well as their followers in the following decades, were blinded by technological pessimism and determinism. They only "saw" the "unholy alliance of capitalism and technocracy"[27] and did not see how both science and technology could be "enframed" and visualized in a complementary (not opposite) way, leading toward salvation (Heidegger) and empowerment and emancipation (Feenberg). This "enframing" and visualization call for alternative and different approaches when it comes to defining "facts" and "values." What is a "fact" in the rhizome of becoming, and what is a "value" in the spatio-temporal, production of meaning? We have to enter into the agora where facts and values are constants and variables at one and the same time. A fact might change due to negotiations and temporal constructive alterations and variations, but it still remains a fact in the way that it is bound to the historicity of what it is and the way we deal with it in our present occupations. A value is in the same way a constant and a variable in the workings of reality. This means that it makes no sense to talk about a set of values that are common to humankind, but rather of constructing, creating, and shaping a framework that upholds, preserves, rejuvenates, invigorates, enhances, empowers, and emancipates what it means to be human, and what it means to be together as human/technological assemblages, on this earth that we are given.

Here we return to the fact that there is a "givenness" at hand, and we should respect that things are given. It is not that some god gave us this earth/universe, and we should act according to laws and rules that were instantiated by this god. Rather we should respect the fact that something is given, hence act and react based on values that abide to the fact that here we have a gift. The fact is a gift, and our ethico-political discussions on how to deal with that gift, which is always the result of the work of human/technological assemblages, should have a direction and indication toward what is prudent (*phronēsis*) and the following of the best possible way (serendipity)—that is, guided and steered by our co-constructed, co-created, co-shaped, and co-produced "plans" for how to survive and thrive.

As indicated at the beginning of this chapter, we make many plans in order to save the earth and the environment. We produce reports, such as the Brundtland report, and we meet at global venues (COP 1-21) and agree or disagree on future action. We set up goals for future action like the SDGs (2015) that are meant to be fulfilled by 2030, but we lack ways of dealing with these aims and goals because no one or nothing can be held accountable. We just have to confide or trust in each other and think that of course we all (as humanity) want to fulfill the aims of, for instance, SDG. Who would not?

Lucy A. Suchman wrote in relation to plans and planning: "A central feature of *planning* in this sense is that it is among the many everyday practices that we, as participants in Euro-American cultural traditions at least, call out as *foundational for the rationality of our actions.*"[28] Following the plans, reports, agreements, and manifestos such as the Paris Agreement or/and the SDG is rational and logical, but nevertheless we choose to let them stay in the background because we are caught in the loop of conversion, production, and consumption. It is not as if we forget or neglect recommendations and good intentions, but we need to reflect on how to deal with our practices as *planners*, because, as Suchman also writes: "'Planning' is an imaginative and discursive practice (now underwritten by a wide range of more and less effective technologies) through which actors project what they might do and where they might go, as well as reflect on where they are in relation to where they might have imagined that they might be."[29] So, in our agreements that are represented in reports and manifestos, we declare and clarify where we are and where we want to go, and we make projections into the future. But what we need is to think of the multiplicity and multistability of things because this is the "only" way that we are able to deal with the instability, variability, and hybridity as things are "enacted" on the way. We have to focus on the steps and the movements as we proceed and be aware of our choices in relation to conversion, production, and consumption, because this is true creativity and mastery of our being together with technology. Suchman, as a true social constructivist, points at the fact that *planning* is a social imaginative and discursive everyday practice, where technology is supporting, more or less effectively, these practices.

Postphenomenology, in my perspective, points at the fact that technology is an integrated part of these practices, hence partaking in planning itself. This means that what happens in the agora/arena of communication, imagination, reflection, and projection is the "work" of becoming. In this way of understanding reality, it becomes obsolete to talk about "new beginnings" and disruptions, but rather we should think of sustainability and the future in the framework of human/technology hybridizations where the "gift" of the future is received in sustainable and responsible ways, which means that we cherish, nourish, care, and share as we project our techno-hybridizations into the rhizome of becoming. This again means that even though we are not capable of calculating and controlling how our plans will affect the outcomes of our dealing with the gift—this earth that is given to us—it is our technologically mediated actions and practices that impact the world, and we should "enframe" our plans in this particular perspective. Technology, or rather technologies, is in the center of this "enframing," and we cannot think of any kind of solution to the environmental and climate crisis without addressing technologies in this center. Technology accordingly brought us to the threshold of disaster and distinction, and technology will in multiple and multistable ways structure our paths toward liveable and acceptable conditions for life.

REFLECTIONS

The *objective phenomenon* of progress and growth (Jonas) seems to be the main issue to be addressed when we talk about possible multistable enactments of conversion, production, consumption, and creation (Mumford). We have to give up upon the economic models that have almost exclusively dominated the twentieth and twenty-first century because these have lead us to the point where our globe and climate can no longer stand the consequences of the *objective phenomenon* of progress and growth. The British economist Tim Jackson, professor at the *Centre for the Understanding of Sustainable Prosperity* at the University of Surrey (UK), points at the fact that we have to replace growth and expansion with opposing values like low growth; even as his fellow economist Peter A. Victor, professor emeritus at York University in Canada, argues, modern Western economies must find new ways to deal with the fact that growth and progression is not an *objective phenomenon*. Victor, as an economist, points toward management and design tools that should enhance and assure values such as calmness and slowness as replacements for growth. We should not design by disaster, where through our models, plans, and technological solutions, we try to prevent an imaginary disastrous future, but rather model and plan in order for calm and slow societies to prosper. Jackson and Victor, along with a large group (243) of European development, environment, and planning researchers (2018), point in an open letter to the EU Commission at possible paradigmatic changes and movements in a post-growth reality, where we have to think anew and replace

Keynesian moral imperatives for constant growth, that solved the problems of the past such as structural massive unemployment in the 1930s, but that are no longer viable policies. The same thing goes for the opposing neoliberal economic model of the past century that guaranteed growth and wealth by letting the market free, because the *trickle-down* effect would ensure the good life for producers and consumers. Paradoxically we are stuck with two economic models of the past, and even though efforts have been made during the past century to replace neoliberal and classical economic models, these have seemingly been in vain. As I am writing these lines, there are discussions and negotiations in a European context where planning and development research environments are trying to engage with decision-makers on an institutional and governmental level (the European Union), and this is evidence of a common concern, which is present in these research environments, but also reflects what is going on in the current public debate and simultaneously also in the realm of philosophy of technology, which this anthology is proving.

We are stuck with economic and political models of the past that are increasingly seen as ineffective as we try to solve problems of the present, in order to have a possible future. In many ways our situation is similar to the 1930s that was a confusing decade of radicalism, absolutism, pragmatism, and simultaneous extreme models for optimization and purification on micro, meso, and macro level. Current transhuman "singularity" visionaries of a techno-future can be compared to similar visionaries and programs of the 1930s where for instance racial hygiene programs were promoted by political systems of very diverse character. Both current posthumanist and transhumanist metamorphic approaches to what it means to be human, and how subsequent possible societal models can be thought, are utopian and elitarian visionaries of the future, where concepts such as responsibility and sustainability are reduced to accountancy and efficiency. These are not the paths toward finding possible ways for common, egalitarian, and democratic gatherings and solutions. New *ecological* models for thinking planning and development toward sustainable futures have to be open, multiple, and organic, cognizant of the fact that it is risky and messy to be together with the begetter twins of science and technology. Jacques Ellul wrote that we have finally managed to technically tame and master the world, but it seems as if he was wrong on that note, because now the world is turning its forces against us. "Man knows himself to be more and more free, for technique has eliminated all natural forces and in this way has given him the sense of being master of his fate. The new man being created before our eyes, correctly tailored into the artificial paradise, the detailed and necessary product of the means which he ordains for himself—that man is I."[30] Technique has not "eliminated all natural forces," on the contrary we are in some sort of agreement on how technique and technological development has let uncontrollable natural forces free, and now we have to confide in a different new technological "man" that is made up by components that transcend efficiency and exploitation, if not we are doomed to succumb and at least a good part of us disappear from the surface of a new and different earth.

There is no one model or one plan to meet the challenges of a future that seems gloomy for most and paradisiac for few, but still we have to model and plan in order to create platforms and arenas for human/technology assemblages, and sometimes we have to make up *imperatives* for these assemblages that point toward more just, more fair, more sustainable, and more responsible co-creations. If not we are doomed to tragedy and disaster or to be left alone with ourselves in a techno-utopia of singularity. Postphenomenology has recently complemented and expanded empirical descriptions of human-technology-world relations, and it is beginning to question what it actually means to mediate technologically and how this mediation should be framed ethically and politically.[31] There is direction, sense, and meaning to be dealt with as mediations take place, and multistable mediations are the results of this kind of phenomenological intentionality (direction, sense, meaning) or "nonconsciuous cognition," which we try to project into a future which is unpredictable and uncontrollable. So our models and plans for a sustainable future together with technology, where we try to meet the environmental challenges and fulfill the goals that we make up together, have to respect the fact that mediations are multistable, metamorphic, dynamic, and organic, and we can only tentatively *create* possibilities for better conversion, production, and consumption.

NOTES

1. *Plan 9 from Outer Space*, directed by Edward J. Wood Jr. 1959. Distributors Corporation of America.

2. See Mikael Hård and Andrew Jamison, *Hubris and Hybrids. A Cultural History of Technology and Science* (London: Routledge, 2005).

3. Andrew Jamison, Steen H. Christensen, and Lars Botin, *A Hybrid Imagination. Science and Technology in Cultural Perspective* (London: Morgan & Claypool Publishers, 2011).

4. Herbert Marcuse, *One Dimensional Man. Studies in the Ideology of Advanced Industrial Society* (London and New York: Routledge Classics, 1964/2006).

5. Thomas S. Kuhn, *The Structure of Scientific Revolutions* (Chicago: The University of Chicago Press, 1962).

6. Bruno Latour, *We Have Never Been Modern* (Cambridge, MA: Harvard University Press, 1991).

7. Raymond Williams, *Politics of Modernism: Against the New Conformist* (London: Verso Books, 1989), 43.

8. Hans Jonas, *The Imperative of Responsibility. In Search for an Ethics for the Technological Age* (Chicago: University of Chicago Press, 1984), 168, my italics.

9. See, for example, Jacques Ellul, *The Technological Society* (New York: Vintage Books, 1964); Paul Virilio, *Speed and Politics: An Essay on Dromology* (New York: Semiotext[e], 1977); and Hartmut Rosa, *Social Acceleration: A New Theory of Modernity* (New York: Colombia University Press), 2015.

10. Martin Heidegger, "The Question Concerning Technology," in *Basic Writings* (Harper San Francisco, 1977), Frontispiece.

11. Lewis Mumford, *Technics and Civilization* (San Diego, London and New York: Harcourt Brace & Company, 1934/1963), 375.

12. Inge Røpke et al., *Økologisk Økonomi* (Ecological Economy). http://www.ecomacundervisning.dk/?lang=en, 2018.

13. Mumford, *Technics and Civilization*, 388.

14. Ibid., 387.

15. Ibid., 431.

16. Ibid., 432.

17. Ibid.

18. Ibid., 433–34.

19. N. Kathrine Hayles, *Unthought: The Power of the Cognitive Nonconscious* (Chicago: University of Chicago Press, 2017), 216.

20. Ibid., emphasis mine.

21. Don Ihde, *Technology and the Lifeworld*: *From Garden to Earth* (Bloomington: Indiana University Press, 1990).

22. Peter-Paul Verbeek, *Moralizing Technology: Understanding and Designing the Morality of Things* (Chicago: The University of Chicago Press, 2011).

23. Hayles, *Unthought*, 216.

24. Sylvano Bussotti, *Five Pieces for Piano for David Tudor* (Milano: G. Ricordi Milan, 1960). Image below, *Piano Pieces for David Tudor*, Music by Sylvano Bussoti, Copyright © 1958 by Casa Ricordi S.r.l., Via Benigno Crespi, 19 – 20159 Milan, Italy, All Rights Reserved. International Copyright Secured, Reproduced by kind permission of Hal Leonard Europe S.r.l. – Italy.

25. Martin Heidegger, *Holzwege* (Frankfurt am Main: Vittorio Klostermann, 1950/2003).

26. Nolen Gertz, *Nihilism and Technology* (London and New York: Rowman & Littlefield International, 2018).

27. A. Feenberg, "What I Said and What I Should Have Said: On Critical Theory of Technology," *Techné: Research in Philosophy and Technology* 17, no. 1 (Winter 2013): 164.

28. Lucy A. Suchman, *Human-Machine Reconfigurations: Plans and Situated Actions* (Cambridge: Cambridge University Press, 2007), 13, my italics.

29. Ibid.

30. Ellul, *The Technological Society*, 227.

31. See Robert Rosenberger and Peter-Paul Verbeek, eds., *Postphenomenological Investigations: Essays on Human-Technology Relations* (Lanham, MD: Lexington Books, 2015); and Robert Rosenberger, *Callous Objects: Designs against the Homeless* (Minneapolis: Minnesota University Press, 2017).

BIBLIOGRAPHY

Brundtland, Gro H. *Report of the World Commission on Environment and Development: Our Common Future.* http://www.un-documents.net/our-common-future.pdf, 1987.

Bussotti, Sylvano. *Five Pieces for Piano for David Tudor.* Milano: G. Ricordi Milan, 1960.

Deleuze, Gilles and Felix Guattari. *A Thousand Plateaus.* London and New York: Continuum, 1987/2007.

Ellul, Jacques. *The Technological Society.* New York: Vintage Books, 1964.

Feenberg, A. "What I Said and What I Should Have Said: On Critical Theory of Technology." *Techné: Research in Philosophy and Technology* 17, no. 1 (Winter 2013): 163–78.

Gertz, Nolen. *Nihilism and Technology.* London and New York: Rowman & Littlefield International, 2018.

Hård, Mikael and Andrew Jamison. *Hubris and Hybrids. A Cultural History of Technology and Science.* London: Routledge, 2005.

Hayles, N. Kathrine. *Unthought: The Power of the Cognitive Nonconscious.* Chicago: University of Chicago Press, 2017.

Heidegger, Martin. *Holzwege.* Frankfurt am Main: Vittorio Klostermann, 1950/2003.

Heidegger, Martin. "The Question Concerning Technology." In *Basic Writings*, edited by D.F. Krell, 311–341. Harper San Francisco, 1977.

Ihde, Don. *Technology and the Lifeworld. From Garden to Earth.* Bloomington and Indianapolis: Indiana University Press, 1990.

Intergovernmental Panel on Climate Change. *Global Warming of 1,5 C.* http://www.ipcc.ch/report/sr15/, 2018.

Jackson, Tim. *Prosperity without Growth? The Transition to a Sustainable Economy*, http://www.sd-commission.org.uk/data/files/publications/prosperity_without_growth_report.pdf, 2009.

Jamison, Andrew, Steen H. Christensen, and Lars Botin. *A Hybrid Imagination. Science and Technology in Cultural Perspective.* London: Morgan & Claypool Publishers, 2011.

Jonas, Hans. *The Imperative of Responsibility: In Search for an Ethics for the Technological Age.* Chicago: University of Chicago Press, 1984.

Kuhn, Thomas S. *The Structure of Scientific Revolutions.* Chicago: The University of Chicago Press, 1962.

Latour, Bruno. *We Have Never Been Modern.* Cambridge, MA: Harvard University Press, 1991.

Marcuse, Herbert. *One Dimensional Man: Studies in the Ideology of Advanced Industrial Society.* London and New York: Routledge Classics, 1964/2006.

McLuhan, Marshall. *Understanding Media.* London and New York: Routledge Classics, 1964/2006.

Mumford, Lewis. *Technics and Civilization.* San Diego, London and New York: Harcourt Brace & Company, 1934/1963.

Post-Growth Open Letter to EU institutions signed by over 200 scientists: "Europe, It's Time to End the Growth Dependency." https://degrowth.org/2018/09/06/post-growth-open-letter, 2018.

Røpke, Inge et al. Økologisk Økonomi (Ecological Economy). http://www.ecom acundervisning.dk/?lang=en, 2018.

Rosa, Hartmut. *Social Acceleration. A New Theory of Modernity.* New York: Colombia University Press, 2015.

Rosenberger, R. and Peter-Paul Verbeek, eds. *Postphenomenological Investigations: Essays on Human-Technology Relations.* Lanham, MD: Lexington Books, 2015.

Rosenberger, Robert. *Callous Objects: Designs against the Homeless.* Minneapolis: Minnesota University Press, 2017.

Suchman, Lucy A. *Human-Machine Reconfigurations: Plans and Situated Actions.* Cambridge: Cambridge University Press, 2007.

Sustainable Development Goals. https://sustainabledevelopment.un.org/post2015/tra nsformingourworld, 2015.

Verbeek, Peter-Paul. *Moralizing Technology: Understanding and Designing the Morality of Things.* Chicago: The University of Chicago Press, 2011.

Victor, Peter A. *Managing without Growth. Slower by Design, Not Disaster.* Cheltenham: Edward Elgar Publishing, 2008.

Virilio, Paul. *Speed and Politics: An Essay on Dromology.* New York: Semiotext(e), 1977.

Williams, Raymond. *Politics of Modernism. Against the New Conformist.* London: Verso Books, 1989.

Chapter 11

Beyond Naturalism

A Personalist Integral Humanism

Thomas M. Jeannot

This chapter responds to Pope Francis's call in *Laudato si': On Care for Our Common Home* for the renewal and development of an "integral humanism."[1] Francis writes, "We urgently need a humanism capable of bringing together the different fields of knowledge, including economics, in the service of a more integral and integrating vision."[2] Humanism, like happiness or truth, is one of those things that everybody's for, as long as it remains undefined, and Francis's humanism has pointed consequences, for it underwrites his call for "ecological conversion,"[3] a call both like and unlike Naomi Klein's in *This Changes Everything: Capitalism vs. the Climate* (2014). My thesis in this chapter is that only a humanism that recognizes the full reality of the person, identifies the "person as [the] key to reality," and takes "personal living" as its philosophical "starting point,"[4] can be a fully adequate, integral humanism—and thus provide the philosophical basis for an adequate response to our environmental crisis. The movement from Marx, through the mid-century naturalist humanisms of Leopold, Dewey, and Maritain, toward a convergence—never complete—with Francis, not only reveals the truth of this claim but traces an outline of what this personalist philosophy might look like.

What makes any philosophy an "integral" one, provided that it's coherent, is a general way of conceiving things inter-disciplinarily in nature. An integral philosophy is not the conclusion of any particular disciplinary or scientific field of specialization or research program. By virtue of its technical and specialized character, no one empirical or positive science logically entails the sought-for generality of a coherent, integral philosophy. Or to put it the opposite way, the positive conclusions of technical, specialized inquiries are logically consistent and compatible with a diversity of philosophical outlooks, even when such outlooks themselves lead to wildly different and mutually incompatible ways of conceptualizing the world. As valuable as it is, especially in a "post-truth" world of "alternative facts," the price that expert knowledge pays in any specialized domain of inquiry is its lack of philosophical generality. No philosophy necessarily follows as an inference from any specialized field of knowledge. For instance, no single philosophy necessarily follows from the positive sciences of physics, biology, or economics. Here we begin to sense the pathos of the call for "a more integral and integrating vision."

It is true that over the past century and a half, philosophical investigations themselves have become increasingly technical and specialized, more or less by design. Technical specialization, especially in mathematical logic, went hand in glove with the attempt to work out a putatively "scientific philosophy," from Bertrand Russell's logical atomism to the logical positivism of the Vienna Circle, and from logical positivism to contemporary analytic metaphysics, which pivots on the approach of possible worlds semantics, based on the rehabilitation of modal logic beginning in the 1970s.[5] This type of specialized investigation aims to discover whether any "truths" are necessarily true for all possible worlds. "Physicalism" is the dominant view in this philosophical discipline. The idea that "everything is physical" is easy enough to state but extraordinarily difficult to work out and defend. The term, "physicalism," is a higher-order philosophical synonym for the commonplace secular outlook we know as materialism.

In his book *Physicalism* (2010), Daniel Stoljar starts out by charting the philosophical itinerary of the physicalist idea of things, from its decidedly minority status in the second half of the nineteenth century and even well into the twentieth to its present-day preeminence. He writes: "If materialism wasn't popular in 1925 . . . the contrast between then and now could not be more extreme. Far from being viewed with professional contempt, materialism became something like a consensus position within analytic philosophy in the 1960s and has remained so . . . ever since. . . . [Physicalism] is in many ways the Weltanschauung of modern analytic philosophy."[6] The word itself "was introduced into philosophy in the 1930s by Otto Neurath and Rudolf Carnap."[7] In his first chapter, Stoljar represents "the standard [physicalist] picture," "a high-level empirical hypothesis,[8] by the conjunction of five theses, "(1) physicalism is true—the *basic thesis*; (2) physicalism summarizes the picture of the world implicit in the natural sciences—the *interpretative thesis*; (3) it is most rational to believe the picture of the world implicit in the natural sciences, whatever that picture happens to be—the *epistemological thesis*; (4) physicalism is, prima facie, in conflict with many presupposition of everyday life—the *conflict thesis*; [and] (5) the way to resolve these conflicts is to propose views about how to interpret the presuppositions of everyday life so that they are compatible with physicalism—the *resolution thesis*. These claims form a system."[9] It turns out in subsequent chapters that the simplicity of the physicalist idea, the starting point of the "standard picture" is inversely proportional to the complexity of the logical and conceptual knots that have to be disentangled in order to work it out as a "system." These tangles too are technical and specialized in nature and beyond the scope of this chapter. But there's one Gordian knot in the physicalist program that we may be able to loosen by way of contrasting it with its humanist rival.

It may not appear obvious that physicalism and humanism are mutually incompatible, but we can eliminate confusion right away once we specify that the humanism in question is the personalist, integral humanism of Pope Francis, and that what is at stake is a philosophical understanding of the relation between humans and the natural world that could ground an environmental ethic. Introducing the standard picture, Stoljar writes: "While physicalism is a thesis we have overwhelming reason to believe . . . [it] is on the face of it incompatible with, or at least in some tension with, various claims that are central to ordinary or common sense views about humans and what they are like."[10] He lists a number of common sense claims and then writes:

> In order to appreciate [their] importance . . . try to think for a moment how things would be if they were false—that nobody thinks or feels, or says anything meaningful, or that ordinary physical objects are not solid or colored, or that there is no freedom of action or social agency or mathematical knowledge. It is obvious when you think about it that these claims and others like them are central to life as we live it; they are . . . *the presuppositions of everyday life.* So in effect what we are being asked to accept by the standard picture is the idea that there is a prima facie conflict between the presuppositions of everyday life on the one hand, and a thesis we have overwhelming reason to believe—i.e. physicalism—on the other.[11]

Stoljar calls this tension "the conflict thesis," which therefore requires a "resolution thesis" in order to achieve the requisite aim of systematic closure. The argument of this chapter begins with the assumption that there is indeed a prima facie conflict, but that its successful resolution, alternative to physicalism, would bring us into the orbit of the humanist Marx of the *Economic and Philosophic Manuscripts of 1844*, the Marx who wrote the aphorism, "One basis for life and another basis for science is a priori a lie."[12]

But I'm getting ahead of myself. There's no question of the disparity between Marx's and Francis's humanism. However, in the reception of the encyclical, the suggestion that the Argentine Jesuit Pope is a liberation theologian whose thought is inflected with Marxism is neither hard to find nor difficult to profile.[13] It is a reasonable question to ask whether Marx, who is a "naturalist," is or must be a "physicalist" too. If the answer is no, as I will suggest, then it's possible to establish a relation between a naturalist form of humanism and a personalist form without slurring the identity of either one. The flash point concerns the defining commitment of a personalist outlook in conversation with alternative views: a conversation about the stakes of the conflict thesis, whether an integral humanism is required in order to preserve the presuppositions of everyday life, and if so, how to go about it.

The problem Francis addresses is not a technical, specialized problem in the specialized empirical sciences, natural or social. Rather, it is an interdisciplinary problem, a problem of philosophy and theology, and a question of one's general conception of things or a worldview. Perhaps the leanest and sharpest way to come to the point is to say that Francis has a sacramental conception of reality, and that the metaphysics of physicalism or materialism, which recurs through the history of European thought, is radically and irreconcilably inconsistent with a sacramental world; from the ancient Greco-Roman atomism of Democritus, Epicurus, and Lucretius, to the Anglo-French materialism of the seventeenth and eighteenth centuries; to the dialectical materialism of Friedrich Engels's presentation of Marxism in the nineteenth century, which was subsequently integrated into the thought of the Second International and then passed on to Russian Marxism and canonical Marxism-Leninism; and also to the scientific materialism of most of the English-speaking twentieth century, which still dominates mainstream philosophy of science in the English-speaking world.[14]

If all this observation means is what everyone already knows, that secular intellectuals are predisposed to materialism, still, the reference to secularism is not incidental. Following the philosophical precedents of Hegel and Peirce, wherever we find a pair—physicalism and secularism—we should look for a trifecta: the third term in my profile is economism,[15] with an eye to Francis's inclusion of the economic in his call for ecological conversion. In this spirit, the first thesis is that Francis's humanism is Catholic, sacramental, and personalist. The second thesis is that this worldview is ruled out of intellectual bounds—and we might as well call it superstition—if physicalism is true (Stoljar's "basic thesis"). Third, we may assume that Stoljar is right that there's a prima facie conflict between the presuppositions of everyday life and the physicalist's standard picture of the world; and that a physicalist's metaphysics would be unable to achieve systematic closure if it failed to work out a resolution of this conflict.

To get ahead of myself again, the fourth thesis in order would be this: inasmuch as our aim philosophically would be to work out an understanding of the world, we actually inhabit—the world of our actual personal and social experience—what Stoljar calls the "presuppositions of everyday life" would take not just linguistic but also explanatory priority over the abstract modal-logical worlds of possible worlds semantics.[16] One way of stating this relation of explanatory priority would be to follow Marx again: one basis for life and another basis for science is a priori a lie. This is the slogan of this chapter. However, we will not turn directly to the critique of economism in Marx and Francis, and the hostility to this move among American Catholic economists.[17] First, it is necessary to address directly the question of what relation a humanism, and the economics it would entail, could have with naturalism. After all, if naturalism and humanism are mutually exclusive then the type of robust environmental ethics that we are after would be impossible.

While some papal encyclicals are addressed to the internal forum of Catholic believers, the tradition of social encyclicals that Francis inherits and develops is addressed, not to believers alone but to the people of the world, based on "reading the signs of the times." The addressee of *On Care for Our Common Home* is ourselves in our common humanity, the humanity we share together, personally and interpersonally, socially and historically, just as much as we share it—it almost goes without saying—quite naturally.

In relation to environmental philosophy, this personalist humanism of *Laudato si'* presents a vision of our common and shared humanity that sublates or transcends what may be a stalemate in the contemporary literature, a standoff between anthropocentrism, on the one hand, and biocentrism or ecocentrism, on the other hand. The alternatives seem to be either humanist, but anthropocentric and speciesist; or biocentric or ecocentric, but species-egalitarian, contra humanism. For Francis, this is a false dilemma. The central nervous system of the encyclical letter goes to "the human roots of the ecological crisis" and the critique of "anthropocentrism" in chapter 3.[18] The fundamental argument of the encyclical reasons that the human community is inseparable from what Aldo Leopold called "the biotic community."[19] Francis calls this higher viewpoint a "universal communion."[20] It is the presupposition of an "integral ecology."[21] An integral humanism, then, requires and includes an integral ecology.

Leopold's land ethic could be thought of as a naturalistic version of an integral ecology, while Francis's is a sacramental one. In philosophy, the extent of their convergence can be measured by the distance of Leopold's "religious naturalism"[22] from Francis's personalism. Personalism would be the breaking point.

Leopold writes that the land ethic's "extension of ethics, so far studied only by philosophers, is actually a process in ecological evolution. Its sequences may be described in ecological as well as philosophical terms. An ethic, ecologically, is a limitation on freedom of action in the struggle for existence. An ethic, philosophically, is a differentiation of social from antisocial conduct. These are two definitions of one thing." He continues, "The first ethics dealt with the relations between individuals; the Mosaic decalogue is an example.

Later accretions dealt with the relation between the individual and society. The golden rule tries to integrate the individual to society; democracy to integrate social organization to the individual." Writing in 1949, he continues,

> There is as yet no ethic dealing with man's relation to land and to the animals and plants which grow upon it. Land, like Odysseus' slave-girls, is still property. The land-relation is still strictly economic, entailing privileges but not obligations. The extension of ethics to this third element in human environment is . . . an evolutionary possibility and an ecological necessity. It is the third step in a sequence. The first two have already been taken. Individual thinkers since the days of Ezekiel and Isaiah have asserted that the despoliation of land is not only inexpedient but wrong.[23]

In this passage, the references of Leopold's characterization of moral development are to the decalogue, the golden rule, and the prophets Ezekiel and Isaiah, sources that clearly provide grounds for convergence with Francis.

The great American naturalist philosopher John Dewey belongs to the same intellectual milieu as Leopold in the prewar and postwar United States rather than Europe and the world of Guardini and Maritain, two important personalist sources for Francis's tradition. Dewey shares Leopold's basic commitment to democracy, the purpose of which, according to Leopold, is "to integrate social organization to the individual."[24] Leopold's land ethic extends this deep underlying commitment to democracy to include the biotic community within the human community and vice versa. For Dewey as well as Leopold, the commitment to democracy, not only in ethics but across the dimensions of human experience, is as crucial as it is irreducible. Dewey's essential philosophical commitment is his commitment to "democracy as a way of life." This is one way of condensing his version of naturalistic humanism or humanistic naturalism into a single statement.[25]

Marx's philosophical naturalism, like Dewey's, is also a humanism.[26] His outlook upon the natural world bears a striking family resemblance to Dewey's. It is the vision of a "*humanized* nature."[27] In his *1844 Manuscripts*, Marx writes, "Here we see how consistent naturalism or humanism distinguishes itself both from idealism and materialism, constituting at the same time the unifying truth of both."[28] In this view epistemology and ontology are fundamentally intertwined and both open onto an integrated view in which "*society is the consummated oneness in substance of man and nature—the true resurrection of nature—the naturalism of man and the humanism of nature both brought to fulfilment.*"[29] This philosophical outlook, in turn, underwrites the *Communist Manifesto*. Marx concludes the second section, "Proletarians and Communists," by writing, "In place of the old bourgeois society, with its classes and class antagonisms, we shall have an association, *in which the free development of each is the condition for the free development of all.*"[30]

We should notice the similarity of this conditional claim to Leopold's, concerning the complementarity of the golden rule and democracy: the former integrates the individual to society, while the latter integrates the form of social organization to the individual. A social theory like this aims toward an integral humanism that recognizes the mutuality, complementarity, and reciprocity of relations of individuals to society, of society to individuals, of the human community to the biotic community, and of the biotic community to the human community. Marx conceivably formulates the correct principle of social justice in his *Critique of the Gotha Program* (1875), when he famously writes, "only then can the narrow horizon of bourgeois right be crossed in its entirety and society inscribe on its banner: From each according to his ability, to each according to his needs!"[31]

We might expect the Rhinelander Karl Marx to be too far afield from the Midwesterners Leopold and Dewey[32] to be relevant to an American conversation about humanism and ecology, but in her book, *The Ruling Ideas: Bourgeois Political Concepts*, the philosopher and social theorist Amy E. Wendling provides the grounds for staging them together. The "bourgeois political concepts" Wendling elaborates are ways of thinking about labor, time, property, value, and crisis.[33] The allusion of Wendling's title is to Marx's claim in *The German Ideology* that "the ideas of the ruling class are in every epoch the ruling ideas: i.e., the class which is the ruling *material* force of society, is at the same time its ruling *intellectual* force."[34] Among the many aspects of these ruling ideas, which Wendling presents as a concrete dialectical totality, two are especially relevant to our consideration—namely, "the turning of private property into an ontological foundation of selfhood, and the reduction of all morality to exchange value."[35] This is a good definition of economism.[36] Wendling develops several brilliant and genuinely Midwestern illustrations of this ontological reduction of self and morality. Jointly they have the effect of making Marx's relevance plain to a conversation between Leopold and Dewey. Wendling's thesis is that the ruling ideas saturate the political, social, and natural body as a whole, leeching into every pore, including fugitive resources that might have seemed beyond their reach, such as the crisis of the Olgallala Aquifer.[37] In another illustration, Wendling observes "a kind of hysteresis" in "the temporal cultures of agricultural communities, which are less minutely regulated by the clock and the calendar than other communities."[38] She writes, "This hysteresis points to a general truth . . . . Non-capitalist, proto-capitalist, or quasi-capitalist pockets of activity persist within capitalist life." Nevertheless, just as the concept of property, the subject of Wendling's third chapter is "poorly equipped to deal with water resources," but the Texan "water pirate" T. Boone Pickens still shows up to enforce his property rights on the management of the aquifer, so too the hysteresis of a vanishing agrarian way of life, still at least partially outside the "field of abstract time," can hardly evade the logic of the industrial production of corn for ethanol, in another of Wendling's illustrations, this time of "the paradox of value."[39] This is what a "ruling idea," a "bourgeois political concept," is like: "To be bourgeois is always to be on the knife's edge between progress and nostalgic conservatism: to use green technologies on an organic farm falsely imagined as being like those of our ancestors."[40] "All that is solid melts into air."[41]

Clearly, neither Leopold nor Dewey nor Marx nor Wendling is doing theology (let alone writing a papal encyclical), whereas the theological component is indispensable to Pope Francis's argument. However, in principle, its philosophical component should also be defensible on philosophical grounds. Moreover, a philosophical defense of Catholic social teaching needs not be reactionary. Just as obvious as the fact that Francis is not a materialist is the fact that there are many secular humanists, across a broad range of predispositions, atheists included, who resonate with the message of *Laudato si'*. In this regard, Francis shares a great deal with Maritain, the personalist author of *Integral Humanism*. Writing in *The Nation* after World War II, Maritain found himself in a circumstance analogous to our own. He found himself in agreement with the erstwhile Marxist Sidney Hook, who was also a student of the naturalist John Dewey's, on the grounds of what we will call the principle of practical convergence. Maritain wrote that people "possessing quite different, even opposite, metaphysical or religious outlooks, can converge, not by virtue of any identity of doctrine, but by virtue of an analogical similitude in practical principles, toward the same practical conclusions, *and can share in the same practical democratic faith*, provided that they similarly revere, perhaps for quite diverse reasons, truth and intelligence, human dignity, freedom, brotherly love, and the absolute value of moral good."[42] Dewey's only book on religion, *A Common Faith*, could be thought to affirm Maritain's principle of practical convergence from the other side. What places them in an obverse/inverse relation in the first place is that they "share in the same practical democratic faith." Suppose we now endorse Maritain's principle in order to take a fifth step in our argument beyond naturalism and toward a personalist, integral humanism.

It's evident that no serious philosophy can be all things to all people. Practical convergence extends to a limit. If it rules in bounds for Catholic believers, we should also investigate what it rules out of bounds, based on the provisos of Maritain's formulation. First of all, personalism rules out physicalism. There is no Catholic world in which physicalism can be the correct metaphysics. But the next step to take, in the spirit of Maritain's ecumenism and pluralism, would be to reinscribe physicalism within the boundary conditions of philosophical naturalism. It is a commonplace of philosophical discussions of naturalism to distinguish two broad types.[43] Physicalism is the reductive type. What it reduces or eliminates are human subjectivity and experience in their own right, in favor of a theory that relies on "Hume's dictum,"[44] the principle of "causal closure," and the "causal completeness of the physical." In his 1908 book, *Personalism*, the American personalist Borden Parker Bowne called this way of thinking about things in general "impersonalism."[45] But there are non-reductive, pluralist types of naturalism as well. Some methodological naturalists hold that this is a distinction without a difference. The only remedy is to demonstrate that the difference between these two types of naturalism is genuine and important.

But once again, the point of our present considerations is not to resolve technical and specialized philosophical debates that can be successfully resolved only on the level of their specialist presentation. Our purpose instead is to wonder what Marxists are doing in the near neighborhood for the reception of *Laudato si'*. We have already identified the philosopher Marx as a naturalist, in the same mix with Leopold and Dewey. They are naturalists of the non-reductive, pluralist type. Thus, we can profile Marx and Dewey as a way of testing the limit-situation for the personalist outlook of an integral humanism, in order to discover how far Catholic ecumenism and Maritain's personalist principle of practical convergence extend.

We are familiar with urban legends about Jesuits and Marxists and about "cultural Marxists" infiltrating and subverting American higher education. There are comic-strip versions; for example, the editorial line taken by John Neumayr in *The New Spectator*, appealing to conservative American Catholics. Or, for an example that appeals to a still larger American public, consider the recent statement issued by the NRA's Wayne LaPierre in response to the Stoneman Douglas High-School shooting: "On college campuses," he said, "Karl Marx is the most assigned economist."[46] Many Americans tend to think of the papacy in the same way they think of the presidency. Through this distorting lens, John XXIII and Pope Paul VI look like John F. Kennedy and Lyndon Johnson, while John Paul II and Benedict XVI look like Ronald Reagan and George W. Bush. For the past five years, the first Jesuit, the first Latin American, and the first pope to take the name Francis has been likened to the first black president. In this diminished conceptual universe, the universal categories of assessment are "liberal" and "conservative." Constituencies are "blue states" and "red states." John Paul II and Benedict XVI appealed to a Republican palate; Francis is a pope for the Democrats. In this climate, rants like Neumayr's or LaPierre's, written in Richard Hofstadter's "paranoid style,"[47] are intellectually on the same level as the conspiracy theories that litter websites like Infowars.

Apart from this hysteria, a more disciplined and intellectually serious version of the urban legend appears in journals like *First Things* and *Crisis*

Magazine. The editorial line of periodicals like these tends to lend academic credibility to the idea of a Marxist pope, even when their authors try to be careful. Last November, in *Crisis Magazine*, John Horvat II reviewed *Pope Francis and the Caring Society* (2017), a collection of essays edited by the economist Robert Whaples, with a "Foreword" by the late Michael Novak,[48] the conceit of which is to engage in "a civilized debate carried out with great respect and reverence for the papal office." Horvat's review explicitly links *Pope Francis and the Caring Society* to *Laudato si'*. He brings Novak's thinly disguised subtext out into the open: Pope Francis knows nothing about the science of economics, which leads him in the encyclical to adopt an anti-capitalist, pro-socialist attitude to the looming ecological crisis. But Horvat's conclusion is wide of the mark: *Laudato si'* is neither a "postmodern narrative" nor a treatise of economics; it is neither a blue state nor a red state encyclical; it is neither liberal nor conservative; but most importantly of all, it is neither in thrall nor chained to "the bottom line." It is a social encyclical deeply consonant with the whole social teaching of the Catholic tradition going back to 1891 and Pope Leo XIII's *Rerum novarum*.

As Francis's teaching in *Laudato si'* is consonant with the Catholic intellectual tradition as a whole, in his "Foreword" to *Pope Francis and the Caring Society*, Novak, the conservative American Catholic belletrist and well-known author of *The Spirit of Democratic Capitalism* (1982), also reaches back in time to retrieve the tradition of Adam Smith, which serves him as a stand-in for orthodox neoclassical economic theory.[49] In his "Foreword," Novak informs us that the economists represented in the new book seek "constructively to engage and educate civic and business leaders and the general public to understand the legacy and meaning of the natural law, moral and economic principles of liberty, personal responsibility, enterprise, civic virtue, family and community, and the rule of law." Moreover, "The education of each pope begins anew when he is elected to office" (xix). Novak would thus lift the scales from Pope Francis's eyes. His subtitle could have been: "Blame Argentina!" Likewise, Novak informs us, the pope who grew up in communist Poland also initially confronted a steep learning curve, but by *Centesimus annus* (1991), he came around to the right idea of things; in effect, for Novak, the view that private property plus unregulated markets equals human happiness and prosperity. For Novak and his fellow-travelers, private property and free markets are the solution; for Leopold and Dewey, on the other hand, property relations and the program of economism are the problem.

Likewise, Marx's spiritual father was the German philosopher Hegel, who appropriated the achievement of the classical political economists Adam Smith and David Ricardo in his *Philosophy of Right* (1820)—Hegel's book of ethics, social theory, and politics. When Marx, a lifelong Hegelian who "openly avowed [himself] the pupil of that mighty thinker,"[50] set out to criticize his mentor in 1844, he discovered "a double error in Hegel," "latent in [Hegel's *Phenomenology of Spirit*] as a germ, a potentiality, a secret, the uncritical positivism and the equally uncritical idealism of [his] later works."[51] Marx's insight into the "double error" of an "uncritical positivism" swimming in the same lane as an "equally uncritical idealism" can be extrapolated to Novak's "Foreword" and his appeal to the legacy of Smith. An uncritical positivism accepts the given order of things within an essentially static conceptual framework. Hence, economics is an empirical, positive science as "scientific" as any other, the aim of which would be to discover the "laws of motion" of economic activity.[52] Novak appeals to the science of economics in order to criticize what he takes to be Pope Francis's misunderstanding of the way things work in practice. In this way, he transposes an empirical, positive science into the key of a critical, evaluative, normative, and prescriptive science (or what one school of Marxism calls a "critical theory" of society).[53] The Scottish philosopher David Hume, a close friend of Smith, in his *Treatise of Human Nature* (1739–1740), classically posed the "is/ought" problem that has dogged ethical theory ever since. In a right-theological reading of Hegelian philosophy, we are tempted to draw the conclusion from Hegel that whatever happens to be the case as a matter of fact ought to be the case concerning the ideal of social justice.

Dewey agrees that this is directly related to their materialism. He writes that "scientific economists," who appeal, like Novak et al., to "natural law" and "laissez-faire, individualistic liberalism" do not make the mistakes of the neo-Medievalists.

But in their own peculiar "scientific" ways, they also fly in the face of facts. The subject-matter of full-fledged "scientific" economics has been identified with aspects of life economists designate as *material*. The consequence of this identification or definition is to separate and isolate the economic from the moral and political. . . . Scientific economists are inspired by a dehumanized conception of the nature of science, still widely prevalent. The great majority of those who now attribute the scientific backwardness of social subjects to absence of proper methods of inquiry advocate, as the remedy for this grievous state of affairs, the outright adoption of techniques of inquiry that have proved themselves in dealing with physical subject-matter. They are unmindful of the fact that these techniques have worked successfully just because they were designed for experimental operations with subject-matters from which human (value) considerations were explicitly ruled out.[54]

In other words, one way to solve Hume's problem is to collapse it. The upshot of such a collapse would be an "uncritical positivism" that coincided with an "equally uncritical idealism." Someone could hold that like any other science, economics also aims for prediction and control. In the not too distant past, it was also held that properly scientific investigations are "value-free" or "value-neutral." Although this view may be less insistent today, the question still arises how an empirical, positive science could also be a critical, evaluative, normative, and prescriptive science at the same time, otherwise than by way of collapsing Hume's distinction and slurring the difference between the facts of the matter and the ideal values and norms we uphold for a truly decent, truly humane, and truly just society.

We began with the conflict thesis of Stoljar's physicalist picture—the conflict between "the presuppositions of everyday life" and a physicalist philosophy—which requires a resolution in order for the physicalist hypothesis to compose an analytic metaphysical system. Physicalism solves for the logically best model and demotes the presuppositions of everyday life to the subordinate position of explanandum.[55] This is what would require it, for example, to reinscribe "thinking" inside the positive science of neurology. In contrast, personalism resolves the conflict thesis in just the opposite direction, in favor of the explanatory priority of "personal living" or the presuppositions of everyday life.

If persons are not presupposed among the primitive terms of a philosophy going in, then neither will they be derived, going out, from the empirical, positive, technical, and specialized sciences of evolutionary biology and psychology; or anatomy, physiology, and neurology; or primatology; or computational methods. Moreover, a successful physicalism would override the boundary conditions of the social or human sciences and history as well. On the other hand, there is nothing in a personalist philosophy that is inconsistent in principle with the leading conclusions of any positive science.

While personalism is irreconcilable with physicalism—the reductive form of naturalism—non-reductive, pluralist forms of naturalism, such as Leopold's, Dewey's,[56] and Marx's, may fall within the scope of the principle of practical convergence. A contemporary representative of the latter may be the French-Brazilian Marxist sociologist Michael Löwy, author of *Ecosocialism: A Radical Alternative to Capitalist Catastrophe* (2015). Löwy reviewed "Laudato Si—The Pope's Anti-Systemic Encyclical," in *Monthly Review*,[57] and his appreciation is in one way the mirror opposite of Novak's critique: Novak cares about being Catholic, while Löwy's secular reception brackets religious belief. For him, what serves as the criterion is not Catholic fidelity, but the fact that the pope invited Naomi Klein to speak at a conference on *Laudato si'* in Rome, and that this was "probably the first time a 'secular Jewish feminist,' as she was described by the Church's official press, was invited to a discussion at the Vatican." Despite his secular criterion, Löwy's reading is hermeneutically superior to readings like Novak's just because it's not chained to economism.

First of all, Löwy recognizes that *Laudato si'* is not about capitalism *versus* socialism. He also recognizes that "Bergoglio is not a Marxist"; the urban legend is a dog whistle. But, more importantly, staying close to Francis's text in his response, we also find him taking the view that an integral humanism requires an integral ecology. He writes: "Always connecting the ecological question with the social question, Francis insists on the necessity of radical measures and profound changes in order to confront this double challenge. The main obstacle to this is the 'perverse' nature of the system." He quotes Francis directly: "The same mindset which stands in the way of making radical decisions to reverse the trend of global warming also stands in the way of achieving the goal of eliminating poverty."[58] Whereas Novak et al. insist that under capitalism, poverty will take care of itself, as well as the global warming that Novak comes as close as he can to denying, conscience permitted.

If the hypothesis were correct that physicalism, secularism, and economism belong to a common intellectual horizon, it may seem odd that some conservative American Catholic writers implacably embrace economism, while secular progressives, liberals, and socialists welcome the once censored, silenced, and suppressed theology of liberation, just as they also extend a warm welcome to Pope Francis and *Laudato si'*. Progressives, liberals, and socialists don't need to be physicalists, but secular economists, within the boundary conditions of their technical, specialized discipline as it is presently practiced, certainly are. This is one of the disciplinary constraints with which we began: the authority of the science of economics is not identical with an authoritative philosophy. So the right question to ask, it seems to me, is how Catholicism would come to be nailed to the rock of John Locke and Adam Smith to start with; or Robert Nozick, Friedrich Hayek, and Ludwig von Mises[59]; or, if the Catholic Speaker of the House of Representatives Paul Ryan is to be believed, all the way down to Ayn Rand, as savage an icon for the conjunction of physicalism with atheism, secularism, and economism as the imagination can conjure.[60] The two climates are so mutually inhospitable that a special apparatus would be required to breathe in their common air.

Without attempting a full genealogy of this pathology, it is enough to see that a rejection of this economism reinvigorates the possibility of a genuine humanism that interweaves a commitment to social justice and care for the marginalized with a non-reductive naturalism that is worth protecting in a robust environmental ethics. As Francis writes, "Today, it is the case that some economic sectors exercise more power than states themselves. But economics without politics cannot be justified, since this would make it impossible to favour other ways of handling the various aspects of the present [environmental] crisis. The mindset which leaves no room for sincere concern for the environment is the same mindset which lacks concern for the inclusion of the most vulnerable members of society."[61] This is the heart of a convergence between Francis's view and a secular environmental ethics, and its most important contribution is to remind ecologically oriented philosophers of the importance of including concern for the poor and vulnerable as a central part of any proper conception of sustainability. For a personalist, this concern for humanity and concern for the environment are united in a nonreductive naturalism: a nature of which humans are a part. Francis, however, goes further and integrates the two in a wider theological horizon.

Ignacio Castuera concludes his small and elegant essay, "The Jesuit Pope," writing, "The concept of the divinization of the universe permeates *Laudato si'* because its author, though named Francis, is thoroughly Ignatian." This is "finding God in all things," and on this note, we can conclude. For the personalist Jesuit Pope, a deep inner accord between Ignatian spirituality and personalist philosophy is axiomatic. But in sympathetic writers from Löwy to Castuera, the missing moment is personalism itself, the dimension that not only brings *On Care for Our Common Home* into profound alignment with Francis's immediate predecessors Benedict XVI and John Paul II, but also signifies the "unity of hearts and minds" in Catholicism itself, in its integral and integrating sacramental vision of the personal nature of reality, and in its integration of an integral humanism with an integral ecology in their universal communion.

In Jesuit education, this integral humanism is expressed in the maxim, "care of the person." This "whole person" is an integral unity of body, mind, and spirit. It is the integral unity who is acted upon and who acts in the world of "lived experience," on the presuppositions of everyday life. The whole person (an integral psychophysical unity) is the starting point of a philosophy that aims to receive and transform the world by virtue of personal action, which is personal, interpersonal, social, and entirely natural all the way through. The person in question is John Paul II's "acting person," which serves as a prelude to his "theology of the body."[62] In Maritain's vision, "society" is therefore "a whole whose parts are themselves wholes."[63] The interweaving implications for a critical theory of society, the struggle for social justice, and renewed understanding of nature are momentous.

In order to indicate the general outline of these implications, let's consider one final coupling, joining the personalist Pope Francis with the personalist Dr. Martin Luther King, Jr. When Francis addressed the Congress on September 24, 2015, he singled out four great American figures, Abraham Lincoln, Martin Luther King, Thomas Merton, and Dorothy Day, the personalist founder of the Catholic Worker movement. In this light, *Laudato si'* can be read as a Catholic workers' encyclical. The personalist Emmanuel Mounier, a member of Maritain's salon, strongly influenced Day and her coworker, Peter Maurin. Thus, a personalist line of descent is clear and distinct.

Therefore, let's come straight to the point by turning again to the personalist Maritain. In 1933, in *Freedom in the Modern World*, Maritain takes up the saying, *"The social revolution will be a moral revolution or not at all."*[64] It is a call to Catholic workers to take social and political action. First, he issues one of his many scathing critiques of "Godless Soviet Russia."[65] Then, like King, Day, and Merton, he calls for "the heroism of love."[66] Concluding his call to social action, he writes, "Those only will be astonished at the apparent paradox [of mixing 'the temporal' with 'the spiritual'] who fail to appreciate the intrinsic and essential dependence of the political and social with regard to the moral, of the temporal on spiritual things; and who do not see that the evils of which mankind is suffering in our time are incurable *if divine things are not brought into the depths of the human itself* and of the profane and secular order."[67]

In 1967, in his speech, "Beyond Vietnam" at New York's Riverside Church, Dr. King too, influenced by the personalist school centered at Boston University while he was in doctoral studies, calls for a "revolution of values," at a time when he was actively discouraged from speaking out and then universally reviled by the American press when he did—before his reputation was transformed into the stature of a national holiday. He writes, "I am convinced that if we are to get on the right side of the world revolution, we as a nation must undergo a radical revolution of values. We must rapidly begin the shift from a 'thing-oriented' society to a 'person-oriented' society. When machines and computers, profit motives and property rights are considered more important than people, the giant triplet of racism, materialism, and militarism are incapable of being conquered."[68] King gave this speech a year to the day before he was assassinated in Memphis. From the perspective of a personalist integral humanism, his convergence with personalism is obviously practical, in the spirit of Maritain's principle, but it also comes from the same deeply humanist source. King prophesied:

> There is something seductively tempting about . . . sending us all off on what in some circles has become a popular crusade against the war in Vietnam. I say we must enter the struggle, but I wish to go on now to say something even more disturbing. The war in Vietnam is but a symptom of a far deeper malady within the American spirit, and if we ignore this sobering reality we will find ourselves organizing clergy-and laymen-concerned committees for the next generation. They will be concerned about Guatemala and Peru. They will be concerned about Thailand and Cambodia. They will be concerned about Mozambique and South Africa. We will be marching for these and a dozen other names and attending rallies without end unless there is a significant and profound change in American life and policy. Such thoughts take us beyond Vietnam, but not beyond our calling as sons of the living God.[69]

In our time, King would surely add climate change to his list of names. His call to enter the struggle is even more resonant and urgent today.

NOTES

1. *Laudato si'*, 2015.
2. *Laudato si'* #141.
3. *Laudato si'* #216–21.
4. I take these formulations from Thomas O. Buford in his "Introduction" to "American Idealism and Personalism," as represented by Borden Parker Bowne, in *Pragmatism and Classical American Philosophy,* ed. John J. Stuhr (Oxford University Press, 2000): 646–52. The selection that follows from Bowne's 1908 book *Personalism* carries the title, "The Failure of Impersonalism" (see pp. 653–66). Bowne discovers this failure by way of a critique of naturalism, pp. 653–61, as well as a critique of idealism, pp. 661–65.
5. The recuperation of metaphysics inside analytic philosophy can be called the move from Quine to Kripke.
6. Daniel Stolar, Physcialism (Routledge, 2010), p. 2.
7. Ibid., p. 10.
8. Ibid., p. 13 ff.
9. Ibid., p. 26.
10. Ibid., p. 13.
11. Ibid., p. 15.
12. Karl Marx, "Private Property and Communism," in *The Marx-Engels Reader*, ed. R. Tucker (Norton, 1978), p. 90.
13. In this chapter, I avoid two extreme views: the view that the social teaching of the Church is unrelated and even diametrically opposed to "Marxism" (whatever "Marxism" might prove to be or mean); and the view that "liberation theology" is a "Marxist" wolf in sheep's clothing. In the mid-twentieth century, avoiding these extremes was the point of departure for a "Marx/Christian dialogue" (see Aptheker and McGovern), related to the "third-way" approach of Catholic social teaching. Assuming the way is still open, there are grounds for a contemporary iteration of this "dialogue" with *Laudato si'*. The object of Pope Francis's critique is "the globalization of the technocratic paradigm" (#106–14). His source for the "technocratic paradigm" is Guardini (see notes 83, 84, 85, 87, 88, and 92). In other words, the object of his critique is not capitalism and Marx is not his source. Nevertheless, in the section on "Politics and Economy in Dialogue for Human Fulfillment" (#189–98), in Pope Francis's characterization of the "economy," we can discern several "Marx-like" features, including the following: (1) it is an economy "[where] profits alone count" (#190); (2) it is an economy in which "economic variables . . . assign to products a value that does not necessarily correspond to their real worth" (#189; and see also #190); (3) it is an economy liable to crises of "overproduction" and "productive" and "financial" bubbles (#189); (4) it entails "a magical conception of the market" (#190); (5) Pope Francis calls for the development of a "new economy" (#189); (6) this "new economy" would open "a path of productive development, which is more creative and better directed" and which "could correct

the present disparity between excessive technological investment in consumption and insufficient investment in resolving urgent problems facing the human family. . . . Productive diversification offers the fullest possibilities to human ingenuity to create and innovate, while at the same time protecting the environment and creating more sources of employment. Such creativity would be a worthy expression of our most noble human qualities, for we would be striving intelligently, boldly and responsibly to promote a sustainable and equitable development within the context of a broader concept of quality of life. On the other hand, to find ever new ways of despoiling nature, purely for the sake of new consumer items and quick profit, would be, in human terms, less worthy and creative, and more superficial" (#192). Finally (7): "For new models of progress to arise, there is a need to change 'models of global development'; this will entail responsible reflection on the meaning of the economy and its goals with an eye to correcting its malfunctions and misapplications.' It is not enough to balance, in the medium term, the protection of nature with financial gain, or the preservation of the environment with progress. Halfway measures simply delay the inevitable disaster. Put simply, it is a matter of redefining our notion of progress. A technological and economic development which does not leave in its wake a better world and an integrally higher quality of life cannot be considered progress" (#194; internal quotation from Pope Benedict XVI, *Message for the 2010 World Day of Peace*).

14. For the sake of greater precision, it's necessary to distinguish between "ontological" and "methodological" naturalism. See David Papineau, "Naturalism," in the *Stanford Encyclopedia of Philosophy* (2015). We'll return to the term "naturalism" below. Concerning physicalism, Stoljar writes, "The word 'physicalism' was introduced into philosophy in the 1930s by Otto Neurath and Rudolf Carnap, both of whom were key members of the Vienna Circle . . . . It is not at all clear that Neurath and Carnap conceived of physicalism in the same way, but one thesis that is often attributed to them . . . is the linguistic thesis that every statement is synonymous with (i.e. it is equivalent in meaning with) some physical statement. On the other hand, 'materialism' is traditionally construed as denoting, not a linguistic thesis, but a metaphysical one, i.e. it tells us about the nature of the world as such. Hence Neurath and Carnap had a good reason for distinguishing physicalism (a linguistic thesis) from materialism (a metaphysical thesis). Moreover, this reason was compounded by the fact that, according to official positivist doctrine, metaphysics is nonsense" (p. 10). Similar considerations could be extended to Russell's neutral monism, Quine's neopragmatism, or Davidson's anomalous monism. Stoljar also argues that there is a sense in which "physicalism" and "idealism" amount to the same thing; that is, the claim that "everything is physical" is not only consistent with but tantamount to the claim that "everything is mental," as, for example, in "mind-brain identity theory" (see pp. 43–44).

15. Let's define "economism" as the view that all solutions to human problems are subordinate to the economy and its requirements; in philosophical anthropology, it is also the reduction of a "person" to *homo economicus*.

16. Marx's way of putting this point is to write, "But *man* is not an abstract being, squatting outside the world." See "Contribution to the Critique of Hegel's *Philosophy of Right*: Introduction," in Tucker, ed., p. 53.

17. See Section IV below.

18. *Laudato si'* #101–36.

19. See Aldo Leopold, *A Sand County Almanac* 2/e (Oxford University Press, 1987; orig. 1949).

20. *Laudato si'* #89–92.

21. *Laudato si'* 137–62.

22. On her website, "The Great Story," which promises "An Immense Journey: Religious Naturalism and the Great Story" (2003), Connie Barlow includes Leopold in her "Tribute to Julian Huxley, Paul Martin, Aldo Leopold, Thomas Berry, Brian Swimme, Annie Dillard, and Loren Eiseley"; she also includes Charles Darwin, James Lovelock, and Edward O. Wilson in her pantheon (http://thegreatstory.org/Reli giousNaturalism.html, retrieved December 4, 2018).

23. Leopold, *A Sand County Almanac* 2/e, pp. 202–203.

24. Note the family resemblance to the principle of subsidiarity, which is basic to Catholic social teaching.

25. For John Dewey's humanistic naturalism or naturalistic humanism, see *Experience and Nature* (Dover Publications, 1925); and *The Later Works*, v.1, esp. Ch. 1, "Experience and Philosophic Method" (Southern Illinois University Press, 1981), pp. 10–41. I will argue below that while Dewey is a naturalist, he is not a physicalist or a materialist.

26. The "Marxism" in the background of this chapter is "Marxist-Humanism" rather than Marxism-Leninism and its offshoots. Marxist-Humanism is based on Raya Dunayevskaya's attempt to "recreate the original Marxism of Marx for our age."

27. See Marx, "Private Property and Communism," in Tucker, ed., p. 89; emphasis Marx's. He also writes, "But man is not merely a natural being: he is a *human* natural being. That is to say, he is a being for himself. Therefore he is a *species being* and has to confirm and manifest himself as such a being both in his being and in his knowing" (p. 116).

28. Marx, *Economic and Philosophic Manuscripts of 1844*, in Tucker, ed., p. 115. While it would be odd to qualify Marx's humanistic form of naturalism as "religious," we have already noted that Leopold can be characterized as a "religious naturalist." Concerning Dewey, among the best book-length treatments of his thought as a whole is Steven C. Rockefeller's, *John Dewey: Religious Faith and Democratic Humanism* (Columbia University Press, 1991). Rockefeller characterizes Dewey's outlook as a "religious humanism." Arguably a "religious humanism" and a "religious naturalism" would be obverse and reverse of the same coin, on the premise of a humanistic naturalism or a naturalistic humanism.

29. Ibid., p. 85.

30. Marx, *Manifesto of the Communist Party*, in Tucker, ed., p. 491; emphasis added. On a Lonerganian interpretation of the meaning of Marx's conditional claim, "the free development of *each*" is the condition of a "conditioned," "the free development of *all*." In this formulation of an "each/all" relation, "each" takes priority over "all." Also see William James, "The Types of Philosophic Thinking" (1909) in Stuhr, ed., pp. 151–61; James distinguishes between the "*each*-form" from the "*all*-form" in his decades-long dispute with his Harvard colleague and friend, Josiah Royce.

31. Marx, *Critique of the Gotha Program*, in Tucker, ed., p. 531.

32. Leopold hails from Wisconsin. Dewey, a Vermonter, took his first job at the University of Michigan. During his tenure at Michigan, he also took a sabbatical year

at the University of Minnesota; then he moved on to the University of Chicago, where he first established his enduring philosophical reputation and became famous.

33. See Amy E. Wendling, *The Ruling Ideas: Bourgeois Political Concepts* (Lexington Books, 2012). Wendling devotes a chapter apiece to the bourgeois form of these ideas and a Marxian critique.

34. See Marx, *The German Ideology*, in Tucker, ed., p. 172.

35. Wendling, *The Ruling Ideas*, p. 118.

36. Since Lenin used the term, "economism," in connection with his critique of a tendency called "legal Marxism," perhaps it should be said that my use may be called "Marxist," but not necessarily "Marxist-Leninist." The principal feature to notice for our purposes is the reductive nature of an economistic outlook.

37. Wendling, *The Ruling Ideas*, pp. 66–67.

38. Ibid., pp. 18–19.

39. Ibid., pp. 93–98.

40. Ibid., p. 29.

41. Marx, *Manifesto of the Communist Party*, in Tucker, ed., p. 476.

42. Jacques Maritain, included in *The Range of Reason* (Charles Scribner's Sons, 1952), p. 167; emphasis added. Also see my essay, Thomas Jeannot, "A Post-Secular Exchange: Jacques Maritain, John Dewey, and Karl Marx," in *Philosophical Theory and the Universal Declaration of Human Rights*, ed. W. Sweet (Ottawa University Press, 2003), pp 83–95.

43. See Papineau, "Naturalism."

44. Stoljar defines "Hume's dictum" in his "Glossary" as follows: "The thesis that there are no necessary connections between distinct existences." Hume's dictum, in effect, rules out the theory of internal relations. It is close to Russell's "doctrine of external relations" as he directs it against F. H. Bradley in "Logical Atomism," included complete in F. E. Baird and W. Kaufmann, eds., *Twentieth-Century Philosophy* 3/e (Prentice Hall, 2003; orig.1924), pp. 67–79. Russell writes, "What, then, can we mean by the doctrine of external relations? Primarily this, that a relational proposition is not, in general, logically equivalent formally to one or more subject-predicate propositions. Stated more precisely: Given a relational propositional function 'xRy,' it is not in general the case that we can find predicates α, β, γ, such that, for all values of x and y, xRy is equivalent to $x\alpha$, $y\beta$, $(x, y) \gamma$ (where (x, y) stands for the whole consisting of x and y), or to any one or two of these. This, and this only, is what I mean to affirm when I assert the doctrine of external relations; and this, clearly, is at least part of what Mr. Bradley denies when he asserts the doctrine of internal relations" (p. 74; italics omitted).

45. See Borden Parker Bowne, *Personalism* (New York: Houghton Mifflin, 1908).

46. *Democracy Now*, (02/23/18).

47. See Richard Hofstadter, "The Paranoid Style in American Politics," *Harpers* (November, 1964).

48. Novak passed away on February 17, 2017.

49. See Michael Novak, "Foreword," *Pope Francis and the Caring Society* (Independent Institute, 2017), pp. xix–xxvii (retrieved from http://www.independent.org/pdf/book_excerpts/Foreword_Novak.pdf, October 4, 2018).

50. In the second German edition of Volume One of *Capital* in 1872; see Marx, *Capital* 1, trans. Ben Fowkes (Penguin, 1976), pp. 102–103.

51. See Marx, *The Marx-Engels Reader*, pp. 110–11.

52. A quick observation: there is no chapter in the introductory physics textbook explaining why physics is a science; but there is typically a chapter in the introductory economics textbook explaining why economics is a science.

53. See Max Horkheimer, "Traditional and Critical Theory" (1937).

54. Dewey, *Experience and Nature*, p. 359. Dewey also maintains this perspective in the famous manuscript he lost in a cab in 1947 (painstakingly reconstructed by Philip Deen from manuscripts dated mainly from 1941–1942), *Unmodern Philosophy and Modern Philosophy* (Southern Illinois University Press, 2012), p. 143.

55. The physicalist program confers explanatory priority on an abstract, modal-logical explanation and demotes the presuppositions of everyday life to a subordinate position. A personalist resolution thesis, by contrast, confers explanatory priority, not on conceptual models, but on the presuppositions of everyday life themselves, to which any merely abstract model is philosophically subordinate.

56. In *Experience and Nature*, Dewey distances himself from physicalism; see, for example, pp. 143, 180, 189–90, 195–96, 200–201, and 228–29). For concerns most relevant to this chapter, see "Appendix XIII," pp. 356–59.

57. See Michael Löwy, "Laudato Si—The Pope's Anti-Systemic Encyclical," *Monthly Review* 67 (December 2015).

58. *Laudato si'*, #175.

59. See note 49 above.

60. For example, see "Paul Ryan and Ayn Rand," *The Washington Post* (August 13, 2012).

61. *Laudato si'*, #196.

62. The "theology of the body" refers to a series of 129 lectures given by John Paul II between 1979 and 1984. Despite the controversial nature of his teaching on human sexuality, marriage and family life, and reproductive rights, his deep insight concerns the immanence of the divine in the human, which is the theological key to self-transcendence. The traditional Catholic way of putting this is that the Holy Spirit is "indwelling" and our bodies are "temples of the Holy Spirit."

63. See J. Maritain, *The Rights of Man and Natural Law* (New York: Charles Scribner's Sons, 1943), p. 7.

64. See J. Maritain, *The Collected Works of Jacques Maritain* v. 11, *Integral Humanism, Freedom in the Modern World, & A Letter on Independence* (University of Notre Dame Press, 1996), pp. 74–79.

65. Ibid., pp. 74–75.

66. Ibid., pp. 75–77.

67. Ibid., p. 79 (emphasis added). Whereas Novak et al. make "spiritual things" depend on a capitalist success story.

68. Martin Luther King, *The Essential Writings and Speeches of Martin Luther King, Jr.* (HarperSanFrancisco, 1986), p. 240.

69. Ibid., pp. 231–44.

BIBLIOGRAPHY

Bergoglio, Jorge Mario. *Laudato si': On Care for Our Common Home.* http://w2.vatican.va/content/dam/francesco/pdf/encyclicals/documents/papa-francesco_20150524_enciclica-laudato-si_en.pdf.

Bowne, Borden Parker. *Personalism.* New York: Houghton Mifflin, 1908.

Dewey, John. *Experience and Nature.* Dover Publications, 1925.

Dewey, John. *The Later Works,* v.1, esp. Ch. 1, "Experience and Philosophic Method." Southern Illinois University Press, 1981.

Dewey, John. *Unmodern Philosophy and Modern Philosophy.* Carbondale: Southern Illinois University Press, 2012.

Jeannot, Thomas. "A Post-Secular Exchange: Jacques Maritain, John Dewey, and Karl Marx." In *Philosophical Theory and the Universal Declaration of Human Rights,* edited by W. Sweet, 83–95. Ottawa University Press, 2003.

King, Martin Luther. *The Essential Writings and Speeches of Martin Luther King, Jr.* San Francisco, CA: Harper, 1986.

Leopold, Aldo. *A Sand County Almanac* 2/e. Oxford, UK: Oxford University Press, [1949] 1987.

Löwy, Michael. "Laudato Si—The Pope's Anti-Systemic Encyclical." *Monthly Review* 67 (December 2015).

Maritain, Jacques. *The Collected Works of Jacques Maritain* v. 11: *Integral Humanism, Freedom in the Modern World, & A Letter on Independence.* Notre Dame, IN: University of Notre Dame Press, 1996.

Maritain, Jacques. *The Range of Reason.* New York: Charles Scribner's Sons, 1952.

Maritain, Jacques. *The Rights of Man and Natural Law.* New York: Charles Scribner's Sons, 1943.

Marx, Karl. *Capital 1.* Translated by Ben Fowkes. New York: Penguin, 1976.

Marx, Karl. "Private Property and Communism." In *The Marx-Engels Reader,* edited by R. Tucker, 81–93. Norton, 1978.

Novak, Michael. "Foreword." In *Pope Francis and the Caring Society.* Independent Institute, 2017. https://www.independent.org/pdf/book_excerpts/Foreword Novak.pdf.

Rockefeller, Steven C. *John Dewey: Religious Faith and Democratic Humanism.* New York: Columbia University Press, 1991.

Stoljar, Daniel. *Physcalism.* New York: Routledge, 2010.

Stuhr, John J. ed. *Pragmatism and Classical American Philosophy.* Oxford University Press, 2000.

Wendling, Amy E. *The Ruling Ideas: Bourgeois Political Concepts.* Lanham, MD: Lexington Books, 2012.

Chapter 12

The Ethics of Sustainability, Instrumental Reason, and the Goodness of Nature

From the Abstractions of Despair Back to the Things Themselves

Daniel O'Dea Bradley

CONTEMPORARY ENVIRONMENTAL ETHICS: CONTEXTUALIZING THE PROBLEM OF INTRINSIC VALUE

Environmental philosophy is always already environmental ethics. It is allied, both conceptually and historically, with the rise of "applied philosophy" and the renewed desire that our intellectual work help change the world for the better. As one of the early pioneers of the movement J. Baird Callicott puts it, "The post-sixties 'applied' movement in late twentieth-century philosophy has been an attempt, on the part of many academic philosophers to descend from the ivory tower and directly engage real-world issues." Motivated by this desire, at "the advent of business ethics, bio-medical ethics, animal welfare ethics, engineering ethics, and environmental ethics . . . an attempt was deliberately made to reorient philosophy so as to apply its rich heritage of theory and powerful methods of argument to illuminate and help solve real-world problems."[1] This hunger to have an impact on society and the world gives environmental philosophy much of its dynamism and intensity. However, in my view, along with that of Callicott and most of the other early practitioners of the discipline, the hope that philosophy would work to effect progress on environmental issues, and thus to radically change our world, was intimately interwoven with the hope that our experience of nature as threatened would teach us important truths about ourselves, the world, and

193

our relationship to it; that is, the environmental movement would change philosophy as much as it would change the world.

It seemed that the prospect of loss—the loss of species, the degradation of habitat, the destruction of ecosystems, the pollution of rivers and lakes, and so on—was teaching us something about the nature of what we were losing that had not been noticed before in modern Western philosophy. For some thinkers, this dawning environmental awareness challenged the exclusion of plants and other non-sentient beings from moral concern in deontology and utilitarianism. For some, it challenged the nominalism of modernity by recognizing not only individuals but kinds or species as ontologically significant. For some, it challenged the substance metaphysics of modernity by recognizing not only things but ecosystems and other relations between things as fundamental. These challenges to modernity[2] overlapped in various ways in different thinkers, but there was a shared sense that the core realization of the new environmental philosophy was an axiological one; put negatively, the more-than-human world does not have merely instrumental value derived from its possible uses for humanity. Put dialectically, challenging the anthropocentrism that had dominated recent thinking allowed us to see the natural world as intrinsically worthy of appreciation, thereby opening grand vistas of value, beyond the instrumental, that had been forgotten or never discovered by modern philosophy. So, while early environmental philosophers certainly wanted to bring the tools they had gained in their philosophical training to bear on environmental issues, it was a two-way relation in which they had perhaps even higher hopes for what their engagements with nature would do to transform their discipline. This meant that environmental philosophy would be about changing policies, but also about changing ourselves and our relation to nature. For the early environmental philosophers, including Arne Næss, J. Baird Callicott, Richard Routley, John Cobb, Gary Snyder, Wendell Berry and their forerunners John Muir, Aldo Leopold, Rachel Carson, and others, there was great sadness at environmental loss and urgency in the need to protect ecosystems, but there was also great purpose and meaning in finding ourselves in a world that was a home, threatened as that home was, and in the vocation of trying to give a philosophical account of the value they found in nature.

From the late 1960s and throughout the 1970s, it seemed as if the energy and enthusiasm behind the environmental movement, as manifest both among academics and the culture at large, would lead to a radical overturning of the atomistic ontology and anthropocentric axiology of much of modernity. These thinkers found the modern assumption that meaning was a product of human acts of valuation intolerably lonely, for it meant that the universe was a cold, dark, and meaningless place until imbued with *our* meaning. This had made the world transparent to our will and given us nothing to which we could respond outside of ourselves. But now it seemed that philosophy would be forced to confront the startling but vivid (re)discovery of the intrinsic value of nature and thus be able to reestablish a less alienated relationship to it.

There was considerable diversity among the early environmental philosophers about how to give an account of this value that we discover in nature, rather than impose with our own imperialistic acts of valuation. For example, Næss drew inspiration from Spinoza and Hinduism, Rolston from Incarnational Christianity, Cobb from Whitehead and process philosophy, Berry from agrarianism, Routley and Callicott from the sentiments of belonging to a biotic community evoked by ecology, and Snyder and others from Buddhism. But they all agreed that the (re)discovery of "intrinsic value" was the great breakthrough of environmental thinking. In reflecting back on the significance of what his generation had achieved, Callicott is clear; "At the heart of the new discourse is the concept of intrinsic value in nature."[3] For Callicott this means that while environmental philosophy is an applied ethics like others, it is also very different, for it not only puts philosophical tools to work, but in the process radically reframes philosophical thinking.

> In environmental ethics, the concept of *intrinsic value* in nature functions similarly to way the concept of *human rights* functions in *social ethics*. Human rights has had enormous pragmatic efficacy in social ethics and policy. The prospective adoption of the Earth Charter by the General Assembly of the United Nations may have an impact on governmental environmental policy and performance similar to the impact on governmental social policy and behaviour of the adoption by the same body in 1948 of the Universal Declaration of Human Rights.[4]

On this reading environmental philosophy begins with an experience of the goodness and value of the natural world which nourishes and inspires a full life (intellectual, political, social, etc.), a life of praxis that moves back and forth between trying to protect the value it discovers and trying to develop an account which allows us both to celebrate that value and to make better decisions about competing claims. The comparison with Kant is instructive. Not only does Kantian ethics inspire us to overcome racism, gender inequality, and so on, it does so because it is *first* an inspiring expression of praise for the intrinsic value of the human being (the starry skies above and the moral law within) that cascades over into, and is supported by, a humanism in the arts, interwoven with a new respect for human reason and human rights in politics, philosophy, and religion, by-way-of-which superstition and oppression would be overcome. Similarly, not only does environmental ethics inspire us to overcome, for example, habitat destruction; it is an expression of praise for the intrinsic value of the diversity of life and the integrity of ecosystems, which cascades over into and is supported by a poetic aesthetics of nature interwoven with a new respect for the more-than-human world in politics, philosophy, and religion, by-way-of-which anthropocentrism would be overcome.

To the disappointment of the first generation of environmental philosophers, these ambitious hopes for the transformation of society and philosophy have not come to fruition. In some ways that failure should not be too surprising. It took a full 200 years after Kant for Germany to definitively embrace a political and social order based on respect for the dignity of every human person, and while Kant was writing close to the first early American experiment with the ideas of a liberal political order, it would take two more centuries to profess the equal standing of women and people of color in the United States. Social transformation takes a long time as the metaphysics and philosophical anthropology of one epoch slowly gives way to another. What is more worrying is that there has been considerable pushback against the idea of the intrinsic value of nature *from within the community of environmental ethicists, itself.* From the beginnings in the 1970s, there had always been a minority of thinkers, including John Passmore and others, who believed that the anthropocentric tools and frameworks of modern philosophy were perfectly adequate for addressing the environmental crisis. Nonetheless they constituted a small minority and were motivated by a prior commitment to Kantianism that they hoped to continue to apply to environmental problems.

Since that time, two succeeding movements have arisen from a more internal connection to the development of mainstream applied environmentalism itself and with successively more urgency and influence. The first is a movement called "environmental pragmatism" that arose in the 1980s and 1990s. The second, "ecomodernism," arose in the early 2000s and has been gathering steam in the last decade.

In this chapter, I introduce environmental pragmatism and ecomodernism partly in light of my ongoing polemic in defense of the intrinsic value of the natural world as the root of environmental ethics, but also, more positively, to highlight two important and interwoven themes that they are right to suggest have not been dealt with adequately in environmental philosophy, namely: despair in the face of climate change and the pessimism of our recent focus on *l'homme incapable,* a philosophical anthropology with an excessive emphasis on the negative aspects of human existence—limited knowledge, finitude, selfishness, apathy, violence, greed, and the intersectionality of environmental destruction, sexism, and racism. Thus, meeting their challenge, and thereby finding a credible way to defend the intrinsic value of nature, will require both dealing with despair and making a place for the creative potential of human beings and their positive experiences of vitality and ability. We are helped in this task by looking at the twin virtues of hope and joy as developed in the work of Brian Treanor in his criticism of what is lacking in contemporary philosophy, although it is important to note from the beginning that this will be a tragic-hope and a tragic-joy that retains a place for the heart-rending losses and the wretchedness that are also part of the human condition—aspects forgotten by the ecomodernists in their hasty inversion of twentieth-century pessimism.

Certainly there are good reasons for despair and wretchedness, on both the practical and theoretical level. Chief among these reasons is the looming threat of climate change. Our newspapers and documentaries are full of reports of imminent widespread death through increasingly violent storms, drought, and wildfire (too much and too little water in the wrong place at the wrong time) and the general disruption of ecosystems and loss of habitat. But as bad as this natural destruction will be, this is not merely a natural disaster. What Stephen Gardiner's book *A Perfect Moral Storm: The Ethical Tragedy of Climate Change* reveals particularly well is that our underlying sense is not only despair about the prospects for so much of life on the planet. It is a despair about our moral competence as we not only cause, but fail to find a way to stop *continuing to cause*, this catastrophe. As Rolston puts it in his review of the book, "Gardiner's challenge is to make sense of a tragic mess at global scales, one with impending disaster. This is something like doing ethics in a hurricane, only this natural disaster has anthropocentric causes."[5] It is one thing to commit a moral crime and to be repentant about it. It is quite another to commit a moral crime, realize what we are doing, and nonetheless continue right on ahead. Further, the reasons for our failure are quite unflattering for a moral anthropology. Because the effects of the disaster will be felt most by those who contribute least—future generations, poorer countries, and the poorest within each country—"there is no one to properly hold us accountable."[6] And so we do nothing to avert the tragedy.

There are also political reasons to despair of a transformation of our philosophy around a new recognition of the intrinsic value of nature. Rather than reorienting a new ethical-political reality the way the concept of human rights has done, the ideas of deep ecology seem to have crumbled under a renewal of the older anthropocentric ethics. As Bill Devall writes in "The Deep, Long-Range Ecology Movement," "the major world environmental conferences held during the 1990s, including the *Rio Summit on Development and the Environment* (1992) and the *Kyoto Conference on Global Warming* (1998) presented documents that retreated from deep ecological statements found in the *World Charter for Nature*"[7] and instead promoted the idea of the "sustainable use of natural resources,"[8] thereby returning to an anthropocentric emphasis on the need to preserve the natural world as a collection of instrumental values for the use of human beings.

Increasing moral and political despair at our inability to unite around a conception of the intrinsic value of nature and avert the disasters of global warming lie at the heart of the criticisms of the traditional environmental movement. Already in the 1980s, a new defense of the anthropocentric ground of environmental ethics had been mounted by the "environmental pragmatists." This was spearheaded by young philosophers such as Andrew Light and Bryan Norton who explicitly linked the failure of the environmental movement to its insistence on the intrinsic value of nature. Norton begins his overview of the discipline in "Integration or Reduction: Two Approaches to Environmental Values" by claiming that "environmental ethics has been dominated in its first twenty years by questions of axiology . . . an assessment of the contributions of environmental ethics to environmental policy in its first two decades is *accordingly* bleak."[9] His solution is clear; "the assumption that environmental ethics must be nonanthropocentric in order to be adequate is mistaken" for "an environmental ethic cannot be derived . . . from the rights or interests of nonhumans."[10] The thrust of his argument, developed more fully via the "convergence hypothesis" in his book, *Unity among Environmentalists*, is that we all basically agree about what needs to be done to protect the environment. Thus, we should stop wasting our time on abstract metaphysical debates about the intrinsic value of nature and put our intelligence, intensity, and philosophical training to use in working out policy positions that do the most good.

There is a large, and in my view compelling, body of literature responding to these claims made by environmental pragmatists.[11] For my contribution to this book, I want to turn a little more closely to "ecopragmatism's" younger cousin, "ecomodernism," for two reasons. First, environmental philosophy has always wanted to engage those outside the academy who are working on the ground as activists, policy makers, journalists, and so on—a desire pursued perhaps even more intently by the postphenomenology movement with which this publication series is associated—and ecomodernism is comprised mostly of nonacademics who are working in precisely these positions. Second, and relatedly, because ecomodernism is housed outside the academy, it poses new challenges that can be useful in renewing the sedimented and, therefore, narrowed, tendencies within academic thinking—even if I hope we find many of their solutions inadequate.

Ecomodernism shares certain traits with ecopragmatism.[12] Both are rooted in a deep existential despair at the failure of the environmental movement, and both blame the emphasis on the intrinsic value of nature for inspiring an anti-humanism that is the cause for this failure. On the first page of the movement's inaugural essay, "The Death of Environmentalism" (2004), Shellenberger and Nordhaus write, "The environmental movement is no longer capable of dealing with the world's most serious ecological crisis. Over the last 15 years environmental foundations and organizations have invested hundreds of millions of dollars into combating global warming. We have strikingly little to show for it."[13] Similarly, an important 2012 article by Kareiva, Marvier, and Lalasz opens abruptly with the line: "By its own measures, conservation is failing."[14] We could repeat these citations *ad naseum*; throughout the literature, we hear the refrain: the old environmental philosophy was able to motivate the preservation of beautiful places in the park system and to clean up our rivers and air—but it is impotent in the face of global warming. Thus, the need for a more human-centered approach less at odds with our contemporary values that will be more pragmatically successful in effecting political solutions for reducing human activities that release carbon dioxide and methane into our atmosphere.

Despite these common motivations, there are also significant differences between ecomodernism and ecopragmatism. The ecomodernists accept that a more human-centered approach, in contrast to the old wilderness-centered approach, will lead to *different* policy goals, thus refuting Norton's convergence hypothesis. In particular, the ecomodernists suggest we need to spend less resources preserving wilderness and more on creating jobs in the green-energy sector and integrating nature into our urban areas. As Kareiva, Marvier, and Lalasz explain, "21st century conservation is changing. Conservationists have taken steps to become more 'people friendly' and to attend more seriously to working landscapes."[15] They end claiming that "the conservation we will get by embracing development and advancing human well-being will almost certainly not be the conservation that was imagined in its early days."[16]

Further, the ecomodernists disagree with the ecopragmatist claim that in order to be more effective we need to stop talking about theoretical questions of value, about which we disagree, and instead focus on policy questions, on which we do agree. Rather, it is on pragmatic grounds, themselves, that the ecomodernists argue we must turn to questions of what makes environmental policies worth pursuing, for they argue that what effectively drives political action is not policy considerations but what Nordhaus and Shellenberger call "vision and values." They directly link this to their assessment of the movement as a whole—and its failure. "The environmental movement's technical policy orientation has created a kind of myopia: everyone is looking for short-term policy pay-off. We could find nobody who is crafting political proposals that, through the vision and values they introduce, create the context for electoral and legislative victories down the road."[17] This call to embrace "values" is related to the rejection of the convergence hypothesis, for Nordhaus and Shellenberger recognize that these more theoretical discussions will create disagreement, but that the price to pay for avoiding conflict is the inability to present a movement that has the motivation to produce any real political success; "Political proposals that provide a long-term punch by their very nature set up political conflicts and controversy on terms that advance the environmental movement's transformative vision and values. But many within the environmental movement are uncomfortable thinking about [this conflict]."[18]

The ecomodernists are right that for a long time environmentalists have been far too heavy-handed in scolding people and demanding policies that restrict human freedom and activity while providing no moving vision that would inspire us to want to make those sacrifices. This gloom has colored all aspects of our understanding of ourselves and our relation to nature. Every *National Geographic* article and even every children's nature show and zoo exhibit seem unrelentingly full of despair, a despair that the ecomodernists are right to worry yields nothing but hopelessness and inaction.

According to ecomodernists, this nihilism of despair is problematic first of all not as a metaphysical question but as an applied problem, a stumbling block to achieving progress in achieving legislative victories in combating climate change. Further, this is a direct response to despair in the face of climate change—and the apathy that despair breeds. As Shellenberger and Nordhaus put it, "Talking about the millions of jobs that will be created by accelerating our transition to a clean energy economy offers more than a good defense against industry attacks: it's a frame that moves the environmental movement away from apocalyptic global warming scenarios that tend to create feelings of helplessness and isolation among would-be supporters."[19]

As always, however, applied questions of strategy and policy are interwoven with our most fundamental understanding of reality and our place in it. Kareiva, Marvier, and Laslasz argue that beginning in the 1970s and 1980s, focusing on the fragility of nature became a ploy to convince people of the need for environmental policy. But they go on to suggest that this threat of total collapse of "spaceship earth" has failed as a practical motivator for driving environmental policy *and* has blinded us to the truth about the resilience of nature. For example, "Books have been written about the collapse of cod in Georges Bank, yet recent trawl data show the biomass of cod has recovered to pre-collapse levels. It's doubtful that books will be written about the cod recovery since it does not play well to an audience somehow addicted to stories of collapse and environmental apocalypse."[20] This is just one of many examples that for them point to the idea that once we are set free from our ideological blinders, we will see that nature is much less fragile than we have tended to suppose.

For these writers, and for ecomodernists in general, the conclusion of this reorientation away from paralyzing despair is a new humanism that celebrates the creative potential of the human and the resilience of nature and produces a political agenda that would shift environmental policy work away from biodiversity and toward cultivating a thriving natural world that fulfills human needs.

> If there is no wilderness, if nature is resilient rather than fragile, and if people are actually part of nature and not the original sinners who caused our banishment from Eden . . . [then] Conservation should seek to support and inform the right kind of development—development by design done with the importance of nature to thriving economies foremost in mind.[21]

Shellenberger and Nordhaus are even more insistent on the way that this new "vision- and values-oriented" strategy for achieving real results in environmental policy will lead to a rethinking of our philosophical anthropology. They explain their approach thus: "Our strategy was to create something inspiring. Something that would remind people of the American dream: that we are a can-do people capable of achieving great things when we put our minds to it. [Our institute's] focus on big investments into clean energy, transportation and efficiency is part of a hopeful and patriotic story that we are all in this economy together."[22] For the ecomodernists this revised, more positive, philosophical anthropology that would undergird a renewed environmentalism is closely tied to a return to classical liberalism in economics. In the "Death of Environmentalism" we hear that "the first wave of environmentalism was framed around conservation and the second around regulation . . . . We believe the third wave will be framed around investment."[23] Similarly, Kareiva, Marvier, and Lalasz tell us, "Instead of scolding capitalism, conservationists should partner with corporations in a science-based effort to integrate the value of nature's benefits into their operations and cultures. Instead of pursuing the protection of biodiversity for biodiversity's sake, a new conservation should seek to enhance those natural systems that benefit the widest number of people."[24]

There is a great deal that is correct, and indeed a needed corrective, in this ecomodernism, and I agree that economic questions have been neglected by environmentalists, thus impoverishing the project. However, like its ecopragmatist forerunners, it still misses much of the greatest promise within the environmental movement. The issue comes to a sharp focus over what we mean by the "Anthropocene." This word is at the forefront of the thinking of the ecomodernists and appears in the titles of some of the movement's leading books and articles, including *Love Your Monsters: Postenvironmentalism and the Anthropocene*, (a collection edited by Shellenberger and Nordhaus in 2009); Kareivera's article, "Conservation in the Age of the Anthropocene" (2012); and *An Ecomodernist Manifesto: A manifesto to use humanity's extraordinary powers in service of creating a good Anthropocene* (signed by eighteen leaders of the movement in 2015), among others.

Kareivera gives us a good sense of how their understanding of the term is related to the call for a rethinking of the environmental movement: "Scientists have coined a name for our era—the Anthropocene—to emphasize that we have entered a new geological era in which *humans dominate* every flux and cycle of the planet's ecology and geochemistry."[25] This reveals a problematic constellation of ideas about science, economics, and a dualist human anthropology, by-way-of-which ecomodernism could be taken to support the worst excesses of Cartesian modernity, the very ideas the early environmentalists thought would be undermined by a bourgeoning love of the natural world. It begins to look as if the humanist strands that celebrate human creativity can be reduced to a view of *homo economicus* correlated with nature understood in a "truly scientific way" as a value-free and inexhaustible supply of resources, a relation understood as one of domination. This would be to accept a Cartesian view of humbeing as the "masters and possessors of nature,"[26] an inescapable truth grounded now not only in the indubitability of metaphysical insight but in the massive inevitability of geological time. I do not have the space to rehearse the criticisms of this Cartesian view, stemming from Marx's theory of labor relations, Weber's thesis of the disenchantment of nature, or Guisani's critique of the desacralization of the material world, let alone a complete catalogue of the critics of modern alienation. Nor do I want to try to claim that there is no other possible metaphysical reading of the ecomodernists' suggestions; I hope the ample quotes above will reveal the implicit dangers phenomenologically. Rather, I want to turn directly to the twin motivations that lie at the heart of the movement—the need to deal constructively with despair over climate change and the need to develop a more positive philosophical anthropology—in order to provide a solution that addresses these real needs but provides an alternative to the ecomodernist solution that I find so disturbing. For in my view, the ecomodernists are correct to suggest that facing and addressing these lacunae will yield a transformation of the discipline. However, this need not mean giving up on the original promise that environmental ethics will overcome modernity's axiological anthropocentrism and reduction of nature to merely instrumental value. Instead we must find an alternative way of dealing with the overwhelming emphasis on despair and human brokenness that dominates contemporary thinking.

HOPE IN THE AGE OF THE ANTHROPOCENE

We find important resources for this project in Brian Treanor's attempt to redirect contemporary philosophy toward the intertwining virtues of hope and joy, without denying suffering and destruction. For Treanor, it is with a full recognition of the darkness of despair that, in response to the signs of our times, we must begin;

> Today we are faced with all the traditional reasons to despair: poverty, loneliness, tragedy, death. . . . However, heaped on top of these headline issues—or perhaps dwelling in the background—environmentally aware people discern potential catastrophes the depth, breadth and complexity of which are cause for despair even in those with generally more sanguine natures.[27]

Further, like Gardiner in *A Perfect Moral Storm* and following Ricoeur, Treanor recognizes that this epic destruction reveals not only tragic losses in nature for which we mourn, but a tragic brokenness at the heart of the human condition for which we must repent. The sixth great extinction event of our planet's history is not just *happening*, we are *causing* it. This makes the problem particularly hard to bear and is, thus, the cause of an even more intimate sense of despair. As Treanor points out, unlike most other tragedies, climate change "accelerates not when things go wrong, but when things go right."[28] As our economy grows and people are lifted out of poverty and the middle classes are given more discretionary spending, the resulting consumption all contributes to the imminent destruction of so much life on our planet. Thus, all our greatest innovation and hard work seems tainted with corruption and selfishness, and all our inability to organize a response seems to reveal a magnification of our failures, limitations, and weaknesses.

In the face of the scope of this tragedy, we are led not only to *fear* for certain bad outcomes but to *despair* of the goodness of our humanity and the meaningfulness of the world. As Treanor explains,

> When a person despairs, he or she loses faith in existence as such. Properly speaking, a person does not "despair" of the loss of a job, a home or even his or her life (though he or she may fear any of these). To despair is to come to the belief that, as Auden puts in in his *Twelve Songs*, "nothing now can ever come to any good." . . . Despair is not the consequence of the loss of any one particular being or object in the world, but rather the loss of one's orientation in the world, the loss of one's *sense* of the world.[29]

For us this despair is fundamentally a question of "applied ethics." It emerges not from abstract speculation but from a response to a particular crisis that emerges at a specific historical time and is in fact bounded by a singular (if highly complex) problematic: the destruction caused by climate change. However, as we are already beginning to see, it is also, and at the same time, an ontological or metaphysical problem in that it touches on our most fundamental understanding of ourselves and the reality we inhabit. In a footnote

Treanor explains that when he claims we have lost our sense of the world, he is using "sense" the way Czech philosopher Erazim Kohák understands it, "as a kind of foundational, global impression based on experience (and later reflection). [Thus] 'Philosophy can claim to be the *scientia generalis* because it seeks to see and articulate the sense of being as it presents itself primordially.'"[30]

As always, in its characteristic way, environmental philosophy is both an applied philosophy, tied to the most pressing concrete problems of the day, and an ontology, opening onto the deepest questions about the meaning of being. Here, however, we see a direct inversion of the way these two aspects of environmental thinking were related in the early days of the environmental awakening. For the first environmentalists, it was in working to save wilderness from development or in cleaning up our local rivers that we have experiences of the beauty and goodness of nature that vividly reveal the inadequacies of the previous mechanistic philosophies of nature and their instrumental axiologies, opening onto whole vistas of meaning never dreamed of by the philosophies they were taught in school. In those early days, the applied questions of environmental ethics were like opening windows on the old musty and cramped anthropocentric philosophies of Cartesian modernity and letting in the warm sunshine, fresh breezes, and exuberant birdsong of a spring morning. Today, the applied question (the singular, abstract, reductive question of climate change, measured in Δ °C) of environmental ethics now seems to do the opposite and to lead ineluctably to the nihilism of despair.

Treanor agrees with the ecomodernists that overcoming despair is the central problematic for an environmental philosophy facing climate change. He also agrees that the question of this overcoming is fundamentally interwoven with the question of the Anthropocene. Treanor accepts that climate change is a determinate, if complex, problem potentially amenable to concrete technical solutions (e.g., geoengineering). Nonetheless,

> precisely because climate change accelerates, magnifies and extends the Anthropocene, it also calls into question accounts of the order and meaningfulness of the world. It is both a physical threat and an existential/spiritual threat: the age of the Anthropocene is heralded by alarm at the "end of nature," the "disenchantment of the world" (Weber) or our loss of our sense of creatureliness (Treanor, Benson and Wirzba). And these narratives court despair as surely as the "death of God." Therefore, the novel and terrifying problem leads us inexorably to the mystery of the Anthropocene.[31]

Further, Treanor agrees that this move from the practical problem of despair in the face of climate change to a reassessment of our philosophical anthropology, under the heading of the Anthropocene, will involve a renewed appreciation of the positive aspects of human existence. For Treanor this involves a shift in emphasis away from the dominant themes of recent philosophy. In "Joy and the Myopia of Finitude," he argues that contemporary philosophy and literature, particularly in the European tradition, "suffers from an imbalanced temperament, an excess of 'black bile,' which takes the form of a profound melancholy."[32] This affects the tradition's reading of all of reality, but it seems to be particularly focused on a negative assessment of the human condition, leading to a preoccupation with "evil, finitude, fallenness, sin, absurdity, loss, limitation, tragedy, and the like,"[33] thus echoing what we heard above from Nordhaus, Shellenberger, Kareiva, et al.

In fact, we might say that for the first generation in the 1960s and 1970s, environmental thinking reveals the limitations of an anthropocentric modern philosophy, while for the current generation, it reveals the limitations of an anti-humanist postmodern philosophy. Nonetheless, Treanor shows us how an overcoming of despair toward a more affirmative philosophy of the human person does not force us into a return to a view of nature as a resource, the efficient use of which is to be maximized by instrumental reason and incentivized by private property rights and the distribution of commodities in free markets.

For Treanor this must begin with the cultivation of hope as a necessary response to environmental despair. As he explains, desire is an orientation toward this or that particular good, the way that fear is an orientation toward this or that particular evil. Similarly, just as despair is a general sense of the meaninglessness and negativity of being as a whole, hope is an affirmation of the meaningfulness and goodness of being. These two pairs of terms (desire-fear/ despair-hope) have a structural similarity, but an inverted existential primordiality. As Francis of Assisi pointed out so dramatically, I can only fear the thief, if I already, and more primordially, desire possession of my things. In the relation between hope and despair this relation is inverted, despair being the more primordial. "If despair is the denial of worth, hope is an affirmation that is a response to this denial; it is only in the context of the temptation to despair that we can respond with hope."[34]

As a general orientation toward reality, hope is not awaiting some definite good outcome for which we desire nor can it be defeated by the arrival of some definite evil which I fear. Rather, it is rooted in "a faith that, despite the apparent lack of worth, the untrustworthiness, the underlying tragedy of reality, there are nevertheless compelling reasons to affirm and endorse it: beauty, goodness, wonder, joy."[35] As a "faith" it is not amenable to a quantitative empirical study by which we add up all the good and evil in the universe and affirm being on the basis of the preponderance of the former over the latter. As such, Treanor says, "Where despair denies that anything is ultimately worthy, hope wagers—hermeneutically, not calculatively—that reality is worthwhile."[36] This wager, however, is not the untestable disregard for experience and reason of a "leap of faith" that we often, perhaps unfairly, associate with Kierkegaard and Pascal. As hermeneutic, it is the claim that by adopting this viewpoint, new aspects of reality will be revealed to our experience that would otherwise be foreclosed. "To focus incessantly on sorrow and suffering is to *miss something* essential about this life and this world. True, we cannot ignore the sorrow and suffering, which climate change will magnify horribly, but neither can we ignore the beauty and wonder that shine out even in lives of extreme hardship (and, given our finitude, all lives eventually come up against extreme hardship)."[37] Attuned in this way we can experience dramatic moments of the goodness of being, while still facing the tragic nature of reality. Treanor quotes from a Jack Gilbert poem, "To hear the faint sound of oars in the silence as a rowboat / comes slowly out and then goes back is truly worth / all the years of sorrow that are to come."[38]

Hope is an orientation toward the world, but as the early environmentalists remind us, it is not an attitude that we choose to adopt but is rather a response to experiences of great meaning and beauty that touch us. In fact, sometimes these moments come as a dramatic shock to our expectations and a reversal of our philosophical presuppositions, particularly when this is opened by experiences of loss. The most famous example of this comes from an account of his early days as a forest manager that Aldo Leopold gives in *A Sand County Almanac*, when he shot a wolf and, "watching the green fire die in its eyes," was moved to change from a sustainability ethic based on thinking like a resource manager to a land ethic based on "thinking like a mountain." Not many write with such poignancy as Leopold or perhaps have an encounter with nature that engenders quite such a dramatic reversal, but many environmentalists have been spurred to action when some place was threatened with development. They may not have known just how much they loved a stream or lake, forest or farmland, prairie or valley, until it was threatened with the construction of a strip mine or strip mall (which would lay the land bare as commodity for our consumption as surely as any strip club).

Thus, as Treanor notes, this recognition of the goodness of nature is not separate from a call to human action. Hope is an orientation toward the goodness and beauty of being, but as hope it involves an existential urgency that means this goodness and beauty are never guaranteed. This marks the vast gulf between the *cogito* and the *spero*. While the one is marked by indubitability, thetic self-grounding, synchrony, and abstractness, the other is marked by contingency, relationality, diachrony, and concreteness. While for the one, epistemology is first philosophy, for the other philosophy is always already contaminated with being. As Treanor puts it: "That hope consists in an assertion indicates that it is both a way of viewing things and a way of acting. . . . Therefore to hope is to adopt a certain way of being-in-the-world; it is an active, not passive, disposition. Marcel makes this clear when he notes that the affirmation of being is 'an affirmation which I *am* rather than an affir-mation which I *utter*.'"[39] This "humanism" of Treanor's shares significant affinities with the ecomodernists. It refuses an anthropology that focuses exclusively on human weakness, sinfulness, and banishment from Eden, for one that celebrates humanity's active and creative potential as a part of the natural world.

Coming at least partially from outside the academy, the ecomodernists are not burdened with the culture of staid sobriety and self-congratulatory seri-ousness that dominates those of us within it. Treanor's work is not marked by their exuberance, but it is almost as radical in its insistence that we recognize the positive aspects of life. This is particularly true if we see his essay, "Hope in the Age of the Anthropocene," as coming to its fruition in "Joy and the Myopia of Finitude." Seen in this light, it is not too strong to say that for Tre-anor the rehabilitation of the capacities of the human person is the movement from despair to hope that finally results in the movement from hope to joy. Significantly, however, while this joy involves a feeling of the plenitude of one's being and capacities, it also draws the self away from itself toward the other. This other is beautiful and radiant and thus fulfills my life in a way that goes beyond being taken hostage by Levinas's *autrui* or the constant deferral of Derrida's *tout autre est toute autre*. Nonetheless, if it is not a fetishization of absolute alterity, it is still ecstatic in a way that the ecomodernist move-ment is not, and it embeds one in relationships of responsibility, even sober obligation, not amenable to the ecomodernist agenda.

Shellenberger and Nordhaus also explicitly link ecomodernism to joy,[40] thus revealing how generational affinities can nonetheless be manifest in deeply divergent claims about reality. For them, joy draws us beyond merely material needs to the goods that satisfy higher needs. But these higher goods still remain exclusively linked to *our* needs and are conceptualized in exclu-sively instrumental terms. For Treanor, on the other hand, joy is marked by the "recognition, appreciation, and gratitude for the unwarranted goodness of being."[41] So while Treanor critiques the overemphasis on passivity and incapacity in contemporary philosophy, his anthropology of joy remains a relational and a responsive one, thus retaining an ethical orientation always already at work in his philosophy from the beginning (rather than one that will need to be analogically projected, later, onto beings like myself).

This interweaving of ontology and ethics is also maintained by the insepa-rability of an anthropology of joy in response to the goodness of being and the question of time. Treanor succinctly states the connection of these three themes in a summary of what he takes from Kohák; "(1) being is intrinsically good; (2) human being is distinguished by its ability to recognize this good-ness and its responsibility to foster it; and (3) when humans recognize this goodness, 'eternity' intersects normal time."[42]

The word eternity is put in scare quotes in order to emphasize that it refers first of all to a phenomenological description, rather than to a developed metaphysics or religion. But it is retained to point to an experience of something that draws us beyond the ordinariness of our everyday preoccupation with understanding causal sequences of events in order to procure our needs against the ravages of time—with relation to our theme this would entail the need for sustainable use of resources so that they will not *run out* and thus be unavailable to our future selves and future generations. In contrast to this utilitarian mind-set, "the order of value is revealed when we glimpse the present 'not in its relation to what preceded and what will follow it, but in its absolute being—in its relation to what, clumsily, we call eternity'"[43]

Because of this phenomenological methodology, the only way of proceeding is to point to some paradigmatic examples of this experience of the "eternal" within the temporal. For Treanor one of these comes from Michelle Serre's experience of rock climbing. In his account Serre reproduces a fairly raw experience, not yet even fully processed into ordinary grammar; "I was suddenly inundated, filled, saturated, satiated, flooded over, thunderstruck with such lofty elation, continuous . . . present in all the space of the world entire present in me. Pleroma of exultation . . . a supernatural joy."[44]

Significantly for our theme, these encounters with a fullness that transcends our ordinary experience of time are often precipitated by close participation in the natural world. A paradigmatic example in my own work comes from Janie's famous encounter with a pear tree in *Their Eyes Were Watching God*.

> It had called her to come and gaze on a mystery. From barren brown stems to glistening leaf-buds; from the leaf-buds to snowy virginity of bloom. It stirred her tremendously. How? Why? It was like a flute song forgotten in another existence and remembered again. What? How? Why? This singing she heard that had nothing to do with her ears. The rose of the world was breathing out smell. It followed her through all her waking moments and caressed her in her sleep. It connected itself with other vaguely felt matters that had struck her outside observation and buried themselves in her flesh. Now they emerged and quested about her consciousness. She was stretched on her back beneath the pear tree soaking in the alto chant of the visiting bees, the gold of the sun and the panting breath of the breeze when the inaudible voice of it all came to her.[45]

Janie encounters something dramatic in *this* pear tree. But it takes her out of her usual experience of temporality and opens onto something in which she participates as an incarnate being deep in her flesh and that makes all things quiver with beauty and goodness, but in a way normally hidden from ordinary consciousness within the flow of ordinary time.

Another paradigmatic example for Treanor comes from a meal prepared by Mrs. Ramsey that serves as one of the focal points of Virginia Woolf's *To the*

Lighthouse. Woolf draws our attention carefully to the juxtaposition of the "eternal" and the "ordinary," or rather of the eternity apparent in the ordinary when transfigured. Mrs. Ramsey's experience

> partook, she felt, carefully helping Mr. Bankes to a specially tender piece [of *boeuf en daube*] . . . that there is a coherence in things, a stability; something, she meant, is immune from change, and shines out (she glanced at the window with its ripple of reflected lights) in the face of the flowing, the fleeting, the spectral, like a ruby; so that again tonight she had the feeling she had had once today, already, of peace, of rest. Of such moments, she thought, the thing is made that endures.[46]

From *Babette's Feast* to *In Search of Lost Time*, from *A Christmas Carol* to *The Brothers Karamazov*, the meal is often an occasion for these kinds of experiences, for in the cooking and sharing of food we have one our most primordial encounters with the intersection of nature and human creativity, which is, of course, why it is one of the grounds of culture.[47] After Simone Weil, Levinas, and all the critiques of post-structuralism, the consumption of food has become a problematic theme. For Treanor, however, this passage directs our attention to an important aspect of the experience of the eternal that makes it worth tangling with the critics of eating; namely, Woolf's atheism points to the fact that these experiences are metaphysically overdetermined. Later in *To the Lighthouse*, one of guests from Mrs. Ramsey's dinner, Lily Briscoe, tries to understand the origin of these epiphanies. "She admits that the revelation had never come" and realizes that "the great revelation perhaps never did come. Instead there [are] little daily miracles, illuminations, matches struck unexpectedly in the dark; [and] here was one."[48] A phenomenology of "all things shining" does not yet even ask whether things shine with their own or a borrowed light and can thus give rise to philosophies as different as Spinozistic metaphysics, sacramental Christianity, Sufic Islam, Taoism, Heidegger's a-theistic *es gibt*, Wolff's atheistic humanism, and so and on. An environmental philosophy starting from a phenomenology of joy will never agree on a metaphysical account that explains the goodness of being. But it will start with the goodness of being.

This does not mean, however, that a phenomenology of joy is metaphysically and ethically neutral. It will reject any dualistic theories in which reality is made up of matter that is evil (Gnosticism) or at best value-free (materialism) and in which goodness therefore has to come from "spirit," primarily meaning voluntaristic acts of human valuation. Joy, as a response to goodness and beauty, brings us back to responsibility for the particular as something that is good in its being, prior to any acts of valuation. An emphasis on the intelligibility of reality can lead to a disregard for the particular being in favor of the abstract form or genus or genetic information encoding it, but goodness and beauty are irreducibly attached to the embodied being. It is not a coincidence that in the *Phaedo* Plato is drawn toward his most dualistic conception of reality, in which it seems as if a contemplation of the forms will involve a turn away from the materially individuated, while in the *Phaedrus* the philosopher sees the form of the good shining *through* the particular, physical beings it finds so beautiful.

Thus, an ethics rooted in a phenomenology of joy will be attuned to an aesthetics that remains wedded to the temporality of the particular in both its beauty and its vulnerability. Treanor suggests that this idea is revealed in the Japanese phrase *mono no aware*. "Often translated as 'the pathos of things,' the phrase expresses the bittersweet feeling associated with a brief moment of transcendent beauty, echoing in the West, Virgil's *lacrimae rerum*. Here the transcendence (beauty, goodness, eternity) and the brevity (fragile, finite in time, ephemeral) are essential to the experience."[49] This is the tension the ecomodernists miss. They are right to remind us that nature, or being itself, is not as fragile as we have recently imagined, but that insight alone tends to obscure the fragility, the beautiful fragility, of particular temporal beings and relationships—and thus to lead to a myopic insensitivity:

> The American chestnut, once a dominant tree in eastern North America, has been extinguished by a foreign disease, yet the ecosystem is surprisingly unaffected. The passenger pigeon, once so abundant that its flocks darkened the sky, went extinct, along with countless other species from the Steller's sea cow to the dodo with no catastrophic or even measurable effects.[50]

No, the destruction of so many chestnut trees and the extinction of the passenger pigeon, stellar sea cow, and dodo are in themselves not only measurable but tragic effects. This recognition should not plunge us into paralyzing despair and shame, but it should not be so quickly brushed passed in the name of the stability of nature itself. Treanor holds two truths in tension for us. On the one hand, passenger pigeons (as both individual beings and a characteristic way of being) are fragile and finite, and all individuals and the species as a whole will, indubitably, one day be gone, perhaps sooner perhaps later. Yet, on the other hand, in their transient beauty, for a moment, they shine with a precious worth that reveals the eternal goodness of being. To that beauty we are called to respond with wonder and joy—and care.

This will have consequences for our way of proceeding. Environmental philosophy ought to be rooted in a celebration of the goodness of being, a goodness that gives our lives meaning when we participate in and nurture it. This means that the ecomodernists are wrong: we ought not to abandon preservation and biodiversity as core and guiding values for environmental philosophy. This does not mean, however, that we cannot accept their legitimate criticisms about the need to be more attentive to human needs. We ought to spend more effort integrating thriving economies and good jobs into our preservation work, and we ought to focus more on preserving natural areas closer to the urban centers where a majority of our people live and from which those lower on the socio-economic ladder find it harder to escape for weekend trips to our national parks.

Maybe the ecomodernists are even right that we need to put greater emphasis on technological innovation. Perhaps a renewed sense of hope and human ability will get more people out of their cars and onto bicycles—particularly when some enterprising start-up can figure out the software to make it economically viable for Lime Bikes to be accessible throughout the city and new medical technologies to allow more people to remain healthy enough to ride bikes into their old age.

Nonetheless, this new exuberant affirmation of human creativity and potential must be rooted in something outside itself. Unmoored instrumental reason sooner or later always becomes a terror, and we seem even less well-positioned now than thirty years ago to escape instrumentalism. The great and enduring promise of environmental philosophy lies in continually reminding us that the more-than-human world has more than instrumental value—and that this is nowhere clearer than when its existence is threatened. Our anger and despair is a recognition of tragedy, that which may come to pass and that which already has, but it is also an inverted recognition of the beauty and goodness of what is threatened and being lost. This is something I feel lucky to have learned early in my intellectual life from the first great environmental philosophers. They did have tendencies to forget the creative and economic side of human nature, but we ought to hold onto their great insight that environmental thinking begins with a goodness it re-cognizes rather than imposes. For then our creative activity becomes a response to and a participation in the goodness of nature,[51] a goodness that gives rise to beings and relations that are dynamic, enduring, creative, and above all good—but also vulnerable and ultimately finite.

NOTES

1. J. Baird Callicott, "Environmental Philosophy is Environmental Activism," in *Environmental Ethics,* eds. Schmidtz and Willott (Oxford University Press, 2012), 12.

2. These challenges revealed that the individualism of modernity is not merely a moral failing but an ontological blindness that missed the importance of relations—in particular, participation in a species and participation in an ecosystem—as fundamental to a being's nature.

3. J. Baird Callicott, "The Pragmatic Power and Promise of Theoretical Environmental Ethics," *Environmental Values* 11 (2002): 4.

4. Ibid., 3.

5. Holmes Rolston, "'Review' of Gardiner's *A Perfect Moral Storm,*" in *Notre Dame Review of Books,* 2011. https://ndpr.nd.edu/news/a-perfect-moral-storm-the-ethical-tragedy-of-climate-change/.

6. Stephen Gardiner, *A Perfect Moral Storm* (Oxford, UK: Oxford University Press, 2011), 12.

7. Bill Devall, "The Deep, Long-Range Ecology Movement: 1960–2000—A Review," *Ethics & the Environment* 6, no. 1 (2001): 30.

8. Ibid., 28.

9. Bryan Norton, "Integration or Reduction," in *Environmental Pragmatism,* eds. Light and Katz (Routledge, 1996), 105–106.

10. Bryan Norton, "Environmental Ethics and Weak Anthropocentrism," *Environmental Ethics* 6 (1984): 131.

11. I have tried to contribute to this literature by arguing that phenomenology offers a way to overcome the dualism between theory and practice that mars Norton's work in: Daniel Bradley, "Fools Crow and a Phenomenology of the Value of Nature," *Presencing EPIS* 7 (2018).

12. In fact, when the movement was introduced to the world with Shellenberger and Nordhaus's 2004 publication of "The Death of Environmentalism," it made quite a stir in the media, and early discussions among these thinkers were sometimes reported as *"Ecopragmatism."* It was not until the 2012 publication of the *Ecomodernist Manifesto* that the movement coalesced around the label "ecomodernism."

13. Michael Shellenberger and Ted Nordhaus, "The Death of Environmentalism," *The Breakthrough Institute* 2004: 6. https://www.thebreakthrough.org/images/Death_of_Environmentalism.pdf.

14. Peter Kareiva, Michelle Marvier, and Robert Lalasz, "Conservation in the Age of the Anthropocene: Beyond Solitude and Fragility," *The Breakthrough Institute* 2012: 1. https://thebreakthrough.org/index.php/journal/past-issues/issue-2/conservation-in-the-anthropocene.

15. Ibid., 2.

16. Ibid., 7.

17. Shellenberger and Nordhaus, "The Death of Environmentalism," 25.

18. Ibid.

19. Ibid., 30.

20. Kareiva, Marvier, and Lalasz, "Conservation in the Age of the Anthropocene," 5.

21. Ibid., 7.

22. Shellenberger and Nordhaus, "Death of Environmentalism," 26.

23. Ibid., 28.

24. Kareiva, Marvier, and Lalasz, "Conservation in the Age of the Anthropocene," 7.

25. Ibid., 6, emphasis mine.

26. Rene Descartes, *Selected Philosophical Writings*, translated by Cottingham and Stoothoff (Cambridge University Press, 1988), 47.

27. Brian Treanor, "Hope in the Age of the Anthropocene," in *Ecology, Ethics, and Hope*, ed. Brei (Rowman and Littlefield, 2015), 95.

28. Ibid., 96.

29. Ibid., 99.

30. Ibid., 109, note 10.

31. Treanor, "Hope in the Age of the Anthropocene," 102.

32. Brian Treanor, "Joy and the Myopia of Finitude," *Comparative and Continental Philosophy* 8, no. 1 (2016): 7.

33. Ibid., 9.

34. Treanor, "Hope in the Age of the Anthropocene," 99.

35. Ibid., 99.

36. Ibid.

37. Ibid., 106, emphasis mine.

38. Ibid., 106.

39. Treanor, "Hope in the Age of the Anthropocene," 102.

40. "All of this will require a new posture and a new paradigm. We must open our eyes to the joy *and excitement* experienced by the newly prosperous and increasingly free. We must create a world where every human can not only realize her material needs but also her higher needs for creativity, choice, beauty—and wilderness. . . . 'The slogan of a democratic society must be machinery, and more machinery, civilization and more civilization.'" (Michael Shellenberger and Ted Nordhaus, *Love Your Monsters* [Breakthrough Institute, 2009]), Introduction.

41. Treanor, "Joy and the Myopia of Finitude," 17.

42. Ibid., 14–15.

43. Ibid., 15.

44. Ibid., 16.

45. Zora Neale Hurston, *Their Eyes Were Watching God* (Chicago, IL: University of Chicago Press, 1991), 15.

46. Virginia Woolf, *To the Lighthouse* (London: Harcourt Inc., 1988), 105.

47. See also Brian Treanor, "Mind the Gap: The Challenge of Matter," in *Carnal Hermeneutics,* eds. Kearney and Treanor (New York: Fordham University Press, 2015), 69.

48. Treanor, "Joy and the Myopia of Finitude," 21.

49. Ibid., 21.

50. Kareiva, Marvier, and Laslasz, "Conservation in the Age of the Anthropocene," 4.

51. Nature- or Being, or Wakan Tanka, or the Epekeina tes Ousias, or the Second Person of the Trinity, or Allah, or the Tao, Dharma.

BIBLIOGRAPHY

Callicott, J. Baird. "Environmental Philosophy is Environmental Activism: The Most Radical and Effective Kind." In *Environmental Ethics: What Really Matters, What Really Works,* edited by David Schmidtz and Elizabeth Willott, 11–17. Oxford, UK: Oxford University Press, 2012.

Callicott, J. Baird. "The Pragmatic Power and Promise of Theoretical Environmental Ethics." *Environmental Values* 11 (2002): 3–25.

Descartes, Rene. *Selected Philosophical Writings.* Translated by Cottingham and Stoothoff. Cambridge University Press, 1988.

Devall, Bill. "The Deep, Long-Range Ecology Movement: 1960–2000—A Review."
   Ethics & the Environment 6, no. 1 (2001): 18–41.
Gardiner, Stephen. *A Perfect Moral Storm: The Ethical Tragedy of Climate Change.*
   Oxford University Press, 2011.
Hurston, Zora Neale. *Their Eyes Were Watching God.* Illinois: University of Chicago
   Press, 1991.
Kareiva, Peter, Michelle Marvier, and Robert Lalasz. "Conservation in the Age of
   the Anthropocene: Beyond Solitude and Fragility." *The Breakthrough Institute,*
   2012. https://thebreakthrough.org/index.php/journal/past-issues/issue-2/conservat
   ion-in-the-anthropocene.
Leopold, Aldo. *A Sand County Almanac.* Oxford University Press, 1987.
Norton, Bryan. "Environmental Ethics and Weak Anthropocentrism." *Environmental
   Ethics* 6 (1984): 131–148.
Norton, Bryan. "Integration or Reduction: Two Approaches to Environmental
   Values." In *Environmental Pragmatism,* edited by Andrew Light and Eric Katz,
   105–138. Routledge, 1996.
Rolston III, Holmes. "'Review' of Gardiner's *A Perfect Moral Storm.*" In *Notre
   Dame Review of Books,* 2011. https://ndpr.nd.edu/news/a-perfect-moral-storm-the
   -ethical-tragedy-of-climate-change/.
Shellenberger, Michael and Ted Nordhaus. "The Death of Environmentalism." The
   Breakthrough Institute, 2004. https://www.thebreakthrough.org/images/Death_
   of_Environmentalism.pdf.
Shellenberger, Michael and Ted Nordhaus, eds. *Love Your Monsters: Postenviron-
   mentalism and the Anthropocene.* Breakthrough Institute, 2009.
Treanor, Brian. "Hope in the Age of the Anthropocene." In *Ecology, Ethics, and
   Hope,* edited by Andrew T. Bre, 95–110. Rowman and Littlefield, 2015.
Treanor, Brian. "Joy and the Myopia of Finitude." *Comparative and Continental
   Philosophy* 8, no. 1 (2016): 6–25.
Treanor, Brian. "Mind the Gap: The Challenge of Matter." In *Carnal Hermeneutics,*
   edited by Richard Kearney and Brian Treanor. Fordham University Press, 2015.
Woolf, Virginia. *To the Lighthouse.* London: Harcourt Inc., 1988.

Index

About the Editor

Róisín Lally is lecturer of philosophy at Gonzaga University. Drawing on the traditions of phenomenology and metaphysics, she works at the interction of time, technology, aesthetics, and sustainability. She has published articles on identity, culture, and technology. She is currently writing a book titled *Being, Time, and Technology.* Her most recent research is focused on developing an ontology of feminism.

About the Contributors

Babette Babich is professor of philosophy at Fordham University in New York City. Her books include *The Hallelujah Effect: Music, Performance Practice and Technology* (2016); *Un politique brisé, Le souci d'autrui, l'humanisme, et les juifs chez Heidegger* (2016); *La fin de la pensée? Philosophie analytique contre philosophie continentale* (2012); *Nietzsches Wissenschaftsphilosophie* [*Nietzsche's Philosophy of Science*] (2010 [1994]); and *Words in Blood, Like Flowers* (2006). Author of over 250 journal articles and book chapters, she has edited 9 book collections, most recently: *Hermeneutic Philosophies of Social Science* (2017) and since 1996 she has been executive editor of the journal, *New Nietzsche Studies*.

Dana S. Belu is associate professor of philosophy and coordinator of the Women's Studies Program at California State University, Dominguez Hills. She works at the intersection of phenomenology, feminist philosophy, feminist phenomenology, and the philosophy of technology. She is the author of *Heidegger, Reproductive Technology and The Motherless Age* (2017) and several articles, including, "Harnessing Birth in the Technical Age" in *Spaces for the Future: A Companion to the Philosophy of Technology*, eds. A. Shew and J. Pitts (2017); and "The Question Concerning a Vital Technology: Heidegger's Influence on Andrew Feenberg's Critical Theory" in *Critical Theory and the Thought of Andrew Feenberg*, eds. D. Arnold and A. Michel (2017).

Cristina Pontes Bonfiglioli is lecturer at the School of Communications and Arts in University of São Paulo (USP), Brazil. She teaches at a Postgraduate Qualification Program (Postgraduate Diploma) in Digital Networks, Third Sector, and Sustainability of the Centro de Pesquisa Átopos (Átopos Research Center). She is also a member of Society for Phenomenology and

223

Media (SPM) and collaborates with three other research centers: History of Science in Science Education, Institute of Advanced Studies, and Centro Interdisciplinar de Semiótica da Cultura e da Mídia (CISC). Her research interests lie in the relations between philosophy of science and technology, phenomenology and postphenomenology, and epistemology and ontology. Most of her academic production focuses on the connections between scientific discourse and imaging, especially those produced as photography (analog or digital) and cinema. Authors that interest her are Edmund Husserl, Maurice Merleau-Ponty, Hans Belting, Aby Warburg, Vilém Flusser, Hannah Arendt, Walter Benjamin, and Michel Foucault.

Dr. Lars Botin is associate professor at the Department of Planning (research group of Techno-Anthropology & Participation) Aalborg University, Denmark. Along with Theresa Scavenius and Tom Børsen, Botin is involved in the coordination and development of the "Art and Technology" study. They also are involved in the coordination and development of techno-anthropology.

Daniel O'Dea Bradley is associate professor of philosophy at Gonzaga University. He teaches a variety of courses in the areas of phenomenology, hermeneutics, aesthetics, ethics, and the philosophy of technology. His research focuses on questions of desire and illusion, with particular reference to the metaphysical and moral status of nature and the sensuous world.

Jan Kyrre Berg Friis is associate professor of philosophy of science and technology at Department of Public Health Science, University of Copenhagen. Friis has authored, edited, and co-edited numerous books on philosophy of technology, philosophy of time, metaphysics, and philosophy of science, as well as papers on perception, hermeneutics, and measurement. His current research interest is "thinking in light of Nietzsche, the later Heidegger, and Zen."

Trish Glazebrook is professor of philosophy in the School of Politics, Philosophy and Public Affairs at Washington State University. She published extensively on Heidegger and science, environment, and sustainability; eco-feminism, capital, and care; and gender and climate change. She currently researches on women subsistence farmers' adaptations to climate change in Ghana, oil in Africa, and military use of drones.

Don Ihde is distinguished professor of philosophy at the State University of New York at Stony Brook. In 2013 Ihde received the Golden Eurydice Award. Ihde is the author of twenty-two original books and the editor of many others. Recent examples include *Acoustic Technics* (2015); *Husserl's Missing Technologies* (2016); *Embodied Technics* (2010); *Heidegger's Technologies: Postphenomenological Perspectives* (2010); *Postphenomenology and Technoscience* (*Chinese 2008/English 2009*) also in Spanish, Hebrew, and forthcoming Portuguese; *Chasing Technoscience* (2003), edited with Evan Selinger; *Bodies in Technology* (2001); *Expanding Hermeneutics: Visualism in Science* (1998); and *Postphenomenology* (1993). Ihde lectures and gives seminars internationally, and some of his books and articles have appeared in a dozen languages.

Thomas M. Jeannot is professor of philosophy at Gonzaga University. He works on Marxism and critical theory, American philosophy, philosophical hermeneutics, ethics, personalism, and the thought of Bernard Lonergan. His articles and reviews have appeared in *Transactions of the Charles S. Peirce Society, Journal of Speculative Philosophy, International Philosophical Quarterly, The New Scholasticism, Owl of Minerva, Philosophy & Social Criticism, Radical Philosophy Review, Ultimate Reality and Meaning, Historical Materialism, International Journal of Social Economics,* and various edited collections.

Brendan Mahoney is lecturer of philosophy and ethics at the State University of New York Polytechnic Institute. Drawing on the traditions of phenomenology and virtue ethics, his work examines the intersection of ethical and aesthetic issues in environmental philosophy and the philosophy of technology. He has published articles on environmental restoration and aesthetics; environmental ethics and the sublime; Heidegger's philosophy of technology and environmental virtue ethics; and moral sentiment and vegetarianism in *Environmental Philosophy*; *Environmental Ethics*; and *English Language Notes: Environmental Trajectories.* Currently, he is writing a book on the ethical dimension of language in the philosophy of Wittgenstein, Heidegger, and Thoreau.

Galit Wellner is senior lecturer at the NB School of Design Haifa, Israel. She studies digital technologies and their interrelations with humans. She is an active member of the Postphenomenology Community that studies philosophy of technology. She published several peer-reviewed articles and book chapters. Her book *A Postphenomenological Inquiry of Cellphones: Genealogies, Meanings and Becoming* was published in 2015 by Lexington Books. She translated Don Ihde's book *Postphenomenology and Technoscience* (2016) to Hebrew. Recently she co-edited (with Yoni Van den Eede and Stacey Irwin) a collection titled *Postphenomenology and Media: Essays on Human-Media-World Relations* (Lexington Books 2017).

9 781498 584227